The Cambridge Introduction to
Anglo-Saxon Literature

An approachable and stimulating introduction to Anglo-Saxon literature, this book provides indispensable guidance for students on this important and rewarding area of literary studies. The chapters are clearly organized by topic, and significant attention is paid to key individual works, including *Beowulf*, *The Seafarer* and writings by Bede. All textual quotations are translated into Modern English, with the original language texts carefully explained. The *Introduction* synthesizes and develops dominant approaches to Anglo-Saxon literature today, integrating Old English and Latin traditions, and placing the literature in larger historical and theoretical contexts. The structure, style and layout are attractive and user-friendly, including illustrative figures and textboxes, and Magennis provides guidance on resources for studying Anglo-Saxon literature, informing the reader of opportunities for investigating the subject further. Overall, the book enables a thorough understanding and appreciation of artful and eloquent works from a distant past, which still speak powerfully to people today.

Hugh Magennis is Professor of Old English Literature and Director of the Institute of Theology at Queen's University Belfast.

The Cambridge Introduction to
Anglo-Saxon Literature

HUGH MAGENNIS

CAMBRIDGE
UNIVERSITY PRESS

CAMBRIDGE UNIVERSITY PRESS
Cambridge, New York, Melbourne, Madrid, Cape Town,
Singapore, São Paulo, Delhi, Tokyo, Mexico City

Cambridge University Press
The Edinburgh Building, Cambridge CB2 8RU, UK

Published in the United States of America by
Cambridge University Press, New York

www.cambridge.org
Information on this title: www.cambridge.org/9780521734653

First published 2011

Printed in the United Kingdom at the University Press, Cambridge

A catalogue record for this publication is available from the British Library

Library of Congress Cataloging-in-Publication Data
Magennis, Hugh.
The Cambridge introduction to Anglo-Saxon literature / Hugh Magennis.
     p.   cm. – (Cambridge introductions to literature)
   Includes bibliographical references and index.
   ISBN 978-0-521-51947-2 (Hardback) – ISBN 978-0-521-73465-3 (Paperback)
   1.   English literature–Old English, ca. 450–1100–History and criticism.
2. Civilization, Anglo-Saxon, in literature.   3. Civilization, Medieval, in literature.
I. Title.
   PR173.M34 2011
   829.09–dc22
                                                                2010046162
ISBN 978-0-521-51947-2 Hardback
ISBN 978-0-521-73465-3 Paperback

Contents

Illustrations

Preface

This book is primarily for readers with some background in literary studies but little or no knowledge of writings produced in Anglo-Saxon England. It is hoped that the book will also have interesting things to say to more advanced students but its guiding intention, in line with that of the Cambridge University Press series to which it belongs, is to open up the subject of Anglo-Saxon literature for those approaching it for the first time – while endeavouring not to 'dumb down' that subject in the process.

The designation Anglo-Saxon literature is one that encompasses writings in 'Old English' but also includes texts in the other literary language in use in the period, Latin. Latin was always the language of a small elite in Anglo-Saxon England but as the language of learning and of the Christian church it was the medium for some of the most important writers of the period. Old English, the earliest form of the English language, was the vernacular language of the Anglo-Saxons. English has undergone such profound changes in its history that Old English is largely incomprehensible today to those who have not studied it. Hence the need for translations in this book, from both languages. Quotations from the literature are mostly given here in Modern English but some glossed words and phrases in their original language are included and some longer passages are quoted in the original, with explanatory commentary.

Old English literature has always attracted more literary critical attention than Anglo-Latin, and that balance of emphasis is reflected again in this book, but I aim to give more consideration to writings in the latter language than they have usually received in introductions to Anglo-Saxon literature in the past and to integrate treatment of Old English and Latin as much as possible. In the following pages I will also be setting out to give a sense of the issues that have particularly concerned critics, and do so especially today, providing an introduction therefore not simply to Anglo-Saxon literature but also to Anglo-Saxon literary studies.

The first chapter flags up some of the major strands to be discussed later in the book, using a passage from the great Anglo-Saxon historian Bede as a starting point. The chapter also presents a discussion of modern perspectives and perceptions of Anglo-Saxon literature and a concise outline of Anglo-Saxon literary, and cultural, history. Chapter 2 then offers a more detailed overview of what have been seen as the major literary traditions of the period, with sections on Old English poetry and its oral background (emanating as it does from pre-literate times), on traditions of Latin prose and poetry, on prose writings in the vernacular, and on the adaptation of Old English poetry to Christian uses.

Chapters 3 and 4 look at kinds or genres of literature produced, the former chapter treating varieties of narrative, specifically heroic poetry, translations and adaptations of the Bible, history writing, and accounts of those Christian heroes, the saints, while the latter chapter surveys some non-narrative strands – sermons, writings of wisdom and lore, including riddles, and, a particularly attractive 'kind' of Old English literature in modern critical perception, the so-called elegies.

The final chapter considers Anglo-Saxon 'afterlives', later uses and appropriations of Anglo-Saxon England and its writings, from the Middle Ages onwards, including a section on creative writers from Wordsworth and Longfellow, via Tolkien, to Heaney and the present. Each chapter also has a number of text boxes and a 'postscript' on a particular topic related to the content of the chapter. The final postscript takes the form of a new verse translation by the distinguished poet Ciaran Carson.

The volume ends with guidance on resources for studying Anglo-Saxon literature and a bibliography of works cited, both of which components offer possibilities and opportunities for taking the subject further, as I hope many readers will wish to do. In approaching Anglo-Saxon literature we come into contact with and try to understand artful and eloquent works from a distant past, which can still speak powerfully to people today. In a similar way the poet of the short Old English poem *The Ruin* considers the buildings left by a great former civilization and exclaims wonderingly that in creating these works from the past

> A mind instigated its quick-witted idea,
> ingenious in the use of ring(-pattern)s.
> [Mod monade myneswiftne gebrægd,
> hwætred in hringas.]

In the following pages, I hope to introduce readers to the mind(s) and ideas, quick-witted and otherwise, of Anglo-Saxon literature.

Acknowledgements

I would like to thank my friend and colleague Ivan Herbison for many enlightening discussions on topics relating to this book, which is the better for his wise advice. I also wish to thank for their constructive suggestions the anonymous readers for Cambridge University Press of earlier drafts of the book. At Cambridge University Press, I am particularly indebted to Sarah Stanton for her astute general guidance and to Rebecca Taylor and Liz Davey for steering the book through production.

One section in Chapter 3 of this book draws upon material from Hugh Magennis, 'Germanic Legend and Old English Heroic Poetry', in Corinne Saunders (ed.), *A Companion to Medieval Poetry*, © Wiley-Blackwell (2010), reproduced with permission of the editor and publisher.

The List of Illustrations provides descriptions of maps and images used in the book. I wish to thank individuals and institutions for granting permission to include this material. Illustration 1.1 is © The Trustees of the British Museum. 1.3, 3.1, 3.3 and 4.1 are © The British Library Board. 1.5 and 2.3 are reproduced with the permission of The Bodleian Libraries, University of Oxford. 2.5 is reproduced with the permission of Bernard J. Muir; acknowledgement for this image is also due to Exeter Cathedral Library as the custodian of the original manuscript. 3.2 is reproduced with the permission of The Master and Fellows of Corpus Christi College, Cambridge.

I am very grateful to Ciaran Carson for producing translations of the Old English poems *The Husband's Message* and *Riddle 60* for this book. Ciaran Carson retains the copyright for these translations. I understand the quotation of other copyright material in the book to fall within the terms of 'fair dealing' for the purposes of criticism and I have limited such quotation to a small proportion of the text of any one work.

The sources of translations from Anglo-Saxon and related texts are indicated in references in parenthesis. Unattributed translations are my own.

Abbreviations

ASPR   The Anglo-Saxon Poetic Records, ed. Krapp and Dobbie
EETS   Early English Text Society
  OS   Original Series
  SS   Supplementary Series
MS(S) Manuscript(s)
PMLA   *Publications of the Modern Language Association of America*

Chapter 1

Approaching Anglo-Saxon literature

A world of literature has survived from Anglo-Saxon England, wide-ranging in subject matter and varied in literary approach. The literature encompasses (among other things) exciting tales of heroic action about Beowulf and other legendary figures, expressions of Christian teaching, meditations on the great questions of life and death, and ingenious and playful compositions. In it the secular is creatively combined with the spiritual and the unserious can be startlingly mixed with the serious. Developing over the course of half a millennium and composed in two languages, Latin and Old English, Anglo-Saxon literature has proved endlessly interesting to those who know it and offers new horizons for those coming to it for the first time. The present chapter presents an introduction to this *Introduction*, working in the first instance from the particular to the general in the opening section and then going on to put together historical and contextualizing frameworks for approaching the rest of the book.

Beginnings: Bede's story of Cædmon

A famous episode from Bede's *Ecclesiastical History of the English People* may serve to flag up some of the dominant themes in the study of Anglo-Saxon literature that this book explores. The passage tells the story of the poet Cædmon, whom Bede presents as the first person to compose Christian poetry in the English language. For Bede, Cædmon is an originary and transformative figure. Bede (*c.* 673–735), a Northumbrian monk, was an intellectual leader of the early medieval world, a prolific and influential writer, in Latin, in the tradition of Christian scholarship inherited from the great 'fathers' of the church of earlier centuries. In the *Ecclesiastical History* he tells the story of the early history of Anglo-Saxon England and in particular of the conversion of the Anglo-Saxons from Germanic paganism to Christianity, and conversion is at the core of his story of Cædmon.

Bede's account of the poet Cædmon

In the monastery of this abbess [Hild] there was a certain brother who was specially marked out by the grace of God, so that he used to compose godly and religious songs; thus whatever he learned from the holy Scriptures by means of interpreters, he quickly turned into extremely delightful and moving poetry in English, which was his own tongue. By his songs the minds of many were often inspired to despise the world and to long for the heavenly life. It is true that after him other Englishmen attempted to compose religious poems, but none could compare with him. For he did not learn the art of poetry from men or through a man but he received the gift of song freely by the grace of God. Hence he could never compose any foolish or trivial poem but only those which were concerned with devotion and so were fitting for his devout tongue to utter. He had lived in the secular habit until he was well advanced in years and he never learned any songs. Hence sometimes at a feast, when for the sake of providing entertainment it had been decided that they should all sing in turn, when he saw the harp approaching him, he would rise up in the middle of the feasting, go out, and return home.

   On one such occasion when he did so, he left the place of feasting and went to the cattle byre, as it was his turn to take charge of the cattle that night. In due time he stretched himself out and went to sleep, whereupon he dreamt that someone stood by him, saluted him, and called him by name: 'Cædmon,' he said, 'sing me something.' Cædmon answered, 'I cannot sing; that is why I left the feast and came here because I could not sing.' Once again the speaker said, 'Nevertheless you must sing to me.' 'What must I sing?' said Cædmon. 'Sing', he said, 'about the beginning of created things.' Thereupon Cædmon began to sing verses which he had never heard before in praise of God the Creator, of which this is the general sense: 'Now we must praise the Maker of the heavenly kingdom, the power of the Creator and his counsel, the deeds of the Father of glory and how he, since he is the eternal God, was the Author of all marvels and first created the heavens as a roof for the children of men and then, the almighty Guardian of the human race, created the earth.' This is the sense but not the order of the words which he sang as he slept. For it is not possible to translate verse, however well composed, literally from one language to another without some loss of beauty and dignity. When he awoke, he remembered all that he had sung while asleep and soon added more verses in the same manner, praising God in fitting style.

In the morning he went to the reeve who was his master, telling him of the gift he had received, and the reeve took him to the abbess. He was then bidden to describe his dream in the presence of a number of the more learned men and also to recite his song so that they might all examine him and decide upon the nature and origin of the gift of which he spoke; and it seemed clear to all of them that the Lord had granted him heavenly grace. They then read to him a passage of sacred history or doctrine, bidding him to make a song out of it, if he could, in metrical form. He undertook the task and went away; on returning next morning he repeated the passage he had been given, which he had put into excellent verse. The abbess, who recognized the grace of God which the man had received, instructed him to renounce his secular habit and to take monastic vows. She and all her people received him into the community of the brothers and ordered that he should be instructed in the whole course of sacred history. He learned all he could by listening to them and then, like some clean animal chewing the cud, he turned it into the most melodious verse: and it sounded so sweet as he recited it that his teachers became in turn his audience. (Bede, *History*, IV, 24; trans. Colgrave and Mynors 1969, pp. 415–19)

Cædmon the simple cowherd becomes Cædmon the inspirational poet. Bede's chapter goes on to say that he eventually 'sang' (*canebat*) the story of the whole of the Book of Genesis and that he also related many other events from the Old Testament, as well as covering Christ's life and death and many other aspects of Christian teaching. None of these other compositions of Cædmon has survived and we do not know how many of them Bede knew himself, but for him Cædmon's poetry represents a beginning, and a divinely inspired one: many other poets came after Cædmon, Bede reports, though none could compare with him.

Bede's narrative of Cædmon and his poem (the poem is usually referred to as Cædmon's *Hymn*) is an engaging one in which an account of a wondrous episode is combined with a strong element of human interest. For a modern reader new to Anglo-Saxon literature the passage is likely to be somewhat disconcerting in the way that it brings together history and miracle, but this defamiliarizing feature is also useful in suggesting the differentness as well as the accessibility of early medieval writings; we will find that in many ways these writings challenge, and indeed problematize, modern assumptions about literature. Seamus Heaney, whose translation of *Beowulf* has probably done more than any other publication in recent times to stimulate popular interest in the poem, and by extension in Anglo-Saxon literature more widely, refers to *Beowulf* as 'a work of the greatest imaginative vitality, a masterpiece', but also as a 'remote' work (Heaney 1999, pp. ix, xii, respectively). Bede's *History* could also be described as 'a work of the greatest imaginative vitality, a masterpiece', and it too is in essential ways different, and 'remote', from modern experience. One recent commentator on the *History*, while insisting that it is a great work, advises, 'It is far more constructive to read Bede as representative of a quite foreign community, distant and strange, whose thought world should be approached with caution' (Higham 2006, p. 48). In the particular case of the Cædmon story Bede gives us a 'myth of origins' which, though it undoubtedly simplifies the story of the beginning of Christian poetry in Old English, throws interesting light on a key literary development in the period.

The passage may be used conveniently, if somewhat impressionistically, to highlight other important issues of concern to readers of Anglo-Saxon literature as well as that of defamiliarization and accessibility, just mentioned. Points about Anglo-Saxon literature arising from our passage for us to bear in mind from the beginning include the following:

Old English and Latin: The bulk of the texts discussed in this book were composed in Old English, but it is important also to pay attention to Latin literature. Latin too was a literary language in early medieval England; indeed Bede's *History* itself must be seen as one of the great literary monuments of the age. Writings in Old English have certainly been perceived as representing the most distinctive and the most significant body of literature from the Anglo-Saxon world but Latin, the language of learning, produced works that are of the highest interest in their own right as well as providing an important background for Old English literature. In this book the term 'Old English literature' is used to refer to writings in the vernacular, while the broader term 'Anglo-Saxon literature' should be understood to include Latin writings as well.

Translation: This point about two languages alerts us to the central importance of translation in Anglo-Saxon literary culture. Christian Latin texts and Christian Latin traditions are translated, adapted and appropriated by vernacular poets and prose writers. At the end of the ninth century Bede's *History* was itself translated into Old English prose (for the Old English text of the Cædmon episode, see Marsden 2004, pp. 76–85). In our quoted passage we see a notable instance of translation in the story of Cædmon: according to Bede, Cædmon, who has no direct access to religious writings in Latin, is instructed by 'interpreters' and then brings forth sweet poetry 'in his own tongue, that is the language of the English'. Interestingly, however, in Bede we get Cædmon's *Hymn* not in Old English but translated into Latin; some manuscripts of the *History* also include the poem in Old English (written in the margin, and the Old English version also appears in the Old

English translation of the *History*), and indeed scholars still debate whether this Old English text is in fact Cædmon's original poem or a back-translation of Bede's Latin.

As will be brought out particularly in Chapter 3, especially with reference to the Bible, to translate is inevitably to change (a topic touched on by Bede at the end of the second paragraph of our passage above); the process of translation changes the source text, and the effect of the translation is to change the receiving culture, a double-sided 'conversion' taking place. It would not be overstating things to say that the impact of translation decisively shaped Old English literature; translation contributed crucially to the ways in which it developed. And the fact that the study of the Latin sources of Old English texts figures centrally in the work of Anglo-Saxonists (as will be apparent in later chapters) can be seen as reflecting the importance to the discipline of ideas of translation in its broadest sense.

Orality and textuality: A third point that is brought out by the passage from Bede concerns the oral origin and dimension of Old English poetry, a topic to be explored further in Chapter 2. Cædmon performs his poetry orally ('then he began to sing verses which he had never heard before') and he composes it orally. Miraculously in a dream, he acquires mastery of the demanding structures and techniques of an experienced traditional oral poet, including alliterative metre and the formulaic language that makes oral composition possible. In the story of Cædmon orality meets textuality, as the 'interpreters' transmit to him written Christian teaching and he recasts it in 'extremely delightful and moving poetic language'. For Cædmon's poetry to be preserved for posterity it would have had to be written down and we don't know to what extent that happened with his work. But when something is written down it is also largely fixed in a particular form, whereas oral performance is by definition fluid and variable. Old English poetry *was* written down, of course (otherwise we could not read it today), a development that represents a key cultural transition. It is thought that most surviving Old English poetic texts are literate compositions (rather than transcriptions of oral performances) but they still make use of the same kind of oral-derived poetic art that gave form to Cædmon's poetry.

Old English prose: Another point arising out of examination of the Bede passage concerns the tradition(s) of Old English prose. I noted above that Bede's *History* was among the Latin works translated into Old English prose, in the late ninth century. The establishment of Old English prose as a medium for the expression of sophisticated intellectual thought is among the most significant literary developments of the Anglo-Saxon period. As explained more fully in Chapter 2, the instigation of the process is traditionally associated with

King Alfred of Wessex, though the emphasis on Alfred (reflecting what looks like another myth of origins) somewhat oversimplifies the situation. The establishment of literary prose in Old English involves the fashioning of an appropriate vocabulary and syntax and eventually the formation, in a period of great dialectal diversity, of a standard literary language. Bede, a foundational figure in the construction of Englishness, has Cædmon singing poetry in 'English' but the English he composed in was his native Northumbrian; later in the period the language of Wessex would emerge as the literary language for England as a whole, 'England' in the later Anglo-Saxon centuries being a political concept that can be applied more convincingly than in the age of Bede. The surviving corpus of Old English prose is many times larger than that of verse and includes much material of great literary as well as historical interest. And, integrating prose with characteristics of verse, in the writings of the most prolific and accomplished producer of Old English prose, Ælfric of Eynsham (*c.* 965–*c.* 1010), a style lucidly expressive of intellectual discourse combines with rhythmical and alliterative features derived from the indigenous tradition of Old English poetry.

Manuscript transmission: As stated above, written literature is largely fixed, whereas oral literature is fluid and variable. It should be noted, however, that in the manuscript culture of Anglo-Saxon England texts were 'fixed' to a much lesser degree than they are today in the age of print. Even Latin texts are subject to some deliberate variation, not to mention accidental error. For example, some copies of our passage from Bede begin 'In this monastery of Streanaeshalch [Whitby]', not 'In the monastery of this abbess'. With Old English texts the potential for variation is very much greater, since these writings were often, in the case of prose, texts for use which could be changed and adapted to suit particular purposes (we will see that Ælfric tries, unsuccessfully, to insulate his writings from such reappropriation), while in the case of verse the formulaic aspect of the poetic language in itself facilitated variation in copying by scribes who were tuned in to the poetic language. In the copies of the Old English Cædmon's *Hymn*, for example, there is variation at one point between Bede's 'children of men' and 'children of earth' (Old English *ælda barnum* versus *eorðan bearnum*, both of which phrases are metrically and semantically possible); copies of Cædmon's *Hymn* also show dialect variation: we have versions in Old Northumbrian but the poem was also 'translated' into the West Saxon dialect, which became dominant later (see O'Donnell 2005). In practice most Old English poems exist in only one manuscript copy but since there are theoretical issues about the status of texts in the period the modern editorial concept of the 'best' text of a work is difficult to apply.

Christian and secular: Cædmon's poetry also opens the way for the inter-action of Christian and secular values and ideas in Old English poetry, an important theme in the chapters that follow. Cædmon applies the traditional Old English poetic art, inherited from the pagan Germanic past, to a Chris-tian subject matter, thereby giving a new form to the subject matter. As well as providing a metrical form, that art brings with it a repertoire of themes and associations from the secular world. Cædmon's *Hymn* is too undevel-oped to illustrate fully the potential – and indeed the problems – of this interaction, which was one that involved tension and contradiction, reflecting inherent differences between Christian teaching and the views and outlook of Germanic poetry, with its preoccupation with the heroic deeds and values of this world. Old English poetry ranges from purely secular poems of heroism and violence set in a warrior society, the kind of thing that Bede would regard (as he puts it in our passage) as 'foolish and trivial' poetry, to religious narratives and treatises that directly express Christian teaching. In between are writings that incorporate elements from both traditions, and such writings include what have been seen as some of the most interesting works in the Anglo-Saxon corpus. As explained more fully in Chapter 2, poems like *The Dream of the Rood,* which portrays Christ going to his death like a young hero preparing for battle, and *The Seafarer,* which transforms heroic glory into striving for heaven, exploit the intersections and the radical disjunctions between Christian and secular in masterful ways.

A monastic dimension: Bearing upon a number of these previous points (particularly, perhaps, the immediately preceding one) is the fact of the monastic and, more broadly, Christian milieu of much Anglo-Saxon litera-ture. Most of the scribal work in the period was done in monastic *scriptoria,* 'writing-houses'. It is not surprising therefore that religious themes figure so prominently. The Anglo-Saxon literature we have was in a sense self-selected: what got written down and preserved was what was perceived to be relevant to those who controlled and participated in the textual culture of the time. A key figure in the history of Old English prose, King Alfred, came from secular society but even he had his clerical/monastic advisers and guides and much of the writing associated with him has a religious dimension. This monastic milieu is illustrated in Bede's story of Cædmon in his *History.* Bede himself writes his *History* from a monastic point of view, telling an *'Ecclesiastical' History* in which religious figures loom large: his greatest English hero of all is the Northumbrian monk and bishop Cuthbert. The poet Cædmon is absorbed into the monastic life under the maternal care of the abbess Hild, secular becoming religious. This monastic dimension of Anglo-Saxon literature being the case, it is notable that so much secular literature was also preserved. Why were monks interested in reading about the feats of secular heroes, as in *Beowulf*, and why interested in outpourings of grief and longing arising from love between the sexes, as in *The Wife's Lament* and *Wulf and Eadwacer*? Why would they want to preserve in precious books Old English riddles not only about the wonder of the world but also having graphically sexual double meanings? We are glad that they did, but the variety and range of surviving literature should alert us, while taking account of the scribal context in which the literature was produced, to the danger of oversimplifying the culture(s) of the time. The historical picture is one of complexity.

Old English poetry: 'beauty and dignity': A final observation arising from consideration of the Bede passage concerns the aesthetic quality of Old English poetry. Bede insists on the beauty of Cædmon's verse, which is 'extremely delightful and moving'; he acknowledges that his Latin translation cannot convey its 'beauty and dignity' (*decoris ac dignitatis*). Cædmon's poetry may not have survived (apart from, perhaps, the *Hymn*), but Bede's description can fittingly be applied to much of the Old English verse that has come down to us. This verse was deeply appreciated in its own day, being copied and recopied into manuscripts in some cases over many generations. And the qualities of Old English poetry, its power and expressiveness and its cleverness and artistry, are among the chief things that modern readers value in it. The poetry tells us much about the Anglo-Saxon world but it is also deeply appealing as poetry, having richness, variety and artfulness. Now, many readers of the present book will have little or no knowledge of Old English, which means that we have to rely mostly on translations in illustrating the literature. Here we are caught in the bind that Bede identified nearly thirteen hundred years ago: 'For it is not possible to translate verse, however well composed, literally from one language to another without some loss of beauty and dignity.' Translations are necessary but, particularly in the case of verse, inadequate. We have to live with this reality for the purposes of this book but as we proceed I will also include some short passages in the original with explanatory commentary, which I hope will give readers some immediate sense of the distinctive qualities of this enthralling literature.

It would be possible to bring out other important considerations relevant to Anglo-Saxon literature by means of reference to our passage from Bede. The point about Bede's identification of Cædmon's language as 'English' and, more generally, about Bede's role in the construction of Englishness could certainly have been developed further, and perceptions of identity, including linguistic identity, will be a topic that will inevitably come up in later discussion. Related to this question of identity would be the observation that Cædmon's name is actually not Anglo-Saxon but 'British', which opens up the fraught subject of relations between Anglo-Saxons and Britons in the early Anglo-Saxon centuries, and therefore also that of the make-up of the 'English people' in that period. Other features that I could have picked up on in the story of Cædmon include the presence of a female authority figure in a society that is often characterized as strongly patriarchal. Also, a more narrowly literary point, the passage includes a 'dream vision', a type of narrative represented elsewhere in Anglo-Saxon literature, most famously in the poem *The Dream of the Rood*. And indeed there may well be features that readers have noticed that I have not mentioned at all. The passage from Bede is an interesting narrative in its own right but it also provides a suggestive point of entrance into the wider subject of Anglo-Saxon literature. My discussion of it has by no means exhausted its critical possibilities.

Studying Anglo-Saxon literature: perspectives and perceptions

This book is historicist in its approach to the literature that it deals with. It seeks an understanding and appreciation of the literature in relation to the historical context and circumstances of its production and reception. In this respect the book places itself very much in the mainstream of current critical thinking in the field of Anglo-Saxon literary studies, and indeed historicizing approaches of one kind or another have been dominant throughout the history of the discipline. Understanding and appreciation of the literature of the past, especially of the fairly remote past, is inevitably provisional and incomplete, of course, but particularly in recent decades knowledge about Anglo-Saxon England and about its place in the early medieval world has increased greatly, throwing new light on the literature in exciting ways and adding to the foundational work of previous scholarship. As one senior scholar put it, writing in 1995,

> What we know about the Anglo-Saxons has increased so dramatically since 1950 that those of us who became interested in them before then can only blink with astonishment at the advances in our knowledge of their language, their literature, their history, their culture, their material circumstances, their way of life, and their attitudes to life and the mysteries which lie beyond it.   (Mitchell 1995, p. 99)

The Anglo-Saxon period is no longer the 'dark age' to critics that it once was. But of course we still have not stopped learning about it; new discoveries are still being made about the literature and about the historical context – as I write this book the first stunning reports of the newly discovered 'Stafford-shire Hoard' of Anglo-Saxon gold artefacts are coming out – and there is still much to discover. Indeed, even the basic work of the recovery and editing of texts continues: although most surviving texts had been printed and were receiving critical attention by the end of the nineteenth century (and much earlier in some cases), there are still some that have not yet been published or that exist only in very unsatisfactory and out-of-date editions. Anglo-Saxon studies have been going for a long time but for those in the field, with previous work being reassessed, new information being processed and new scholarly tools coming to the fore, it has the feel of a young and expanding subject. And with a literature as inexhaustibly rich, and in many cases as enigmatic, as that of Anglo-Saxon England there will always be issues of cognition and interpretation which will remain open and indeterminate, particularly in the poetry. As explained below, even a short poem like Cædmon's *Hymn* falls into this category in a number of ways.

The basis of a historicist approach to literature is the principle of the 'situatedness' of the literary work in a historical context. What also distin-guishes current historicist thinking, however, is a self-conscious awareness that the critic is also situated in a particular historical context and that history is constantly being revised and reconceived. The emphases of Anglo-Saxon studies in the past have reflected and contributed to larger cultural preoccupations and have changed as these cultural preoccupations have changed. In earlier centuries Anglo-Saxon literary studies participated in ideological constructions of national and religious identity, for example, while today they tend to problematize such constructions. And while much work in Anglo-Saxon studies still follows traditional approaches and meth-odologies, current scholarship also engages productively with contemporary critical and cultural issues and indeed has been in the forefront of key methodological developments, notably perhaps in the area of the application of digital technology and its theory (see, particularly, Foys 2007).

Anglo-Saxon studies have moved on from earlier paradigms, but in some quarters perceptions of them have not moved on in the same way, so that for some critics the discipline remains tarred with the brush of previous reputa-tion. Terry Eagleton has recently written that *Beowulf* 'ultimately retains its pride of place in English studies mainly due to its function, from the Victorian period forward, as the cultural tool of a troubling nationalist romance with an archetypal and mythological past' (Eagleton 1999, p. 16). Eagleton is writing about *Beowulf* in particular but would doubtless apply the same sentiments to Anglo-Saxon literature as a whole. He is seeing *Beowulf* as tainted by dubious nationalist and imperialist associations, whereas in fact it is possible – and indeed essential – to get beyond these in our study of the poem and of the wider literature. It is true to say that from early on in its modern history *Beowulf* acquired a national and institutional status that made it something of a sacred cow of English literary history and that it retains a kind of canonical position in English studies which can be legitimately questioned. For many English students down the generations *Beowulf* was all the Anglo-Saxon literature they encountered and, to quote the critic and translator Michael Alexander, they tended to view it as 'a sort of dinosaur in the entrance hall of English Literature' (Alexander 1973, p. 10).

Beowulf is not conceived of in these ways in today's scholarship. If anything, *Beowulf* and other Anglo-Saxon texts have been used to undermine inherited constructions, including, as illustrated most strikingly in Seamus Heaney's *Beowulf* translation, constructions of nationality and literary tradition. Heaney recognizes the role that *Beowulf* and other early English writings have played in the development of a national, English, literature, but in translating it he makes it something else. He writes from an Irish and a postcolonial experience, not an English one, and he addresses his translation of the poem to the readership of the 'global village' (Heaney 1999, p. xiii) rather than appealing to shared cultural origins. Michael Alexander, writing in the 1970s, reflects unicultural perceptions when he writes of *Beowulf* as standing 'at the beginning of our literature' (Alexander 1973, p. 10); for Heaney such a concept of 'our literature' would be problematic: who is the *our* here? Who does it include, and who does it exclude? Heaney's engagement with *Beowulf* raises issues of language and identity and of cultural connections, and this can be said of the study of Anglo-Saxon texts more widely (see further, Magennis 2011).

A dominant historicist approach of Anglo-Saxon studies as they developed over the past two hundred years, and one that can be seen to have influenced Eagleton's troubled perception, was that of philology. Philology might be defined as the systematic study of the language of the past from a historical and comparative perspective and in relation to other evidence about culture. Philology was conceived of as a science of language. It was interested in language as an autonomous system and sought through rigorous analysis to reveal the underlying 'laws' that operated in it across time and space. Building on the study of Latin and Greek from the Renaissance period onwards, philology came to fruition in the 1800s; its classic methodology was developed in the romantic era and refined thereafter, chiefly in Germany. From Germany it was imported into Britain, with considerable reservations there about the desirability of this 'German-made' science

(Shippey 2005, p. 10), and into America, more enthusiastically (Frantzen 1990; Hall 2001). Philology's project was fostered in Germany by national pride about the past and philology itself fostered such pride, seeing early texts as expressing ethnic origins and ethnic identity; philology played a key role in the development of ideas of Germanness, which were increasingly expressed, with considerable stridency in some quarters, as the century went on (Benes 2008). Philology became increasingly marginalized in the twentieth century, but it served as a basis for more current approaches and its techniques are still seen as providing essential tools for editors and lexicographers. Without philology we would not have recovered Old English literature to the extent that we have, and we wouldn't be able to read it and other medieval literature competently.

The trouble that many twentieth-century and earlier (see Palmer 1965, pp. 79–84) literary students had with philology was that it was not able to discuss literature as literature (an observation, it might be added, that could equally be made of 'new historicism' today). The critic Frank Kermode recalls that when he was studying Old English in the 1940s the interests of the teachers were 'exclusively philological and antiquarian': texts were rarely examined as literature by these teachers but 'provided them with a great variety of complicated scholarly problems, and it was in these that they wanted to involve their students' (Kermode 2001, p. 2). One of the great exponents of philology was J. R. R. Tolkien, who once wrote, 'I like history, and am moved by it, but its finest moments for me are those in which it throws light on words and names!' (quoted in Shippey 2005, p. 18). To unsympathetic outsiders such interest in the minutiae of language could be portrayed as pedantry which failed to see the wood for the trees, but in philology small observations could lead to far-reaching conclusions, and philology demonstrably provided remarkable insight into the study of the past. Tom Shippey has written recently of 'the immense stretch of the philological imagination' (Shippey 2005, p. 21). It has become increasingly recognized, indeed, that nineteenth-century philology provided a foundation for the 'linguistic turn' that brought language to the centre of intellectual debate in the twentieth century. For Michel Foucault philology modified 'the whole mode of being of language' (Foucault 2002 [original edition 1966], p. 306), thereby transforming the basis of knowledge. As Tuska Benes points out, 'The constructivist understanding of language that itself underlies Foucault's philosophy has deep roots in nineteenth-century Germany' (Benes 2008, p. 294) (according to constructivist theories, language shapes human experience and thought rather than being a passive instrument controlled by the speaker).

J. R. R. Tolkien is widely known today as the creator of enduringly popular fantasy literature but he was also one of the major figures in Anglo-Saxon literary studies in the twentieth century, his background in medieval English and in philology providing indeed an essential foundation for his fiction. An academic publication by Tolkien in 1936 proved to be a turning point in the study of *Beowulf* and by extension of Old English literature. This was his essay (based on a lecture) '*Beowulf*: The Monsters and the Critics', in which, arch-philologist though he was, Tolkien argued that *Beowulf* should be read as a great poem, not just as a philologically interesting document. It would be oversimplifying things to say that Tolkien's essay was the beginning of the literary study of Old English texts but it certainly succeeded in getting scholars to think differently about *Beowulf*. It is after the Second World War that concentrated literary study of Old English poetic texts takes off, and literary interpretation becomes a central interest (see Magennis 2011, pp. 73–5).

The period after the Second World War also saw the advent of two approaches to literature that were non-historicist in their underlying principles, formulaic studies and formalism. Formulaic studies taught that Old English poetry was orally composed and that the poets systematically used ready-made verbal formulas and formula systems as an integral part of their compositional technique (Magoun 1953), a theory that presented a considerable challenge to conventional critical assumptions. Formulaic theory was impacting on Anglo-Saxon studies at about the same time as formal criticism became influential in literary criticism, particularly through the writings of the American 'New Critics'. Formal criticism involved the close reading of literary texts as organic unities in which the precise words and their order determined the unique meaning of the work of art. Both of these schools, diametrically opposite in their approach to literature, affected the study of Old English poetry, though in their application both needed to be modified: it came to be recognized that poetry could have a formulaic character without necessarily being oral (Benson 1966), while formalists had to take the formulaic character of the poetry on board in close reading of texts (e.g., S. B. Greenfield 1955). The best critics of Old English poetry writing today are good close readers but also sensitive to the effect of formulaic tradition and indeed, as mentioned in the previous section, of textuality upon that tradition.

In our present period the concern of the New Critics with formal unity and with the idea of the poem as a 'well-wrought urn' (to refer to the title of a classic text of formalism, Brooks 1947) has been replaced for many scholars by an interest in the contradictions, tensions and instabilities that can be discerned in texts. To discern these requires close reading, of course: deconstructionists as well as formalists have to be good close readers. In current historicist approaches to Anglo-Saxon literature close reading is often used to bring out the complexities and frictions of a changing historical picture.

Among other features distinctive of Anglo-Saxon literary studies today is a concern with the manuscript context of particular texts, which tended not to receive due attention in the past; the manuscript context provides crucial information of how texts were used and understood in the period. Today detailed attention is paid too to such prose writings as homilies and saints' lives, which had been relatively neglected by previous scholarship but which were major literary forms in the period and tell us much about Anglo-Saxon 'attitudes', as well as being interesting in their own right. And the Latin literature of the period is being studied alongside the Old English literature to a greater extent than happened in previous generations, reflecting the understanding that both literatures are intimately interrelated and are expressions of a larger common culture. Finally, to mention one other distinctive feature of Anglo-Saxon literary studies today, it used to be thought that texts that came from after 1066 or a bit later were not of much interest to Old English scholars, but it is now recognized that 'Old English' culture continued at some level down to the thirteenth century: post-Conquest English vernacular literature is now being reassessed and is recognized as throwing new light on the history of the time (see Swan and Treharne, eds., 2000; Treharne 2006).

Before concluding this section there is one possible impediment or limitation to historically based criticism of Anglo-Saxon literature that we need to take account of. We *are* able to locate much of the literature, particularly the prose literature, in fairly narrow historical contexts that are defined and reasonably well understood. Granted, there are plenty of anonymous Old English prose texts that we still cannot place temporarily or geographically and some that we may never be able to, but the bulk of the major prose works can be placed confidently in specific contexts, as can most Anglo-Latin literature.

It is, rather, Old English poetry that presents insurmountable problems in terms of origin and provenance. This is partly because Old English poetry is overwhelmingly anonymous and partly because it mostly survives in versions written in 'standard' West Saxon, a form of language in which texts that were non-West-Saxon in origin (like Cædmon's *Hymn*, for example) were transmitted, as well as West Saxon ones. But the crucial difficulty in dating Old English poetry stems from the inherent character of the poetry itself. This character of Old English poetry has recently been well summed up by Elizabeth Tyler, who refers to the 'timelessness' of the poetry (Tyler 2006, p. 3). Rather than seeking to relate their work to a specific time (or place) Old English poets cultivated a quality of timelessness, a quality that is reflected, for example, in an attachment to archaic diction. Poets certainly influenced each other but the underlying poetic diction and stylistic conventions that they employed remained stable over many centuries and poets actively worked to ensure that they continued to be so. As Tyler puts it, this stylistic stability was not just a matter of the passive adoption of tradition on the part of poets: 'the distinctive conventionality of Old English verse was sustained by the active choice of poets to use convention, rather than being generated by tradition' (Tyler 2006, p. 5). We know that *The Battle of Maldon* was composed after 991 since that was the date of the battle that the poem commemorates. There are some features in the language of *The Battle of Maldon* (ed. Marsden 2004, pp. 251–69) which might be seen as reflecting its 'lateness' but generally the poem has that quality of timelessness referred to above: it does not set out to present itself as a post-991 poem. As for *Beowulf*, dates of composition have been proposed ranging from the seventh century to the early eleventh (the unique manuscript of *Beowulf* comes from the early eleventh century) and there is no real consensus on the topic among *Beowulf* specialists today. Agnosticism reigns with reference to the dating of most other poems as well, though some of them must have come before others (there is evidence that the poet of the verse saint's life *Andreas* knew *Beowulf*, for example: Riedinger 1993, Jagger 2002).

We can still apply historicist approaches to Old English poetry in broad terms, however, and can view the poetry as reflecting ideas and ideals which must have continued to be perceived as relevant throughout much of the Anglo-Saxon period. But, becoming more specific, if we cannot identify the date of origin of most Old English poems, we are able fairly precisely to date the manuscripts in which they have come down to us. We can thus identify at least one reception context for any given poem in the period, that of when we know that it was being read (and read out) in a particular manuscript. As it happens, all the major extant manuscripts of Old English poetry date from late Anglo-Saxon England, from the later tenth and early eleventh centuries, a fact that in itself bears out the longevity of the poetic tradition and also provides evidence that the tradition was valued as speaking relevantly to the concerns of that age, including (as we have seen) those of people in religious life. Old English poetry was inherited by the late Anglo-Saxon period, being read, no doubt, in some ways as it had always been read but also perhaps being reappropriated for particular ideological purposes relevant to the time; and, as the example of *The Battle of Maldon*, for one, suggests, it could still provide a living and productive literary medium. Old English poetry can be read historically at a number of levels but one of them has to do with the concerns that can be identified as particularly current in late Anglo-Saxon England (see, for example, Niles 2007, Howe 2008). Questions of the use and audience/readership of Anglo-Saxon literature will be among those to be considered in the course of this book.

Anglo-Saxon literary history: an outline

In our context of historicizing the literature it might be useful at this stage to identify briefly some landmarks in Anglo-Saxon history, with particular reference to their literary significance, relating literature also to aspects of Anglo-Saxon art. To the outside observer Anglo-Saxon England can easily seem a fairly monolithic entity with few features to distinguish one period within it from the next. The quality of 'timelessness' that we have noted to be a feature of Old English poetry might be thought to bear out such a perception. But of course Anglo-Saxon history spans the whole period from the first arrival of Germanic settlers in Britain in the fifth century to 1066 and beyond, a period of more than six hundred years. At the beginning of it the incomers were pagan and pre-literate tribal groups in conflict with the indigenous Celtic kingdoms and with each other. By the end of it, a yet later group of immigrants, the Scandinavians, had been absorbed and a kingdom of England was in place, supported by the doctrines and the structures of the Christian church. By the end of the period too a substantial body of sophisticated vernacular written literature had been produced, while the admired Latin works of the earlier Anglo-Saxon centuries continued to influence writers of the learned language.

Scholars traditionally distinguish a number of phases in the history of Anglo-Saxon England, each of which differs from the others in significant ways. In the following widely accepted construction four periods are identified, though it should be borne in mind that they mostly overlap with each other and that alternative structurings might also be devised, which would bring out different themes. Before sketching our four phases, I supply a timeline giving some relevant dates in Anglo-Saxon history. At the end of this section I will also include a timeline of dates from the wider early medieval world.

Some significant dates in Anglo-Saxon history

449	Bede's date for beginning of settlement of 'Angles, Saxons and Jutes' in Britain
597	Augustine brings Roman Christianity to Kent
625?	Sutton Hoo ship burial
634	King Oswald invites the Irish monk Aidan from Iona to convert the Northumbrians
657–80	Hild abbess of Whitby; according to Bede, during this period Cædmon composes the first religious poetry in Old English
673–735	Life of Bede
687	Death of Cuthbert, bishop of Lindisfarne
709	Death of Aldhelm
757–96	Offa king of Mercia
782	Alcuin at Charlemagne's court
793	Viking raids begin; sacking of Lindisfarne
851	Danes' first winter in England
871–99	Reign of Alfred king of Wessex; the period of the Alfredian translations and the beginning of the *Anglo-Saxon Chronicle*
878	Alfred defeats the Danes at Edington; Treaty of Wedmore, setting up the 'Danelaw'
937	West Saxon victory under King Athelstan at Brunanburh
950–1015	Approximate dates of the four major Old English poetry codices: Exeter Book, Junius MS, Vercelli Book, *Beowulf* MS
959–75	Reign of Edgar, West Saxon king of all England
959–88	Dunstan archbishop of Canterbury
963–84	Æthelwold bishop of Winchester
978–1016	Reign of Æthelred II ('the Unready')
991	Battle of Maldon
1003–23	Wulfstan archbishop of York
1005–c. 1010	Ælfric abbot of Eynsham
1013	Danish Sweyn acknowledged as king of England
1016–35	Reign of Cnut (Canute)
1042	Edward the Confessor king
1066	Battles of Stamford Bridge and Hastings: William I, 'the Conqueror', king

Migration and after

The early Anglo-Saxon period is the period of the immigration and settlement of Germanic tribes in Britain and of the establishment and consolidation of the structures of Anglo-Saxon power over much of the southern and central part of the island. Extending from the middle of the fifth century to the end of the seventh and later, this is largely a pre-Christian

Fig. 1.1 Sutton Hoo: one of an identical pair of small shoulder clasps (width 5.4 cm), gold with inset garnet and glass, with detachable hinge pin

period and also a period – for the Anglo-Saxons – before written literature; and so by definition we have no literary record for much of the time, though archaeologists have plenty to tell us about the period (see, notably, Hines, ed., 1997). The Sutton Hoo Ship Burial, for example, of probably 625, has been shown to reflect a pre-Christian culture but one that may also be at a point of transition to Christianity (Carver 2000).

The treasures of Sutton Hoo, now among the glories of the British Museum, include many gold artefacts of amazing artistry and craftsmanship, often set with garnet and other fine minerals (see Figure 1.1). These artefacts are executed in styles based on animal and other kinds of interlace and on abstract and geometric patterns. The Sutton Hoo objects and the wealth of other such pieces from early Anglo-Saxon England bear witness to the sophistication of the pre-Christian culture of the early Anglo-Saxon kingdoms, and, just as pre-Christian poetry would influence later literary traditions, their designs and techniques were creatively appropriated and adapted by Christian artists.

There was written literature produced in Britain in this period but it was of Celtic not Anglo-Saxon origin. One of the best-known Latin writings from this time is the Briton Gildas's *On the Ruin and Conquest of Britain* (*c.* 540), which presents the pagan Anglo-Saxon conquest of the Christian Britons as a calamity; later Gildas's book would serve as a source for Bede's *History*, which portrays the Anglo-Saxon colonizers as the rightful inheritors of Britannia. Also related to this period are traditions of vernacular Celtic heroic poetry, of which the most famous example is the *Gododdin*. The *Gododdin*, an elegiac celebration of British resistance against the invaders, survives in a manuscript from much later and is in a later form of the British language (Middle Welsh) but the original may date back to the early seventh century.

Although we have no written Anglo-Saxon records from the time, Old English poetic works written down later, or versions of them, may have existed in some oral form in this early period. And although this was not a Christian period, it was one that later, Christian, Anglo-Saxons would look to respectfully as foundational to their culture. It figured centrally in people's consciousness right down to the closing decades of the Anglo-Saxon age (Howe 1989). The Old English poet of *The Battle of Brunanburh* (ed. Marsden 2004, pp. 86–91), another poem for which, unusually, we can supply a date after which it must have been composed (it commemorates a battle that took place in 937), is one who invokes the arrival of the Anglo-Saxons when he exclaims of the famous battle that the poem celebrates,

> Never until now
> has there been greater slaughter
> on this island, never more people felled before this
> with the sword's edges, since the time when,
> as books tell us, ancient authorities,
> the Angles and the Saxons (*Engle and Seaxe*) landed here,
> sought Britain (*Brytene*) across the broad seas,
> proud warriors and noblemen keen for glory,
> defeated the Welsh (*Wealas*) and seized the land.   (lines 65b–73)

The early centuries of Christian Anglo-Saxon England

The period from 597 to about the second half of the eighth century is the period of the conversion of the Anglo-Saxons to Christianity, the period in which Christian culture takes root and Christian institutional structures are developed and strengthened. The year 597 was when the Roman missionary Augustine and his followers first landed in Kent, sent by Pope Gregory the Great to convert the people; Irish missionaries would arrive in Northumbria a few decades later, led by Aidan. Our indispensable source for this period is Bede's *Ecclesiastical History*, though it is increasingly recognized that the

Fig. 1.2 England in the eighth century

process of conversion must have been more complex than Bede's account, written from a particular point of view, suggests. These centuries constitute an important period in secular politics as well as in religion, with continuing contraction of the area still under British rule and a changing balance of power between the developing Anglo-Saxon kingdoms: in the eighth century Mercia, particularly under the long-lived King Offa, becomes the most powerful kingdom, eclipsing the previously dominant Northumbria. As far as literature is concerned, however, it is the coming of Christianity that is profoundly influential in this period. Christianity brought written literature and it brought learning (see Figure 1.2).

To what extent Christianity transformed the life of ordinary people at this time is a good question (see Blair 2005, pp. 135–81) but the period certainly saw major intellectual developments. The seventh and eighth centuries are when many of the most celebrated works of Anglo-Latin literature were produced. As described in more detail in Chapter 2, three names stand out in particular, that of the Northumbrian Bede, biblical commentator, historian and polymath; that of an earlier figure, the West Saxon Aldhelm (d. 709), erudite spiritual guide and formidable stylist in prose and verse; and that of Alcuin of York (*c.* 735–804), theologian, biblical scholar and prolific letter-writer, and a leading member of the intellectual circle of the emperor Charlemagne in Francia. A substantial body of Latin compositions by other writers was also produced, ranging from saints' lives, books of religious instruction and commentaries on scripture to academic riddles.

Discussing the scholarly resources available in England in this early period, one of today's leading commentators writes, 'Anglo-Saxon libraries were stocked to the point where, for several centuries, they could sustain the schools and scholarship which put England in the vanguard of European learning' (Lapidge 2006, p. 30). A particular focal point of intellectual life in the period was the monasteries of Northumbria, which not only produced impressive literature but also art works of the highest achievement, among which are the Ruthwell Cross, a sculpted high cross with a complex scheme of iconography, and the Lindisfarne Gospels, a manuscript in vibrant colour that stunningly integrates Christian and secular artistic traditions. In the Lindisfarne Gospels animal interlace and other types of exuberant 'insular' patterning are transferred to the page and combined with continental artistic models. Learned and imaginative, Northumbrian monasticism drew upon the influence of Irish traditions and maintained links with Italy, but was itself very much in the intellectual forefront of its day (see Figure 1.3).

With regard to vernacular literature, this appears to have been a rich period poetically, though we have few existing compositions that we can confidently date to it. The seventh century is the century of Cædmon, of course, and some of the extant poems may come from this time: Bede says that many other religious poets came after Cædmon, quite apart from his secular counterparts. A text in runes corresponding to part of *The Dream of the Rood* is carved onto the sides of the Ruthwell Cross (probably from the first half of the eighth century) and a short poem from early Northumbria is attributed by a contemporary to Bede (on the Ruthwell and 'Bede' poems, see below, pp. 38–9 and 33, respectively). Aldhelm too is supposed to have performed oral songs in the vernacular, as a way of attracting crowds before turning to more serious religious matter (see also p. 51, below).

Bede is also reported by his contemporary to have been working on an Old English translation of the first six chapters of the Gospel of John at the time of his death (see Colgrave and Mynors 1969, pp. 582–3), presumably into prose; of this, however, no trace remains. This translation by Bede would antedate surviving Old English literary prose considerably, since the literary

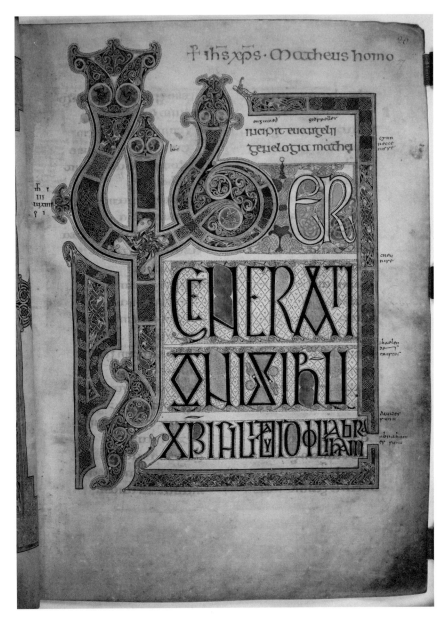

Fig. 1.3 *Liber generationis,* 'The book of the ancestry [of Jesus Christ]' (Matthew I. 1): Lindisfarne Gospels

prose traditions that we know about appear to have their beginnings only in the ninth century. Among prose documents in English that do survive from this early period are laws, the recording of which in writing represents a radical cultural development, from oral to textual. It is significant that this development coincides with the Christianizing of secular authority that marks the post-597 period; the first written laws date from *c.* 614, in Kent. The opening clauses of one of the early law codes, those of King Wihtræd of Kent (695), reflect the extent of the church's political power less than a century after Augustine's arrival: the first two clauses of the code stipulate (trans. Swanton 1993, p. 3):

1. The Church shall have freedom from taxation; and they are to pray for the king, and honour him of their own free will, without compulsion.
2. [Violation of] the Church's protection is to be fifty shillings, like the king's.

Vikings, and the emergence of Wessex

An entry in the *Anglo-Saxon Chronicle*, a collection of annals in Old English covering the whole of the Anglo-Saxon period and beyond, records the beginning of Viking attacks in England and the disturbing portents that preceded the first raid, on a defenceless monastery (trans. Crossley-Holland 1984, p. 39):

> 793 In this year dire portents appeared over Northumbria and sorely frightened the people. They consisted of immense whirlwinds and flashes of lightning, and fiery dragons were seen flying in the air. A great famine immediately followed those signs, and a little after that in the same year, on 8 June, the ravages of heathen men miserably destroyed God's church on Lindisfarne, with plunder and slaughter.

Throughout much of the ninth century and also later, Anglo-Saxons were greatly preoccupied with the threat and the reality of Viking raids and invasion. In 851 the 'great army' arrived, wintering in England for the first time, and by the closing decades of the century the invaders were on the verge of conquering the whole country. Only King Alfred of Wessex held out against them, managing eventually to stem their advance and preserve his own rule, but only at the expense of accepting the setting up of the 'Danelaw', a vast area in the north and east which was administered under Danish law.

The Danelaw reflected the reality of Danish settlement as well as Danish military strength in England; the Scandinavians were feared invaders but many of them were peaceful settlers, who lived alongside and in close relationship with their Anglo-Saxon neighbours, becoming integrated into

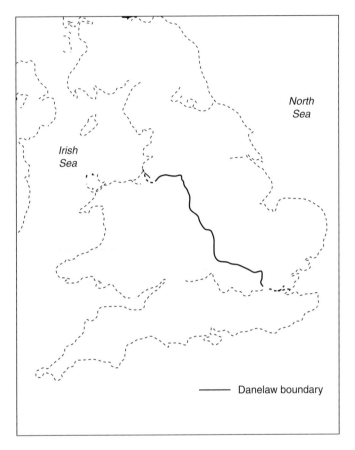

Irish
Sea

North
Sea

——— Danelaw boundary

Fig. 1.4 The Danelaw (boundaries established in 886)

Anglo-Saxon society. The two languages, English and Norse, are thought to have been mutually comprehensible (Townend 2002) and would have co-existed for some time before the Scandinavian settlers adopted English, influencing it permanently in the process with their own linguistic usage. This influence is reflected only minimally in Old English writings because of the stability of English literary conventions in the period, but it comes out strongly in Middle English texts and is still very much apparent in the English language as spoken to this day (see Figure 1.4).

England remained 'partitioned' until well into the following century and the settlement of large numbers of Scandinavians in the Danish area would shape the culture of northern England permanently, but in the tenth century Alfred's successors established their rule over the whole of England, including the Danelaw. A decisive battle occurred at a place called Brunanburh in 937 (as celebrated in a poem mentioned earlier), at which the forces of Wessex, under King Athelstan, defeated a Scandinavian army and secured West Saxon hegemony. It is from this time on that England becomes a reality as a political entity rather than purely as an imagined community. The kingdom of England would, however, have the renewed threat of Scandinavian conquest to face later in the tenth century.

This turbulent period was not a promising one for intellectual and literary activity, with monasteries being despoiled and ecclesiastical life disrupted; and a drop in standards of learning had been perceived even before the effects of the wars with the Danes were being fully felt. Latin cultural life falls away badly in this period and there are few productions either in Latin literature or in art to compare with those of the previous centuries. And yet the later ninth century is one of the most productive periods of all in the history of Old English literature, as it is in this period that vernacular literary prose can be seen to proliferate. The development of Old English literary prose is particularly associated with King Alfred and though other, non-West-Saxon, traditions had also developed in the ninth century (the Old English version of Bede's *History*, for example, seems to have been produced in Mercia rather than Wessex), it is clear that the king was a key influence on and participant in vernacular literary culture at this time. His sponsoring of the English language as a medium for sophisticated literary discourse reflected his commitment to learning and education but must also be seen as stemming from his valuing of the language itself and of the sense of national identity that it expressed for him. We learn from the Latin *Life of King Alfred*, written by his clerical adviser Asser, that the king would learn by heart and recite vernacular poems (ch. 76; trans. Keynes and Lapidge 1983, p. 91). It is Old English prose that Alfred is particularly associated with, however; and indeed, as well as commissioning works from others, he himself engaged in the translation of works in Latin, produced with the help of a group of learned clerics.

Most of the literary products associated with the age of Alfred were translations into English prose. One 'original' prose composition was the *Anglo-Saxon Chronicle*, the first part of which covers the whole of Anglo-Saxon history, in annal form, down to 891; afterwards it would be kept up in various versions until well into the Norman period (a page from a *Chronicle* manuscript is reproduced below, p. 111). While we cannot with certainty link the *Chronicle* to Alfred, it was produced in Wessex in his reign and is strongly 'Alfredian' in outlook, and it is most likely that Alfred commissioned it. In view of Alfred's literary activity he is often referred to as the 'father of English prose'. This large claim on his behalf requires considerable qualification to say the least but he was certainly of great symbolic importance both in the Anglo-Saxon period and later.

Later Anglo-Saxon England: the later tenth and eleventh centuries

The last phase of Anglo-Saxon history was highly productive in literary terms, particularly in English. As has been mentioned previously, we are unable to date most Old English poems with much precision, but we know that the traditions of Old English poetry were still being vigorously maintained in late Anglo-Saxon England, as evidenced by the production of poems which we *are* able to date, by the influence of Old English poetry on prose writers of the time, and by the active transmission of existing poems through manuscript copying. Indeed, the overwhelming majority of surviving Old English poems are preserved, most of them uniquely, in manuscripts that can be dated to the later tenth or early eleventh century, including the four major books that contain most of them (see below, p. 70). It is also the case that most extant manuscripts containing Old English prose belong to the later Anglo-Saxon period as well. This was clearly a period of considerable literary activity and one in which in a sense the promise of the age of Alfred can be seen as at last fulfilled.

Alfred's programme of education and translation was an ambitious one but it seems to have petered out after his death, and the first half of the tenth century, a time of political struggle for hegemony in England, was not a period notable for learning and writing. It is in the second half of the tenth century and later that we get a sudden flowering particularly of religious literature, and this was still going strong when the power bases of Anglo-Saxon culture were shattered by the Normans. Later Anglo-Saxon England is the period of Ælfric, the most prolific vernacular writer of all, of the preacher and purveyor of political thought Wulfstan, archbishop of York (d. 1023), and of a number of other heavyweight named authors (in English and Latin), as well as a host of anonymous ones.

The foundations for much of this literary activity, and certainly for the work of Ælfric, were laid in what is referred to as the 'Benedictine reform' of the second half of the tenth century. As the name implies, the Benedictine reform movement was monastically inspired. Taking its lead from developments on the Continent in the Carolingian period (that of the dynasty of Charlemagne), the movement sought to establish and disseminate, after a period of considerable decline, high monastic, liturgical and pastoral standards in England. The outlook of the reform is to be seen too in the religious art of the period, which contrasts strikingly with that of earlier

Anglo-Saxon England. Later Anglo-Saxon religious art is remarkable for its intellectual and spiritual depth (see, for example, Raw 1997). In it, instead of the exuberance of the emphatically non-classical insular tradition, we see a naturalistic approach to representation, a cultivation of Mediterranean styles of decoration and the adoption of a 'Roman' display script, all of which signal the English church's relationship to the European mainstream, though art, like literature, also develops in distinctively Anglo-Saxon ways. Representative of the art of the period are the image of Christ from 'St Dunstan's Classbook' (see Figure 1.5) and illustrations from a remarkable service-book, the 'Benedictional of St Æthelwold' (see p. 119).

Leadership of the reform is associated particularly with the three dominant ecclesiastical leaders of the time, Dunstan (*c.* 910–88), archbishop of Canterbury (he of the 'Classbook'), Oswald (d. 992), bishop of Worcester and archbishop of York, and Æthelwold (*c.* 905–84), bishop of Winchester (who commissioned the 'Benedictional'); but these three crucially also had the political backing of the powerful King Edgar (943–75; reigned 959–75) – to such an extent indeed that the reform has been described as a 'court-driven' movement (Blair 2005, p. 350).

Ælfric wrote about things eternal but his writings also strongly reflect the times in which he lived, as do those of his contemporary Wulfstan. And, after a period of relative stability under the admired King Edgar, those times were times of political conflict and insecurity. In the reign of the weak Æthelred II (978–1013 and 1014–16) (Æthelred 'the Unready'), Scandinavian attacks resumed with devastating effect. Wulfstan's most famous sermon, the apocalyptic *Sermon of the Wolf to the English*, was written for the English people 'when the Danes persecuted them most, which was in the year 1014 from the Incarnation of our Lord Jesus Christ' (trans. Swanton 1993, p. 178; for the Old English text of the sermon, see Marsden 2004, pp. 209–20). In 1013 the Danish Sweyn briefly became king of England and his son Cnut reigned from 1016 to 1035, later to be followed by his son Harthacnut. Interestingly, however, with Danish rule in England the sky did not fall in. Cnut was seen to conduct himself as a devout Christian king – even going on pilgrimage to Rome in 1027 – and one of his key advisers was the fiery Wulfstan of York. As we are learning in more detail from current scholarship, Scandinavian culture was emphatically represented at the courts of the Danish kings of England, who patronized composers of skaldic verse for example (Townend 2001), but their rule and leadership were integrated into Anglo-Saxon patterns.

The end of Anglo-Saxon culture as politically dominant came not with Danish rule, which ended in 1042 with the accession of the home-grown Edward the Confessor, but with the Norman Conquest of 1066, sweeping aside the existing Anglo-Saxon order both secular and ecclesiastical. Even

Fig. 1.5 St Dunstan's Classbook (mid-tenth century): drawing of St Dunstan kneeling before Christ, with accompanying prayer, both done by Dunstan himself: text (top), 'The picture and the writing on this page seen below is in St Dunstan's own hand'; (bottom), 'I ask you, merciful Christ, to watch over me, Dunstan; may you not allow the Taenarian tempests [tempests of the underworld/hell] to have swallowed me up'.

then, literature in Old English continued to be read and indeed produced throughout the eleventh century and also, intermittently, in the twelfth and even the thirteenth century. The latest surviving Old English poem is either *Durham*, a poem in praise of that city, composed at the beginning of the twelfth century, or, depending whether one classifies its language as Old English or a transitional form of Middle English, *The Grave*, a salutary homiletic piece focusing on the decaying body in the grave, dating from the middle of the twelfth century. We have no fewer than 140 manuscripts from the period 1060 to 1220 containing Old English texts, many of them copied or recycled from pre-Conquest exemplars but some also newly composed. The number of individual Old English texts in these surviving post-Conquest manuscripts has been worked out as being about 800, a stunning figure that prompts a reassessment of the question of when Anglo-Saxon England really ended. The Norman ruling class may not have been studying and reading Old English texts but their subjects were, particularly texts of a religious nature, texts that were needed to cater for the spiritual needs of a population unable to access directly material in Latin or French.

A wider world: some dates in early medieval European history

410	Rome sacked by Goths; Roman legions withdraw from Britain
432	Beginning of St Patrick's mission to Ireland
437	Attila becomes leader of the Huns
493–526	Reign of Theoderic, founder of the Ostrogothic kingdom of Italy
507	Establishment of the Visigothic kingdom of Spain
511	Death of Frankish king Clovis I, who had united the Frankish tribes under one ruler
523	Boethius writes the *Consolation of Philosophy*
537	Dedication of St Sophia church in Constantinople
590–604	Gregory the Great pope
673–8	Muslim siege of Constantinople
711	Beginning of Muslim period in Spain
720	Muslim armies cross the Pyrenees from Spain
734	Image worship condemned by the Greek church (iconoclasm)
771	Accession of Charlemagne as king of the Franks (d. 814)
c. 786	Work begins on the Great Mosque at Cordoba (completed 990)
800	Charlemagne crowned in Rome as Emperor of the West
911	Foundation of Cluny Abbey
912	Norse settlement in Normandy begins
c. 930	Beginning of the period of Cluniac reform in Francia
1096–9	First Crusade

Cædmon's *Hymn*: reading an Old English poem

In this final section of the chapter I wish return briefly to Cædmon's *Hymn*, which we can use to make a few points by way of conclusion. I quote the text of the poem (from Marsden 2004, pp. 80–1) in its West Saxon version (as mentioned above, Cædmon's *Hymn* also survives in the Northumbrian dialect):

> Nu sculon herigean   heofonrices weard,
> meotodes meahte   ond his modgeþanc,
> weorc wuldorfæder,   swa he wundra gehwæs,
> ece Drihten,   or onstealde.
> He ærest sceop   eorðan bearnum
> heofon to hrofe,   halig scyppend;
> þa middangeard   monncynnes weard,
> ece Drihten,   æfter teode
> firum foldan,   frea ælmihtig.

A possible literal translation of this would be:

> Now must we praise (*herigean*) the guardian of the heavenly kingdom,
> the might of the ruler and the purpose of his mind,
> the works (*weorc*) of the father of glory, as (*swa*) he of every wonder,
> the eternal Lord, established the beginning (*or*).
> He first created (*sceop*) for the children of earth
> heaven as a roof, the holy creator;
> then (*þa*) middle-earth the guardian of humankind,
> the eternal Lord, afterwards adorned (*teode*)
> for the people of the earth, the almighty master.

The Old English writing system

With the beginning of written literature in the vernacular in Anglo-Saxon England, scribes adopted the Latin alphabet for Old English texts, on an essentially phonetic basis. Some Old English sounds were not represented in the Latin alphabet, however, and to cater for these some non-Latin letters were used. It is the occurrence of these letters in our texts that makes them look particularly strange to modern beginning readers:

- For the *th* sound (as in Modern English *this* and *thin*) the letters Ð/ð ('eth') and Þ/þ ('thorn') were used; these letters often seem to be used interchangeably in Old English texts: *eorðan, þa* in Cædmon's *Hymn* (but elsewhere we find *eorþan, ða*). Thorn is a letter from the old Germanic runic alphabet, eth is adapted from Latin *d*.

- Old English also made use of an additional vowel, not in the Latin system of sounds, Æ/æ ('ash'), the pronunciation of which falls between *a* and *e*: *æfter*, *ælmihtig*.
- For the sound *w* scribes of Old English texts used the runic letter Ƿ/ƿ ('wyn'): *ƿeard*, *ƿeorc*. By convention, the letter wyn is not used in modern editions of Old English texts, *w* being substituted instead (as with *weard*, *weorc* in our text of Cædmon's *Hymn*). By contrast, thorn, eth and ash are universally used in modern editions.

For a page from a manuscript illustrating the Old English writing system, see Figure 2.5, below (p. 71).
The runic alphabet is briefly discussed and illustrated below, p. 38.

I will give a fuller account of the metrical features of Old English poetry in the next chapter but even from this quotation the structure of the verse stands out clearly, with its strongly differentiated half-lines and each pair of half-lines being bound together by alliteration (in the system of alliteration used in Old English poetry any vowel can alliterate with any other: in line 4, for example, the *e* of *ece* alliterates with the *o* of *or*). Evident here too is a syntactical trait typical of Old English poetry, that of parallelism and apposition, in which phrases in variation with each other create a sense of rhetorical elaboration: in the first sentence four things are identified as the object of praise, forming a series of phrases grammatically parallel or in apposition to each other, and throughout the poem a number of different ways of referring to God provide variation, while also suggesting in an appropriately hymnal manner the breadth of divine power. Variation is facilitated by the wide range of synonyms and near-synonyms that the poetic tradition makes available, with synonyms for God as lord particularly drawn upon in the *Hymn*; and variation is facilitated also by the frequent use of striking compound words (for example, in the *Hymn*, *modgeþanc*, 'mind-purpose', *wuldor-fæder*, 'glory-father'), part of the special vocabulary of Old English poetry. Also illustrated in the passage is the formulaic character of the verse: for example, the phrase *ece Drihten*, 'eternal Lord', appears twice and *heofonrices weard*, 'guardian of the heavenly kingdom', and *monncynnes weard*, 'guardian of humankind', are variants of an underlying formulaic pattern or system; these same phrases are also found widely in other Old English poems.

For Bede, Cædmon's *Hymn* is the result of a wonder: Cædmon has received this 'art of singing' (*canendi artem*), some features of which I sketched in the previous paragraph, and he has received it not by learning it from other poets but spontaneously through the gift of God. The poem itself, a meditation on the beginning of the Book of Genesis, is appropriately about wonder, the wonder of creation and the wonders of creation (*wundra gehwæs*, 'every wonder'), and it *embodies* its theme of creation, being itself the divinely inspired creation of Cædmon.

Cædmon's *Hymn* has been shown to pick up on important issues in theology; in the first sentence, for example, the objects of praise mentioned can be convincingly interpreted as referring to the Trinity, the 'three persons' of God, Father, Son and Holy Spirit. The poem may not be structurally complex in the way that many Old English poems are but it is carefully crafted, following the course of God's work and emphasizing his care for his creation. Notably, it displays interesting and suggestive ambiguity at a number of points. The opening lines could be legitimately construed in a different manner from that reflected in my translation. The translation understands the subject of the opening clause to be *we* even though the pronoun is not expressed: 'Now must [we] praise.' This translation corresponds to Bede's Latin version, which has *laudare debemus*, 'we ought to praise', but the first three lines of the Old English could also be understood to mean 'Now must the works of the father of glory praise the guardian of the heavenly kingdom, the might of the ruler and the purpose of his mind'. The sense can simultaneously be that we must praise God the creator and that his creation must praise him. Another ambiguity comes with *firum foldan* in the last line of the poem: this phrase makes sense as 'for the people of the earth' (as in the translation above), but it could also be taken as parallel to *middangeard*, 'middle-earth' (thus exemplifying variation), in which case the sense would be that the guardian of humankind 'adorned middle-earth, the earth for people'. Audiences in Anglo-Saxon England could have understood the phrase in either way or both ways.

Potential ambiguity is a feature of Old English verse that some poets evidently exploited, a feature that the very light or non-existent punctuation of the manuscripts also facilitated. Ambiguity is sometimes present in prose texts as well but it is particularly in verse that we find it, where it provides richness and depth of meaning. To revert to a point that came up earlier in the chapter, this again makes life difficult for the modern translator and confirms the desirability of engaging with the original text. Even in translation, however, something of the power of the original literature can be got across, and when translation is supplemented with guided quotations in the original, as in the present book, aspects of the subtlety and suggestiveness of the literature can also be brought out (I hope).

Bede celebrates the vernacular poetry of Cædmon. He himself was a scholarly writer of Latin prose and verse. His pupil Cuthbert reports, however, that on his death-bed Bede recited a poem in Old English, noting that he was 'skilled in the art of poetry in our language' (*erat doctus in nostris carminibus*, ed. and trans. Colgrave and Mynors 1969, p. 580). Needless to say, this poem was not 'foolish and trivial'; appropriate to its setting, it is about the soul's departure from the body in death. It is a five-line poem of a single sentence, the sense of which is as follows (for the Old English text, see Marsden 2004, p. 169):

> Before the inevitable journey (*nedfere*, literally 'need-journey') no one
>   will become
> so wise in his mind that there is no need (*þearf*) for him
> to consider, before his going hence (*heonengange*),
> what good or evil (*hwæt godes oþþe yfeles*) may to his soul
> be adjudged after the day of his death.

(This is the West Saxon version: like Cædmon's *Hymn*, Bede's *Death Song* exists in Northumbrian and West Saxon versions, with some variation between the versions.)

Did Bede compose the *Death Song* himself? Perhaps he did, though Cuthbert doesn't quite say so; he could have being reciting a poem he knew. Whether Bede was the composer of the poem or not, it is interesting that the last composition associated with him brings him and Cædmon strikingly together. In these two figures, regarded as foundational by later Anglo-Saxons (and by modern Anglo-Saxonists), the Latin and vernacular traditions of Anglo-Saxon culture intersect in crucial ways.

Postscript: what's in a name?: Anglo-Saxons, Anglo-Saxon and Old English

This book follows the long-established convention of using the term 'Anglo-Saxon' to refer to that period in English history stretching from the first settlement of the Germanic tribes in Britain in the fifth century down to the Norman Conquest of 1066. The composite adjective is a convenient one, though it is also one that, as Susan Reynolds points out in a seminal article published in 1985, 'invites us to beg questions and confuse our own ideas with those of the period we study' (Reynolds 1985, p. 414). The word 'Anglo-Saxon' is widely current in popular usage today, with connotations stretching from the colloquial ('Anglo-Saxon' being a term for speech that is plain, unvarnished and even crude) to the ethnological (aspects of which are further refined in the term 'WASP', for example); as described below (pp. 176–8), in nineteenth- and twentieth-century 'Anglo-Saxonism' the pre-Norman period and its people, wrongly imagined as an ethnically pure group, were appropriated for racialist purposes in Britain and America. It should be added that, as well as 'Anglo-Saxon', the term 'English' used at the beginning of this paragraph begs a few questions as well – notably: when does 'English' history begin?

Forms like *Angli Saxones* began to be used from the ninth century, mostly by continental writers, to distinguish the Saxons who had settled in Britain from those still living east of the Rhine. Among the descendants of the settlers themselves, the compound was never widely in use: Latin *Angli* (Old English *Englisc*) was the norm in the period as the collective adjective/noun for the whole 'English' population, a formulation that generalized the meaning of a word which referred originally to one perceived group among the immigrants, the northern Angles, while the term *Saxones* (Old English *Seaxe*) continued to be used to refer specifically to the inhabitants of the southern kingdoms. As Reynolds notes, the name *Angli Saxones* (and variants) was adopted in their titles by some West Saxon kings, who were 'perhaps using such forms to help them build bridges towards parts of the country that were, or had once been thought of as, quintessentially Angle', but the usage 'had become rare by the later tenth century' (Reynolds 1985, p. 398). Reynolds is thinking of instances such as King Alfred styling himself *Angul-Saxonum rex*, 'king of the Anglo-Saxons', and King Athelstan referring to himself as *Ongol-Saxna cyning*, 'king of the Anglo-Saxons'; such usages are not widely found, however. It is likely that Bede's use of the term *Angli* in the generalized sense, as in our passage about Cædmon, was influential in its widespread adoption in later usage (Wormald 1994).

The compound name (never common) dropped out of use and it did not reappear until it was adopted by the antiquarians of the early modern period who began to study early English history and literature. The terms 'English Saxon' and 'Anglo-Saxon' are found from the beginning of the seventeenth century as referring to the people living in England before the Norman Conquest, with the form 'Anglo-Saxon' soon gaining ascendancy. From the early seventeenth century 'English-Saxon' and 'Anglo-Saxon' also began to be used to refer to the *language* of the pre-Conquest period, first adjectivally, as in one of the citations given in the *New English Dictionary/ Oxford English Dictionary* – 'Folc, the English-Saxon word for people' (1605) – and then it was also used as a noun, so that in the eighteenth and nineteenth centuries 'Anglo-Saxon' was the commonest name for the language. By the end of the nineteenth century, however, 'Old English' had almost entirely displaced 'Anglo-Saxon' in this sense. At a time when modern humanities subjects were defining and establishing themselves, the adoption of the name 'Old English' reflected the desire of scholars to view the language of the Anglo-Saxons as part of English. In the first volume of the *New English Dictionary* (1888) James Murray, while recording instances of 'Anglo-Saxon' being used as the name of the language, writes that the *Dictionary* itself 'uses Old English not Anglo-Saxon to refer to the language'. The issue of the name was part of larger ideological and political debates in the academic world, a legacy of which is that today Anglo-Saxon literary studies are normally pursued in university English departments. Note, however, the continuing (unique) existence of a Department of Anglo-Saxon, Norse and Celtic at the University of Cambridge (on the establishment of the department, see Frantzen 2001, pp. 478–9).

The use of the term 'Old English' for the language of the Anglo-Saxons has long been uncontentious and the present usage is likely to remain normal practice in the future. Language politics live on, however, and even 'Old English' can be seen as something of a loaded term. Recently the suggestion has been made that Old English should be called something else. Specifically, since Old English is just as much the ancestor of modern Scots as of modern English, it has been asked whether scholars might not think of devising a name for the language that did not include the ostensibly privileging word 'English' (Scott 2007). We would be unwise to hold our breath waiting for such a change of nomenclature but this suggestion raises an interesting point about language perception and ownership. What's in a name? Often a great deal.

Chapter 2

Developing literary traditions

Old English poetry and its oral Germanic background

The arrival of settlers from parts of what is today north Germany and Denmark in Britain in the fifth century was part of a larger pattern of migration of Germanic tribes in late Roman and post-Roman western Europe. In the fifth and sixth centuries Germanic tribes, sharers in common social and cultural values and speakers of varieties of what in prehistoric times had been a single language, moved out from east of the Rhine and from Scandinavia and conquered many areas of the Empire, transforming the political landscape in the process. The Romans had already had military dealings with Germanic tribes in previous centuries and indeed our earliest account of Germanic culture comes from a Roman writer of the beginning of the second century, Tacitus, in his ethnographic work *Germania* (trans. Mattingly 1970). Tacitus, drawing an implicit contrast with his own world, which he perceived to be decadent, presents the Germanic tribes as fierce but virtuous barbarians, socially cohesive and with strong bonds of group loyalty. He was not writing about Anglo-Saxons in those days, of course, but Tacitus's account, when carefully sifted, throws some light on values that the colonizers of Britain would have embraced.

In a modern myth of origins nationalists today fondly, if simplistically, look back to this migration period as the time when the Europe of nations has its beginnings (Geary 2002), and this period was idealized too by Anglo-Saxons and other Germanic people in the early Middle Ages. They saw the fourth to sixth centuries as a heroic age and their secular poetry focuses on these centuries as a time of legendary exploits and epic conflicts. Poetry memorializing this time seems to have been composed in England throughout the Anglo-Saxon period – none of it, incidentally, set in Britain – and we have survivals of other traditions of Germanic poetry in Old High German and in Old Norse, the latter of which was still going in the thirteenth century. In all such traditions we see a heroic world displayed, in which the centre of attention is the lord and his retainers, bound together by ideals of reciprocal loyalty, seeking glory and praise on the battlefield and acting out their social life in the context of the hall, the scene of feasting and drinking and of gift-giving.

Most of the migrating Germanic tribes eventually ended up speaking the established languages of the areas in which they settled. The Anglo-Saxons, however, not only replaced existing power structures in the parts of Britain that they conquered but they also dominated linguistically. Scholars debate the question of how many Anglo-Saxons came to Britain in the fifth century and also to what extent the incomers interacted with the Britons (see, e.g., Hills 2003, Brooks 2006) but it is notable that, apart from place-names, only a handful of British (Celtic) words were borrowed into the language of the settlers, perhaps less than a dozen altogether: examples still in use in English are *bin*, *brock* ['badger'] and *crag*. The few loan words from Celtic were introduced alongside more numerous borrowings from Latin in the time before and during the settlement period, borrowings reflective of the influence of Roman cultural sophistication (Latin words introduced into Germanic in this early period include such examples, still current in English, as *wine, pepper, copper* and *mile*). In what was assuredly an ethnically mixed Britain in the early Middle Ages (see Figure 2.1), the minimal influence of Celtic on Old English is an indication of the autonomy of Anglo-Saxon language and culture. The Anglo-Saxons did not assimilate themselves to indigenous cultural practices as happened elsewhere in Europe, bringing instead a new beginning in much of lowland Britain based on their own culture. Their word for the Celtic inhabitants of Britain was *wealh*, 'Welsh', the basic meaning of which is 'foreign, slave'.

The culture that they brought was one of what has been called 'primary orality' (Goody and Watt 1968). In the world in which the early Anglo-Saxons lived, tradition, knowledge, belief and law were normally transmitted

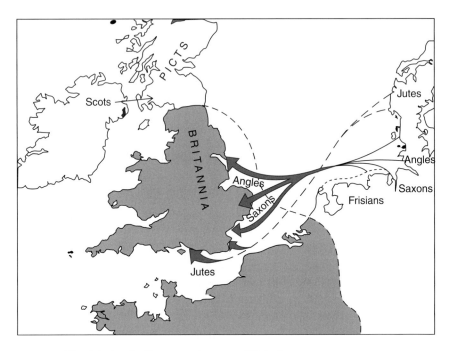

Fig. 2.1 Anglo-Saxon settlement of Britain

entirely by word of mouth, remembered and uttered. Some groups among the early Anglo-Saxons did make use of a writing system, runes, but runic writing represented rare esoteric knowledge; it was known to the few and employed for restricted purposes that did not include the extensive inscription of literary texts. Runes were used for epigraphical statements of commemoration and ownership and perhaps in magic rituals (Page 1999). Later, runic letters would be incorporated into manuscript texts, and one Old English poem, the poem of the cross on the Ruthwell Cross, is carved in runes, but the culture of the early Anglo-Saxons was essentially oral (see Figure 2.2).

The English 'futhork', runic alphabet, called after its first six letters

ᚠ ᚾ ᚦ ᚨ ᚱ ᚲ
f   u   þ   o   r   k

Note the angular character of the letters, which are suitable for carving on wood, stone and bone. Reflective of this kind of writing, the etymological meaning of the Old English verb *writan*, 'write', is 'cut, score' (incidentally, the verb 'to read', *rædan*, has the general meaning 'decide, guess, interpret', and is related to *rædels*, 'riddle, interpretation').

Fig. 2.2 Runes on the west face of the Ruthwell Cross: the top line and beginning of the right side reads + *Crist wæs on rodi*, 'Christ was on the cross'

In a world of primary orality, as explained by Eric Havelock with reference to early Greece, poetry performs a vital social function, 'that of preserving the tradition by which [the members of the society] lived and instructing them in it' (Havelock 1986, p. 8), and the poet is an important figure. In Old English the oral poet is referred to as the *scop* and his primary place of performance is in the aristocratic hall, where he entertains the lord and his family and followers. In the great hall Heorot in *Beowulf*, for example, there is the 'clear song of the *scop*', *swutol sang scopes* (line 90a).

With the coming of Christianity, written literature would develop in Anglo-Saxon England, introducing new literary forms but also adapting existing tradition to new purposes (as we saw in the story of Cædmon). While it is thought that most surviving Old English poetry is literate rather than oral in composition, it is all underlain by oral characteristics inherited from the pre-literate era and actively maintained; and indeed oral features of Old English poetry can be seen to have influenced other literary traditions, most evidently Old English prose. Old English poetry moves beyond the performance of the *scop* in the hall but it retains structural and stylistic essentials that derive from its original non-textual context.

A passage in *Beowulf* (ed. Klaeber 2008, lines 867b–74a) shows us a *scop* in action, spontaneously composing a poem in honour of Beowulf's victory over the monster Grendel. The passage depicts orality and, like all Old English poetry, itself reflects features distinctive of oral tradition:

> At times a thegn of the king,
> a man laden with eloquence, mindful of songs (*gidda gemyndig*),
> who remembered a multitude of stories
> from the whole range of ancient tradition, found new words,
> properly bound together (*soðe gebunden*). The man began again
> artfully to treat of Beowulf's exploit
> and successfully (*on sped*) to relate an apt tale,
> to vary his words (*wordum wrixlan*).

Old English poetry: metre and alliteration

The basic building block of Old English poetic composition is the **half-line**, which consists metrically of two heavily stressed syllables (represented below by the symbol '/') plus a variable number of unstressed syllables (represented below by 'x'); in some lines lightly stressed syllables (represented below by '\') also occur. The heavily stressed syllables are referred to as 'lifts', while each group of one or more unstressed syllables is known as a 'dip'. A half-line consists therefore of two lifts and two dips.

There are five variant metrical structures for the Old English half-line (the 'Sievers Five Types', called after the nineteenth-century scholar who identified them). Poets do not like to use the same type in successive half-lines. The five types are:

Type A, or 'falling rhythm' (/ x / x): *wordum wrixlan* (*Beowulf*, line 874a: 'to vary his words')

Type B, or 'rising rhythm' (x / x /): *hwilum cyninges þegn* (*Beowulf*, line 867b: 'at times a thegn of the king')

Type C, 'clashing rhythm' (x / / x): *ond on sped wrecan* (*Beowulf*, line 873a: 'and successfully to relate')

Type D, or 'falling by stages' (/ / \ x): *þeod-cyninga* (*Beowulf*, line 2a: 'of the people-kings')

Type E, or 'fall and rise' (/ \ x /): *monncynnes weard* (Cædmon's *Hymn*, line 7b: 'guardian of humankind')

These are the main patterns but note that minor variations are allowable within types D and E; there are also rules which allow one or even two unstressed syllables to come before the start of type A or D verses (such syllables being called *anacrusis*).

The metrical rules look complicated in the abstract but they have been internalized by Old English poets and give them scope to generate new lines in composition. As a way of encapsulating the five types, readers might note the following mnemonic (from Mitchell and Robinson 2001, p. 165):

Anna angry: / x / x (A)
And Byrhtnoth bold: x / x / (B)
In keen conflict: x / / x (C)
Ding down strongly: / / \ x (D)
Each one with edge: / \ x / (E)

And in Old English poems we occasionally find passages of 'hypermetric' verse, introduced for special effect, with three instead of two stressed syllables in each half-line.

The Old English 'full' poetic line consists of two half-lines, 'a' and 'b', with a distinct caesura between them (indicated by extra spacing in modern editions):

ond on sped wrecan spel gerade (*Beowulf*, line 873)
[and successfully to relate an apt tale]

Both half-lines making up the full line are bound together by **alliteration**: the sound at the beginning of the first stressed syllable of the second half-line (the 'b' half-line) is always the alliterating one. This syllable can alliterate with the first or the second stressed syllable of the first half line (the 'a' half-line):

*ond on **s**ped wrecan **s**pel gerade*
(here the first stressed syllable of the 'a' half-line alliterates)

*Nu sculon **h**erigean **h**eofonrices weard* (Cædmon's *Hymn*, line 1)
[Now must we praise the guardian of the heavenly kingdom]
(here the second stressed syllable of the 'a' half-line alliterates)

Sometimes (though rarely) both stressed syllables of the first half-line alliterate:

*guma **g**ilphlæden, **g**idda gemyndig* (*Beowulf*, line 868)
[a man laden with eloquence, mindful of songs]

Alliteration can be vocalic as well as consonantal; in vocalic alliteration any vowel alliterates with any other:

*ece Drihten, **o**r onstealde* (Cædmon's *Hymn*, line 4)
[the eternal Lord, the beginning established]

As well as referring to the poet's role as the preserver and transmitter of tradition, our passage from *Beowulf* highlights aspects of his technique of composition – properly binding words together, relying on artfulness and skill, and varying his words. The oral poet has internalized a poetic metre, grammar and vocabulary that enable him to generate new compositions ('new words') in performance and that facilitate memorization. As touched on in my first chapter, the metre combines rule-governed patterns of stressed and unstressed syllables with structural alliteration that 'properly binds together' each pair of half-lines into a full line; the grammar of Old English poetry includes distinctive syntactical patterns but in a wider sense the 'grammar' also involves the use of traditional verbal formulas and formula systems providing phrases that are not only ready-made but also bring with them richness of association and connotation; the vocabulary incorporates words not found in prose and includes a range of synonyms and near-synonyms that allow the same idea to be fitted into different alliterative and formulaic contexts: as well as the prosaic words *mann* and *wer*, for example, Old English poetry has a number of poetic words for 'man', including *beorn*, *eorl* (used in a more restrictive sense in prose), *guma*, *hæleð*, *rinc* and *secg*. The poetry is also rich in compound nouns and adjectives, including kennings (allusive metaphorical phrases); examples of compound words in our passage from *Beowulf* are *gilphladen*, 'laden with eloquence', and *ealdgesegena*, 'ancient tradition' (literally, 'things anciently said').

Grammar and vocabulary are coordinated in patterns of variation and apposition through which the poet is able 'successfully to relate an apt tale'. Such patterns give the verse a highly wrought quality, allowing effects of cumulation and recapitulation to be created, as in the opening sentence of our *Beowulf* passage, which begins with a string of different descriptive phrases referring to the poet who sings in praise of Beowulf. Variation, cumulation and repetition also have the purpose of helping the audience to follow the verse in a performance context. To aid comprehension oral verse has to be stylistically 'copious', with plenty of cues for the audience, an additive syntax and no information overload (Ong 1982, pp. 41–57; see further Magennis 2001, pp. 91–5).

Variation and apposition

The syntax of Old English poetry is one which in weaving patterns of apposition, parallelism, recapitulation and juxtaposition exploits grammatical characteristics of the Old English language. In Old English (unlike Present Day English), word endings rather than, or as well as, word order indicate the relationship between words in a sentence and so there is greater flexibility in placing words and phrases in relation to each other and in constructing interweaving patterns of grammatically related phrases. In our passage on the *scop* in *Beowulf* note the line *guma gilphlæden, gidda gemyndig* (line 868), which provides further description of the 'king's thegn'; the line consists of two phrases in apposition to *cyninges þegn*, with further elaboration coming in the relative clause of the following line and a half; at the end of the passage *wordum wrixlan* is similarly in apposition to *on sped wrecan spel gerade*.

Another poem that presents an image of the *scop* is *Widsith* (trans. Alexander 2008, pp. 105–12). In it we meet a poet, the eponymous Widsith, who is rewarded for his performances in the halls of great men. The beginning of the poem introduces a speech by Widsith (lines 1–4a), with an accompanying account of his life and travels as a *scop*:

> Widsith spoke, unlocked his word-hoard,
> he who among men travelled through most tribes,
> peoples over the earth; often on the floor of the hall
> he received a splendid treasure.

The opening line of this passage, *Widsið maðolade, wordhord onleac*, itself illustrates characteristic qualities of the language of the traditional oral poet, with its formulaic quality and its poetic vocabulary, all of which aid fluency of expression. The verb *maðolade*, 'spoke', is a poetic word which serves as a formulaic way of introducing a speech. It occurs in its past-tense-singular form forty-four times in the surviving Old English poetic corpus, always introducing a speech. It is invariably the second word of its line, the first word always being its grammatical subject, normally a name, and the second half of the line always providing a variation on the first, usually a reformulation of the name, though in *Widsith* it is the verb that is varied. The verb phrase *wordhord onleac*, 'unlocked his word-hoard/treasure-chest of words', is also formulaic, appearing in identical form in four other occurrences, always as a second half-line; and *wordhord* is a distinctively poetic word, a compound noun and, more specifically, a kenning, the metaphorical meaning of which is clarified by the accompanying verb.

The language of the *scop* is 'copious', allowing a competent audience to process it in a performance context, but it is also elaborate and specialized, providing poets with the resources to exercise their craft not only spontaneously but also with virtuosity. The language of Old English poetry has been referred to as 'almost … a language within a language' (Alexander 1966, p. 11); one recent commentator on Old English poetic syntax even goes as far as to declare, 'For the Anglo-Saxons, the language of poetry may have been something analogous to a foreign language or a second native language, which they had to learn separately from their "first" language' (Momma 1997, p. 193).

In Anglo-Saxon England textuality changed the way poetry could be composed: some surviving poems were clearly composed by poets working from books, and some incorporate visual features of layout and design that call to be appreciated on the page. And textuality changed the way poetry was experienced. The poems *Beowulf* and *Widsith*, from which I have quoted, exist as texts in manuscripts of course – to be read, or read out. They preserve the fiction of the poet speaking directly to an audience, as is seen strikingly at the very beginning of *Beowulf* (lines 1–3) with its famous call to attention, *Hwæt*, 'Listen, behold', its communal use of first-person pronoun (*we*) and its appeal to orality (*gefrunon*, 'have heard'):

> Hwæt, we Gar-Dena   in geardagum
> þeodcyninga   þrym gefrunon,
> hu ða æþelingas   ellen fremedon.

> Listen, we have heard in former days
> of the glory (*þrym*) of the kings of the people (*þeodcyninga*)
>   of the Spear-Danes (*Gar-Dena*: emphatically placed in line 1),
> how the noblemen accomplished [deeds of] valour (*ellen*).

But it is not literally the *Beowulf*-poet that most Anglo-Saxon audiences would hear but some reader, and the poem could also be read privately. In *Widsith* the framing narration is impersonal and most of the poem consists of a speech by Widsith – but who is it who tells us that Widsith spoke, and when is this figure imagined as speaking?

Textuality moves the composition and reception of literature to a different level from that of a purely oral world. This is a move that we see fascinatingly illustrated in the development of Old English poetry. In the next sections I wish to consider the textual aspect of literature in Anglo-Saxon England; in concluding the present section I would only emphasize again that the textual Old English poetry that we study today all has its origin and basis in the oral tradition that the Anglo-Saxons migrants brought with them to Britain in the first place and subsequently developed. The alliterative stress-based metre of the passages we have looked at is ubiquitous in the poetry, as is the repertoire of lexical and grammatical features that we have seen, including crucially the enabling framework of formulaic language. Old English poetry is creative and original but it is also highly traditional in essential respects.

Writings in Latin

The coming of Latin literacy to Anglo-Saxon England with Christian missionaries at the end of the sixth century and in the subsequent period represented the beginning of a change from oral to textual culture. Oral culture continued, of course, alongside and interacting with textual culture but Anglo-Saxons became people 'of the book', acquiring the technologies of book production and developing book-based literary traditions. In the first instance such literary traditions were in the medium of Latin and were decidedly learned in character. Latin literature would continue to be produced in England throughout the Anglo-Saxon period, alongside the traditions of vernacular writing that became established later. The present section sets out to provide an overview of writings in Latin, with reference to their linguistic and cultural contexts, and identifying key aspects of their style. It highlights in particular the works of Aldhelm, Bede and Alcuin, and notes their influence on a range of later writers.

The Christian missionaries to England brought a rich heritage of Latin literature with them and they also brought knowledge of Greek (Lapidge 1988): one of the early archbishops of Canterbury was the biblical scholar Theodore of Tarsus (602–90), whose learned writings in Latin reflect his training in the traditions of Greek scholarship associated with the famous school of Antioch. Knowledge of Greek never became widespread in Anglo-Saxon England but an interest in arcane Greek-derived vocabulary is evident in much of the Latin writing produced throughout the period. Greek was also studied later by some scholars on the Continent in the Carolingian period, again influencing Latin vocabulary. Latin grammar and rhetoric and Latin vocabulary, the latter transmitted in elaborate glossaries as well as through literary texts, were taught in monastic schools in England from the beginning of the conversion period and Anglo-Latin texts of considerable sophistication were being produced from the seventh century onwards. One of Theodore's pupils at Canterbury was the brilliant Aldhelm, a descendant of the royal house of Wessex.

Before I turn to specific Anglo-Latin writers, one feature concerning the development of Latin literature in Anglo-Saxon England worth emphasizing from the start is that (as in early Christian Ireland) the Latin language had to be learned there as a foreign language. This was not the case in the areas of the Continent from which the missionaries to England had come or in the Christian centres of learning in the former territories of the Roman Empire with which the Anglo-Saxons would interact over the centuries. On the Continent the Latin of antiquity gradually evolved and separated into the 'Romance' languages of French, Italian, Spanish and so on, but it is recognized that throughout the early medieval period a single speech community still existed in the Romance-speaking world, with regional variation in pronunciation and grammar but an underlying perceived unity across much of Europe. Writing in Latin was thought to represent a formal and 'polished' form of the spoken language and was accessible to the population through being read aloud to them by trained readers who made the formal language comprehensible to their local audiences by pronouncing it so that it could be understood. One leading scholar of early Romance speech goes so far as to insist that translation from Latin into Romance languages begins only in the twelfth century: 'Translations did not occur before, because Latin had not existed separately as a different system from ordinary spoken Romance. A complex but monolingual Romance was all that had existed before' (Wright 1997, p. 27). In England, on the other hand, it was only through translation that most people could gain access to textual culture and indeed to the life of the church, whose liturgies and written teachings were in Latin; it was only through translation, or through learning Latin.

Since Latin was a foreign language to the Anglo-Saxons their approach to it inevitably had a distinctly school-based foundation and there was an emphasis on correct grammar and – a particularly alien idea on the Continent – on correct pronunciation. The erudite Northumbrian churchman Alcuin of York introduced the Anglo-Saxon approach to Latin to the Carolingian world in the late eighth century in his educational role at the court of Charlemagne, attempting to impose new rules of correctness on his Frankish contemporaries. Alcuin's reforms had mixed results but his intervention and that of other Germanic speakers may be seen as contributing to the emerging perception throughout Europe of 'medieval Latin' as a distinct language on its own, separate from the 'vulgar' forms with which it co-existed (Wright 1997, pp. 24–5).

In England, Latin was always a separate, acquired, language anyway. Its academic aspect is apparent in Anglo-Latin style, whether (as we shall see) in the studied obscurities and convolutions of Aldhelm and his successors or in the more restrained gracefulness of Bede and Alcuin. And symptomatic of the perception of Latin as a language studied in the schoolroom is a widespread interest among Anglo-Latin writers and readers in texts that are clever and ingenious, reflected, for example, in a fondness for acrostics and a cultivation of abstruse vocabulary.

The interest in ingenuity in Anglo-Latin writings comes out particularly in the *enigmata*, or riddles, that became something of a speciality among writers of the seventh and eighth centuries and that later would influence vernacular poetry as well, as would other academic aspects of Anglo-Latin literature. Following the example of the late-classical poet Symphosius, there developed a tradition in England of composing collections of metrical riddles, characterized by a learned allusiveness and by clever effects, and sometimes also incorporating acrostic letter patterns. The *enigmata* of Symphosius had basically been playful entertainments – literary 'trifles', as he referred to them – but the Anglo-Saxon ones have a serious religious purpose, expressing theological teaching and emphasizing the diversity of God's creation. Within the collections, patterns of relationship are apparent between the objects described, and a sense of the wonder and complexity of the world is conveyed. Aldhelm instigated the tradition of riddle writing in England, producing a collection of a hundred *enigmata*, and he was followed in the genre by Tatwine, Eusebius, Boniface and other Anglo-Saxon writers (Salvador 2005). In the preface to his collection Aldhelm offers up his *enigmata* to God, through whose aid he is able 'to reveal by Your decree the hidden mysteries of things through my verse' (trans. Lapidge and Rosier 1985, p. 70).

A short sequence of *enigmata* by Aldhelm

(note that the 'answer' is supplied by Aldhelm at the beginning of each piece)
LXXXVII. *Shield*
From the trunk of the willow-tree and from the shaved hide of an ox I am constituted, ready to undergo the bloody encounters of battle. I shall always protect the body of my bearer with my own body, so that Orcus [i.e. the underworld] will not snatch away his life. What (other) warrior sustains such great misfortunes or so many deadly wounds in battle?
LXXXVIII. *Serpent*
More cunning than all other creatures that breathe the air of the atmosphere [cf. Genesis III.1], I scattered the seeds of death far and wide through the world, whence a terrible crop grew up with its deadly harvest, which the Fornicator [i.e. the devil] reaps for wicked purposes with his evil scythe. I greatly fear encounters with the antlered stag. In old age I shall be deprived of my aged skin and once again I shall carry on, sustained with new-found youth.
LXXXIX. *Book-cupboard*
Now my inwards are filled with holy words, and all my entrails support sacred books. And yet I am unable to learn anything from them. Unfortunately, I am deprived by fate of such a gift, since the deadly Parcae [i.e. the Fates] take away the illumination (which) books (provide).
(trans. Lapidge and Rosier 1985, p. 89)

Bede

Bede's elegant prose style is modelled on that of the best ancient authors, particularly Cicero, as learned in the schoolroom. A sense of Bede's carefully constructed sentences in the classical mode is apparent, even in translation, in the passage in the closing chapter of his *Ecclesiastical History*, where he sums up what he has done in the work:

> This account of the history of the church in Britain have I, Bede,
> servant of Christ and priest of the monastery of St Peter and St Paul
> which is at Wearmouth and Jarrow, put together with the help of God
> and to the best of my ability insofar as I was able to glean it either from
> ancient documents or from tradition or from my own knowledge.
>
> (V, 24; trans. Colgrave and Mynors 1969, p. 567 [modified])

The clauses here are balanced, with elaborate use of modifying material, the phrasing is measured, and the elements of the sentence are integrated in an overall unity that sweeps the reader forward.

Bede was a composer of verse as well as prose. He produced a book on the art of metre but he also practised that art himself in an accomplished way, his largest-scale verse composition being a metrical life of St Cuthbert. He also incorporated into the *Ecclesiastical History* a verse composition in praise of St Etheldreda, and a poem on Judgement Day has been attributed to him.

In *De die iudicii*, 'Judgement Day' (ed. Hurst 1955, pp. 439–44), written in hexameters (and later to be paraphrased in an Old English version), the writer draws upon traditional Latin motifs to develop the theme of the necessity for repentance in the face of the coming judgement of God. The opening lines introduce a pensive speaker in a beautiful setting, a conventional *locus amoenus*, 'lovely place', of the kind that Bede has encountered in late antique poetry:

> While among the flowery grasses of the fertile sward
> under the covering of a shade-giving tree, I sat sorrowfully alone,
> with the boughs everywhere resounding to the blowing of the wind,
> suddenly I was overcome by a bitter lament.   (lines 1–4)

The Etheldreda poem, consisting of 54 lines in classical elegiac metre, is a skilful piece of work but comes across as a mannered exercise rather than a profound poetic engagement with its subject. Its 'abecedarian' format (with each couplet beginning with a succeeding letter of the alphabet) allows Bede to show off his competence as a versifier and displays an interest in ingenuity that, as we have seen, represents a widely found characteristic of writing in Anglo-Latin.

Bede is best known to modern readers, of course, for his *Ecclesiastical History*, a prose work tracing in detail the course of Anglo-Saxon history from the time of the settlement down to his own day, with particular emphasis on his native Northumbria and (as brought out in the title) on the growth of the English church. I will return to it in more detail in a later chapter. The *Ecclesiastical History* was also much read in the early Middle Ages, as were the other historical and hagiographical writings (writings about saints) that he produced. He was even better known, however, for his books on scientific and pedagogic subjects (including Latin metre), much of it intended to be of practical use to monastic readers, and above all for his authoritative homilies and commentaries on Scripture, of which he composed a considerable number. Bede, who spent his whole life from childhood at the remote twin monastery of Wearmouth-Jarrow, became regarded throughout western Christendom as one of the great 'fathers' of the church, his interpretations of biblical books being studied down the centuries. We saw in the first chapter that vernacular compositions were also attributed to him.

Alcuin

Alcuin too was a prolific writer and an influential one, though most of his works were produced not in England but on the Continent, where he spent much of his career. His elegant writings, like Bede's following classical models (Brown 2008), consist of more than 200 letters, a wide range of poems, books of biblical exegesis, saints' lives, homiletic and theological material and educational works, and he was also one of the most important textual scholars of the Latin Bible of the entire Middle Ages, producing a major revision of the 'Vulgate' text that included not only the removal of errors in its transmission but also the correction of some of the phrasing of the great translator Jerome himself (Loewe 1969, pp. 133–9). Such was Alcuin's significance to the intellectual and ecclesiastical life of early medieval Europe that he has been called the 'architect of the "Carolingian Renaissance"' (Lapidge 1986, p. 23).

The passage from Alcuin most widely quoted today, his condemnation of the performance of secular poetry as entertainment for a bishop at dinner, combines polished rhetorical embellishment with moral fervour:

> Let God's words be read at the dinner-table of the ordained. It is right that a reader should be heard, not a harpist, patristic discourses, not pagan song. What has Hinield to do with Christ? The house is narrow and has no room for both. The heavenly king does not wish to have communion with pagan and forgotten kings listed name by name; for the eternal King reigns in Heaven, while the forgotten pagan king wails in Hell. The voices of readers should be heard in your dwellings, not the laughing rabble in the courtyards.   (trans. Bullough [modified] 1993, p. 124)

In the exclamation 'What has Hinield to do with Christ' (Hinield, or Ingeld, being a heroic figure who is mentioned in *Beowulf*), the passage even contains a clever and apt allusion to a famous quotation from a work of Jerome, 'What has Horace to do with the Psalter, Vergil with the gospels, Cicero with the Apostle [Paul]?' The disapproving reference to Cicero and other classical writers has ironic overtones given the Ciceronianism of both Jerome and Alcuin.

Alcuin was also a composer of Latin verse following the best ancient models. In his cultivation of classical metre and style he again places himself in the tradition of Bede, whom he referred to as his 'father'. He wrote larger-scale pieces but something of the sophisticated quality of his poetry comes out in his short poem 'Versus de cuculo', 'Cuckoo', which, while containing a moral message about drunkenness, urbanely displays elegant conceits and Vergilian allusions. The speaker laments the absence of the young man 'Cuckoo', who has allowed himself to get caught in the 'destructive whirlpool' of Bacchus:

> Only 'Cuckoo' is absent. Who, I ask, nourishes him?
> Alas, badly, in my opinion, does Bacchus, that impious one,
>   nourish him,
> he whose evil desire is to subvert all hearts.
> Lament now for 'Cuckoo', lament now all for 'Cuckoo'.   (lines 30–3)

Here the classical metre and style give expression to a sentiment that is delicately homoerotic, as comes out notably in Alcuin's use of a pet name for his young disciple.

Aldhelm

Aldhelm was another prolific writer in prose and verse. He wrote on poetry and metre but most of his works are explicitly religious in their subject matter. These works are remarkable stylistically for the highly wrought, ostentatiously learned quality of the writing. Aldhelm's Latin is not only correct and polished (like Bede's and Alcuin's); it is also characterized by its difficulty and its dazzling virtuosity. His vocabulary is self-consciously obscure and recondite, his rhetoric is mannered and his prose sentences are bewilderingly intricate – and lengthy. From today's perspective Aldhelm's writings, particularly the prose, can easily look pedantic and grandiloquent but they impressed his contemporaries, as they were designed to do, and key aspects of his style were enduringly influential not only in Anglo-Saxon England but further afield. As Andy Orchard puts it with specific reference to England, 'The influence of Aldhelm's prose style on later Anglo-Latin is profound and unsurpassed, while in the field of verse his influence is still more extensive, and it would be fair to say that almost every Anglo-Latin poet owes Aldhelm some debt' (Orchard 1994, p. 1).

Aldhelm's most famous composition is the massive double treatise *De virginitate*, 'On Virginity', written in separate versions in prose and verse for a group of (obviously highly educated) nuns at the monastery of Barking. The work is a discussion and celebration of the theme of chastity and it contains a large number of accounts of the lives of famous virgins in history, male and female. At the end of the prose version Aldhelm signals his intention to prepare the second version 'in the heroic measures of hexameter verse'. The passage in which he does so conveniently illustrates his prose style:

> Henceforth, just as I have attempted to honour the glory of incorrupt virginity with applause in my rhetorical narratives, in the same way – if this fleshly prison of the soul does not first pass away, prey to the increasing violence of the Fates, as they say, and the stiff repose of the Parcae and the iron sleep of death do not retard the fluttering of my eyelids – I shall try with artistry to adorn the renown of this same chastity, with Christ's co-operation, in the heroic measures of hexameter verse, and, as if the rhetorical foundation-stones were now laid and the walls of prose were built, so I shall – trusting in heavenly support – build a sturdy roof with trochaic slates and dactylic tiles of metre.   (trans. Lapidge and Herren 1979, pp. 130–1)

This is one of the shorter sentences in the treatise.

Aldhelm notably incorporates poetic effects in his prose, of which the most insistent is alliteration (a feature that is lost in our translated quotation). His poetry itself is, like his prose, highly artificial and ornamental. Traditionally critics, while crediting the technical innovations of the poetry, have not had much to say in its favour, though more recent work has stressed its artistry and its power. Andy Orchard insists that 'while Aldhelm's prose style can be described as a triumph of form over content, his poetic style is the product of a much more even conflict'; Orchard draws attention to the vigour of Aldhelm's poetic language and sees him as 'possessed of a truly poetic imagination' (1994, p. 15). According to the later historian William of Malmesbury, Aldhelm was also a proficient composer of Old English verse and was even considered by King Alfred to be the finest vernacular poet he knew. While no Old English verse by Aldhelm has survived, the importance of Old English poetry as an influence on his Latin verse is now being recognized, an influence apparent not only in his use of alliteration but also in his fondness for formulaic phrasal patterning resembling that of Old English oral tradition

(Orchard 1994, pp. 112–25; Remley 2005). Aldhelm, a foundational figure of Anglo-Latin literature, thus links with the world of vernacular poetry as well as with that of learned Latin tradition, a striking reflection of the interconnectedness of literary traditions in Anglo-Saxon England.

Other writers

The influence of Aldhelm, Bede and Alcuin, but particularly the former, is pervasive in Anglo-Latin literature, though no later figures approach them in literary stature. The most gifted of those influenced by Aldhelm was probably the missionary Boniface (*c.* 675–754), who, like Alcuin, produced most of his writings outside England. Boniface was a pedestrian imitator of Aldhelmian poetry but a prose writer of flair and fluency, whose best work, in his substantial corpus of letters, while clearly influenced by Aldhelm, avoids the excesses of the Aldhelmian style. Some of the letters express fiery moral indignation about various abuses but the writing is cultured and often includes personal touches, as when he writes from the mission fields to an English nun, thanking her for books she has sent him:

> May the Eternal Rewarder of good works give joy on high among the choirs of angels to my dearest sister, who has brought light and consolation to an exile in Germany by sending him gifts of spiritual books. For no man can shed light on these gloomy lurking-places of the German people and take heed of the snares that beset his path unless he have the Word of God as a lamp to guide his feet and a light to shine on his way.   (trans. Talbot 1954, p. 88)

It was clearly tough on poor Boniface in Germany.

Anglo-Latin literature was particularly productive in saints' lives, a genre amply represented in the works of Aldhelm, Bede and Alcuin but also in those of many other writers, mostly in prose but with examples also in verse. Anglo-Latin saints' lives range from early Northumbrian texts like the anonymous *Life of St Cuthbert* (*c.* 700) and *Life of St Gregory the Great* (*c.* 710), Stephen of Ripon's *Life of St Wilfrid* (710 × 720) and the lives by Bede, through lives from later in the eighth century, like Felix's *Life of St Guthlac* (730 × 740), Willibald's *Life of St Boniface* (*c.* 760) and Alcuin's *Life of St Willibrord* (*c.* 780), to later lives such as those of St Dunstan, St Æthelwold and other recently deceased churchmen. Saints' lives will be one of the genres highlighted in the next chapter.

No Latin saints' lives survive from the period from about 800 to about 950 and indeed, as we saw in the first chapter, this seems to have been a lean time for Latin culture more generally. One other Latin prose composition that can be dated to this time, specifically to 893, is Asser's *Life of King Alfred*, a biographical account of the West Saxon king in abstruse ostentatious style by a writer who has been described as 'a man with considerable stylistic pretensions but without any mastery of prose style' (Keynes and Lapidge 1983, p. 54). The *Life* (discussed at pp. 102–3, below) is ostensibly the work not of an Anglo-Saxon but a Welshman, however, and is thought to have been written for a Welsh audience; Asser himself was a monk from west Wales, who became a bishop in Alfred's Wessex.

It is only with the influence of the Benedictine reform of the later tenth century that writing in Latin for an Anglo-Saxon readership revives, some of it produced by visiting continental scholars, some by home-grown churchmen like the prolific Wulfstan of Winchester (whose writings include the *Life of St Æthelwold*, c. 996) and the also prolific Byrhtferth of Ramsey (whose writings include the *Life of St Oswald*, c. 995, and an *Enchiridion*, partly in Old English, c. 1010, the latter being a wide-ranging commentary, with diagrams, on his earlier work, the *Computus*). From this period too comes a Latin prose translation of a version of the *Anglo-Saxon Chronicle*, the *Chronicon* (978 × 988) (ed. and trans. Campbell 1962), written by, or in the name of, the prominent layman Æthelweard, a patron of Ælfric of Eynsham.

The *Chronicon*, like the other works mentioned above, though to a particularly extreme degree, exemplifies the abstruse and extravagant style that we first saw in Aldhelm. The most obscure words, preferably of Greek origin, are sought out and nothing is expressed straightforwardly. The style was given fresh ammunition with the introduction of new Greek words into the West in the Carolingian period and was pretty much *de rigueur* for writers who wished to impress in later Anglo-Saxon England, eclipsing the restrained register of the Bede–Alcuin tradition. The style is generally described today as 'hermeneutic' (the term derives from the *Hermeneutica*, Greek–Latin glossaries, that contain the kind of rare words found in the style). So extensive was its use in later Anglo-Saxon England that there appears to have been only one significant writer who avoided it, Ælfric (Lapidge 1975), whose Old English writings are also known for their clarity and directness of expression.

Writings in Old English prose

One of the best-known literary documents from Anglo-Saxon England is King Alfred of Wessex's *Preface* to his translation into Old English prose of the *Pastoral Care* of Gregory the Great (trans. Swanton 1993, pp. 60–2; for the

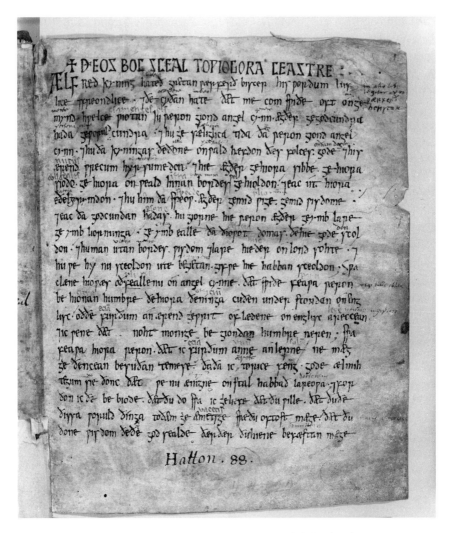

Fig. 2.3 'Ðeos boc sceal to Wiogora ceastre', 'This book is to go to Worcester': beginning of the *Preface* in the copy sent to Bishop Wærferth of Worcester

original Old English text of the *Preface*, see Marsden 2004, pp. 32–6). The document was written by, or for, King Alfred, in the form of a 'covering letter', to be sent out to Alfred's bishops along with the translation; each copy of the letter would have been personalized for the particular bishop receiving it (see Figure 2.3). Written in the first person singular, the *Preface* presents an assessment of the state of learning at the end of the ninth century, and the writer is saddened at what he sees. He perceives a radical decline to have taken place since what he views as an earlier golden age in which England was celebrated for its learning and scholarship. The letter is looking back to the age of Bede and others in the seventh and eighth centuries, admired writers of Latin, and to the culture that they were part of. In the intervening years things have gone downhill, not least because Viking invasions have taken place. The invasions brought peace to an end and brought the destruction of places of learning. The *Preface* dramatically evokes the disruption and chaos of those times, and observes the poor state of affairs of the present.

Alfred laments in the letter that when he came to the throne 'there were very few people this side of the Humber who could comprehend their services in English, or even translate a letter from Latin into English; and I imagine that there were not many beyond the Humber'. He goes on to declare, 'There were so few of them that I cannot even remember a single one south of the Thames when I succeeded to the kingdom' (trans. Swanton 1993, p. 61). He points out that in previous centuries people from abroad used to come to England in search of learning, while in his own day it is the other way round. Scholars debate to what extent Alfred may be exaggerating when he makes these observations – after all, later in the *Preface* he praises the learning of his bishops ('it is uncertain how long there may be such learned bishops as now, thanks be to God, there are nearly everywhere', p. 62) – but it is evident that things have fallen away greatly from what they once were. Alfred's point about getting learning from abroad is borne out by the membership of his own group of clerical advisers, which comprised scholars from Wales and the Continent.

It is in this context of perceived decline in learning that Alfred invites the bishops to join him in his project of teaching the well-born youth of the country to read English, with the most gifted of them also going on to learn Latin, and of translating important Latin works into English: 'Therefore it seems better to me, if it seems so to you, that we also should translate certain books which are most necessary for all men to know, into the language which we can all understand' (p. 62). Alfred here sets the agenda for a textual culture which includes prose writing in English as well as Latin: since Latin literacy has declined he is making written literature available to those who can read English. By extension he is also making it available to those who can have English read to them, though the works translated are learned in nature and are clearly not targeted at a popular audience. Alfred's aim is to provide scholarly writings in English, and in the process he is also valorizing the English language, which is viewed as a worthy medium for intellectual discourse. Alfred portrays himself as leading the way in this educational and literary project, assisted by clerical advisers. His own translation of the *Pastoral Care* is presented as the first book in the project: 'Then when I remembered how the knowledge of Latin had previously decayed through-out the English people, and yet many could read English writing, I began amidst other various and manifold cares of this kingdom to translate into English (*on Englisc*) the book which is called *Pastoralis* in Latin and "Shepherd's Book" in English' (trans. Swanton, p. 62).

The ninth century and writings associated with King Alfred

Much sifting and deconstruction of this famous *Preface* have gone on in modern scholarship. By many commentators Alfred has been taken simply at his word and a grand narrative constructed of him as the begetter of Old English prose through an ambitious literary project (Alfred the 'father of Old English prose'). Others have been less convinced about this, however, and scepticism concerning the extent of the Alfredian project is very much in the current scholarly picture following the publication of an incisive recent article (Godden 2009b).

Most surviving Old English prose does indeed come from the period of King Alfred and after but it is important for us to note that Old English literary prose did not begin with Alfred at the end of the ninth century. The *Preface* itself acknowledges that 'many could read English writing', which implies that there must have been English writings in fairly widespread circulation. We have seen that Bede is supposed to have translated part of the Gospel of John into Old English and have no reason to believe that the report of this is untrue, though the work itself has not survived. But we do have what appear to be pre-Alfredian prose works from the ninth century and these are works written not in Alfred's West Saxon but in Mercian, a dialect of the Anglian variety of Old English (see Figure 2.4). Among these works of Mercian provenance is an anonymous *Life of St Chad*, based on Bede's account of the saint in his *Ecclesiastical History*, and a larger work, the *Old English Martyrology*, a collection (incomplete today) of brief summaries of the lives of some 230 saints, set out in the calendar order of their feast days, and also containing short readings on the six days of creation and other biblical and doctrinal information. No specific source has been identified for the *Martyrology*, which appears to synthesize and rework a number of Latin writings (including some by Bede) – more evidence that Latin texts were being read, and used intelligently, in ninth-century England. These works, like the ones taken to be 'Alfredian', testify to the perceived need for Christian literary texts in the vernacular and in them we see writers striving to devise

Fig. 2.4 Old English dialects

appropriate ways of presenting in English the kind of material that previously could be accessed only in Latin. Another Mercian text of the ninth century or possibly a bit later is the Old English prose translation of Felix's *Life of St Guthlac*, the original having been a product of earlier Anglo-Saxon Latinity. Such works were evidently useful to vernacular readers but do not really come into the category of books 'most necessary for all people to know'.

Works displaying Mercian linguistic forms that have been widely thought to be connected to the Alfredian project are the Old English version of Bede's *Ecclesiastical History* and the Old English *Dialogues* of Gregory the Great, though it must be admitted that the evidence for such a connection is indirect at best. What is certain is that the story of prose writing in ninth-century England was more complicated than that which is offered by too uncritical a reading of King Alfred's *Preface* in its own terms. Literary traditions in Old English prose are establishing themselves in this period and though the political dominance of Wessex would ensure that the

'Alfredian' tradition was the most influential, other centres of activity must also be taken into account. Much scholarly work remains to be done on this fascinating area of Old English studies.

King Alfred's *Preface* sets out a programme in which he presents himself as leading the way by producing the translation of Gregory the Great's *Pastoral Care* (to which the *Preface* is attached), a work which, as the title suggests, deals with matters of responsibility and rule over others, specifically with reference to bishops. The Old English version is relatively faithful in its adaptation of the Latin. This is the only translation which can safely be directly connected to the king himself, though also traditionally attributed to Alfred have been the Old English versions of Boethius's *Consolation of Philosophy* and Augustine's *Soliloquies* and a translation of the first fifty psalms.

These texts may be 'Alfredian' in a broader sense but there are problems about attributing any of them to Alfred. They are unlike each other in approach, and they each display considerable academic learning. The *Psalms*, the most literal of all the translations that have been associated with Alfred, precedes the text of each psalm with a short introduction explaining the psalm in terms of traditional learned biblical interpretation. The treatment of the *Consolation of Philosophy* by contrast is remarkably free and original, with Boethius's great dialogue being recast and overtly Christianized and many reflective passages added; Boethius's metres are translated into prose, though later they were also turned into verse, the verse having been rendered from the prose version. The *Soliloquies*, a philosophical dialogue in three books between Augustine and 'Reason', is very much an appropriation and expansion of its original. Even in Books I and II of the translation there are lengthy added passages, while Book III is based on another work by Augustine and on other Latin texts and, throughout, the translator's own learned reflections are very much in evidence. The preface to the *Soliloquies* develops a famous metaphor in which the translator presents the wide reading on which his writing is based as materials brought back from the forest, which the craftsman uses to construct a new building; this down-to-earth metaphor nicely describes the methodology of the *Soliloquies* translator.

The tools of the (writer's) trade

I then gathered for myself staves and props and tie-shafts, and handles for each of the tools that I knew how to work with, and cross-bars and beams, and, for each of the structures which I knew how to build, the finest timbers I could carry. I never came away with a single load without wishing to bring home the whole of the forest, if I could have carried it all – in every tree I saw something for which I had a need at home. Accordingly, I would advise everyone who is strong and has many wagons to direct his steps to that same forest where I cut these props, and to fetch more for himself and to load his wagons with well-cut staves, so that he may weave many elegant walls and put up many splendid houses and so build a fine homestead, and there may live pleasantly and in tranquillity both in winter and summer – as I have not yet done!

(from the Old English *Soliloquies*, trans. Keynes and Lapidge 1983, p. 138)

The *Boethius* and *Soliloquies* are unlikely to have been directly authored by King Alfred and certainly at least the commentary parts of the *Psalms* must come into the same category, based as they are on a monastic exegetical text. These works may have been produced in Alfred's circle, however, and in connection with his translation programme, though it should be pointed out that it has recently been suggested that the *Boethius* and *Soliloquies* should be detached from an Alfredian context altogether and placed in the tenth century (Godden 2009b, pp. 118–22).

Three other compositions, while recognized by scholars not to be by Alfred himself, have been associated with the Alfredian milieu, the Old English version of Orosius's *History against the Pagans* and two translations of Mercian origin, the Old English version of Gregory the Great's *Dialogues* and the Old English *Bede*. Orosius's work, written in 417–18 shortly after Rome had been sacked by the Goths, is a history of the world from the time of Adam down to the writer's own day, showing in the light of previous world history that the collapse of the Roman Empire was not a unique calamity (as Roman pagans evidently claimed). It fits in well with Alfred's declared translation scheme as it is a learned universal history. Gregory's *Dialogues*, translated by Bishop Wær-ferth and perhaps others, is an edifying compendium of miracle stories, with particular reference to St Benedict, along with a treatise on the afterlife. Apparently written originally for Alfred's personal use, the translation ante-dates the Alfredian project, but it received wider circulation and was even systematically revised in the later Anglo-Saxon period (see further Godden 1997). The Old English version of Bede's *Ecclesiastical History*, another Mercian work, is a major translation of considerable thoughtfulness and intelligence, which slightly recasts Bede for a vernacular audience. The Old English *Bede* may have been produced independently from Alfred's plans but it is conceivable that it was part of them. Alfred collaborated with scholars from outside Wessex and the *Bede*, unlike many of the works discussed in this section, fits the description of a book 'most necessary for all people to know'.

The process of glorifying King Alfred as both a literary and a political figure began in his own day and was continued later in the Anglo-Saxon period, and

Alfred was to achieve an even higher status in the modern era (when he became 'Alfred the Great'). We see the first phase of this process of glorification reflected in the entries in the *Anglo-Saxon Chronicle* relating to his lifetime, in which the king has a heroic role. Alfred is also an exemplary figure in the eulogizing *Life of King Alfred* by Asser, and his own *Preface* contributes to the perception of him as a man of great vision and achievement.

Alfred must be considered an important figure in Anglo-Saxon literary history, who had a key role in particular in legitimizing the English language as a literary medium and in encouraging – though not initiating – the development of Old English prose (Davis 1998; Discenza 2005). But he is also in an important sense a constructed figure, presented to the world by a kind of publicity machine. The output resulting from his translation programme may have been more limited than scholars have assumed and he himself less engaged in its detailed working out. Recently indeed the question has been asked, in what sense did Alfred actually write any of the works associated with him, including the *Preface* and the *Pastoral Care*. Was he hands-on or did his scholars produce his writings on his behalf, under his close, or broad, direction, or even independently from him (Godden 2007)? According to the *Preface* to the *Pastoral Care*, Alfred prepared his translation of Gregory's original with the assistance of a number of scholars: 'Plegmund my archbishop, and Asser my bishop, and Grimbald my mass-priest, and John my mass-priest' (trans. Crossley-Holland 1984, p. 220) – all, incidentally, from outside Wessex (Plegmund was Mercian, Asser Welsh, and Grimbald and John from the Continent). Alfred the author worked in collaboration with these and other figures to produce his writings; his own exact role in the process will continue to be debated, as will the extent of the programme announced in the *Preface*.

One other text that portrays Alfred very favourably from a political point of view is that referred to by modern commentators as 'The Voyages of Ohthere and Wulfstan', even though at first sight Alfred appears to have only an incidental role in this. 'The Voyages of Ohthere and Wulfstan' (trans. Swanton 1993, pp. 62–9) is part of the Old English version of Orosius's *History*. The original Latin text begins with a brief account of the geography of the world, based on classical written sources. This is taken over and even slightly developed in the Old English version, but the geographical part of the Old English *Orosius* is most remarkable for the insertion of several pages of new material, describing the voyages of two ninth-century travellers, Ohthere and Wulfstan. Orosius's account of northern Europe had been sketchy, and it is filled out by these first-hand reports by two experienced voyagers who visited King Alfred's court. Ohthere, a

Norwegian, describes his voyages along the coast of Norway and as far north as Arctic Russia. Wulfstan, perhaps a Dane, tells of his travels in the Baltic Sea. The Old English accounts of the travels of Ohthere and Wulfstan are among the earliest pieces of original (i.e. not based on a Latin source) narrative prose composition in the English language. They are modest and unpretentious in style, but they represent 'documentary' prose of considerable fluency and versatility.

The reports of the two travellers bring a kind of reflected glory on Alfred, who appears in the episode as a great king whose followers report back to him from remote parts. Alfred doesn't control these remote parts but his interest in them suggests an outward-looking world view that his rule represents; and in a sense, 'to know is somehow also to dominate' (Michelet 2006, p. 27). This is no insular, provincial ruler but someone whose vision incorporates remote parts at the edge of the known world. Alfred emerges as an Anglo-Saxon version of the powerful ruler whose representatives explore the margins of the world. For Orosius Britain was itself a place at the edge of the world but in 'Ohthere and Wulfstan' Alfred's Wessex becomes not a marginal place but a centre which travellers report back to. Alfred himself comes across as a grand figure, receiving the reports of these foreign travellers, who acknowledge him as their lord.

Scholars of later generations in England would look back to Alfred as a glorious political leader and an important writer. Ælfric refers to the writings of Alfred (among which, however, he includes the Old English *Bede*) (Godden 2009a) and, unlike most writings in English, he admires them:

> I have seen and heard of much error in many English books, which
> unlearned men, through their simplicity, have esteemed as great
> wisdom: and I regretted that they knew not nor had not the evangelical
> doctrines among their writings, those men excepted who knew Latin,
> and those books excepted which king Alfred wisely turned from Latin
> into English, which are to be had.
>
> (Preface to *Catholic Homilies* I, trans. Thorpe 1844–6, I, 3)

In singling Alfred out for approval, however, Ælfric implicitly indicates that the fruits of the king's endeavours in the field of learning were short-lived: Alfred had no immediate literary successors; his longer-term successors were Ælfric and his contemporaries.

In another of his prefaces Ælfric writes, in words that strikingly echo those of the *Preface* to the *Pastoral Care*, of the continued decline of learning in his own century until the influence of the Benedictine reform was felt:

> It is proper then for God's ministers and monks to take great care that
> divine learning should not cool or fade in our time, as it did in England
> a few years ago, so that no English cleric knew how to compose
> or interpret a letter in Latin, until Archbishop Dunstan and
> Bishop Æthelwold restored scholarship again in the monasteries.
> (Preface to Ælfric's *Grammar*, ed. Zupitza 1880, p. 3)

I referred to the principles of the Benedictine reform in the preceding
chapter and to its leading figures, including Dunstan and Æthelwold. Ælfric
here pays homage to both of them, though he was particularly influenced by
Æthelwold, referring to himself elsewhere indeed as the 'fosterchild' of
Æthelwold.

Ælfric and later prose writings

The Benedictine reform is the key context for the works of Ælfric and other
late Anglo-Saxon writers. It is worth noting, however, that the movement is
now recognized to have been a more diffuse and a more complex phenom-
enon than it was thought to be in the past (C. A. Jones 2009). The 'wing' of
the reform that is particularly relevant to literary studies is that associated
with Æthelwold, whose leadership and example transformed ecclesiastical life
at Winchester and whose promotion of writing in the vernacular influenced
the development of Late West Saxon as a standard literary language. The
writings of Ælfric, the most prolific Old English writer, represent the reform
in a particularly rigorous form – Ælfric's criticism of the (religious) error he
finds in many English books is entirely typical of him – but to what extent the
views of Ælfric are representative of the movement as a whole is debatable:
certainly his insistence on religious orthodoxy is not matched by other
writers.

There were other significant writers associated with the Benedictine reform
working at the same time as him (see above, pp. 27, 53) but Ælfric has
received most attention from scholars, because he wrote a lot, he wrote well,
and what he wrote is perceived to be very interesting. Ælfric's voluminous
writings range from homilies (some 125 of them) and saints' lives
(numbering more than fifty) to biblical translations and paraphrases, to
practical pedagogical works, treatises of various kinds, letters and occasional
pieces, and they constitute a thematically consistent and coherent body of
work; if we did not have them, later Old English literature would look
different, and the variety of its traditions would stand out more.

Ælfric's career and writings

c. 955	Ælfric born
980s	Educated at Winchester, under the influence of Bishop Æthelwold
987	Went to newly founded monastery at Cerne Abbas (Dorset)
989	Completion of *Catholic Homilies I*, a cycle of some forty homilies covering the course of the church year
992	Completion of *Catholic Homilies II*, a second cycle of homilies
992–1002	*Grammar*, *Glossary*, *Colloquy* and other pedagogical pieces, aimed at instructing students; Old Testament translations and *Preface to Genesis*, expressing his qualms about translating the Bible; *Lives of Saints*, a cycle of saints' lives and other edifying material in the order of the feast days covered; miscellaneous other homilies and occasional pieces
1005	Went to new monastery at Eynsham as abbot
1005–10	*Treatise on the Old and New Testament*, an interpretative overview of the books of the Bible; reissue of *Catholic Homilies I* and *II*; pastoral letters
c. 1010	Death of Ælfric

Other prose traditions had developed in the tenth century, notably in the areas of homily writing, biblical apocrypha and hagiography, as represented, for example, by the Vercelli and Blickling collections of homilies. These are pre-reform or non-reform religious writings aimed at a popular audience, intended to instruct the laity in the elements of the Christian faith. Ælfric doesn't mention any of them by name but they represent the kind of religious writings that he objected to, being viewed by him as doctrinally suspect and even dangerous in their influence on their audiences. More learned in character but still not the kind of work that Ælfric would approve of for lay reading is the (Anglian) translation of the *Life of St Mary of Egypt*, which is graphic in its presentation of its heroine's promiscuous early life and unapologetic in its endorsement of her later independence from male spiritual guidance. Ironically, the *Life of St Mary of Egypt* would end up in a manuscript of Ælfric's own writings, an indication that even reform-minded sponsors of his work were less strict in adhering to his principles than he hoped. Ælfric insisted that the integrity of his own works should be respected and that they should be transmitted separately from the writings of others but right from the time of their first release, and in a manner typical of the pragmatic use of preaching texts in the period, his homilies and his saints' lives were appropriated, edited and mixed with other texts in precisely the ways that he had worried about. Ælfric's homilies were still being used at least a hundred years after the Norman Conquest but they very soon lost their association with Ælfric and circulated on an anonymous basis.

Ælfric's mentor Bishop Æthelwold is now thought to have been the author of the seminal *Monastic Agreement* (*Regularis concordia*) (*c.* 973), a 'customary' which sets out the Benedictine *Rule* as the basis of monastic observance in England, and he also translated the *Rule* of St Benedict itself into English, a translation that exists in a version specially tailored for women as well as one for men.

In the translation of the *Rule* and in other writings associated with Æthelwold we begin to see the development of a special standard vocabulary that scholars refer to as 'Winchester' vocabulary, according to which certain Old English words, particularly those for key religious concepts, are consistently preferred over possible synonyms (Hofstetter 1987). This vocabulary became increasingly fixed and is distinctively found in the works of Winchester writers and those influenced by them, Ælfric being strictest and most consistent in his use of it. Æthelwold is also argued to have been the driving force behind a much more widespread literary development, the fashioning of a standard form of Old English based on Late West Saxon. Again Ælfric is a conspicuous proponent of this form of writing, in which we find accepted norms in morphology and orthography being consistently applied, but by the early eleventh century the regularized form of the language was being used not only by rigorists like Ælfric but was to be found in manuscripts from right across Anglo-Saxon England. A striking uniformity of linguistic practice is apparent in late Old English texts, which must have been systematically taught to scribes throughout the country. Mechthild Gretsch traces the genesis of this development to Æthelwold and the closing years of King Edgar's reign in the 970s: 'It is during these years that the English political and intellectual elite south of the Humber appears to have developed a pervasive awareness of what had been achieved in the course of the past decades: a kingdom of the English, unified under West Saxon rule and powerful enough to command the submission of the neighbouring Welsh and Scottish kingdoms' (Gretsch 2009, pp. 125–6).

The creation of a standard Old English, a development that took place at a time of considerable and increasing linguistic diversity and change, must be seen as one of the most remarkable developments in early English literary history. A form of standard English would not emerge again for another five hundred years. The standard English of late Anglo-Saxon is a medium for a vernacular literary culture that was particularly vigorous in the last phase of Anglo-Saxon England, a culture in which Ælfric was certainly a key player but which incorporated too an extraordinary variety of writings, some of which were very different from the products of the monk of Eynsham, ranging from wonder tales to intellectual treatises and from translations of the Bible to romances; and also including poetry.

The literature of late Anglo-Saxon England also ranges from the learned to the popular, having different kinds of intended audiences. Indeed, the writings of Ælfric alone have a spectrum of intended audiences. His Latin works, most notably letters (including his *Letter to the Monks of Eynsham*, based on Æthelwold's *Monastic Agreement*), are addressed to a monastic and clerical audience, as are his pedagogic works in Old English. His homilies, which were intended to be read out in church, seem to be aimed at an audience that includes monks and the laity (Clayton 1985). His saints' lives and biblical translations and treatises were commissioned as reading books for prominent laymen but lend themselves to public performance as well as private reading and would have had a wider lay and religious audience. Ælfric's homilies and saints' lives in particular were soon absorbed into anonymous traditions of popular preaching literature, which is perhaps the most widespread form of vernacular literature of the period both before and after the Norman Conquest.

Before I turn in the final section of this chapter to Christian traditions of Old English poetry it is important to note that the metrical features and style of Old English poetry had an impact too on Old English prose. As we might expect, the prose was influenced by syntactical and rhetorical features of the esteemed language of Latin (though not by its 'hermeneutic' flights), but patterns and techniques derived from the vernacular poetic tradition are also widely apparent. From Alfred's *Preface to the Pastoral Care* to anonymous homilies we find alliterating phrases reminiscent of ones that occur in the poetry (Orchard 1997), and some writers go further, taking over rhythmical structures from the poetry in a systematic way and thereby 'heightening' their register and giving it a strong aural dimension.

Particularly notable in this respect are Ælfric and his contemporary Wulfstan of York. Wulfstan's powerful prose is largely made up of two-stress phrases, often alliterating, which are structurally similar to Old English verse half-lines. Ælfric experimented with his prose style and while always aiming for an elegant clarity of expression he developed a medium that is very verse-like indeed in its structure, to the extent that some scholars would even argue that what he writes is a form of verse rather than, as I would prefer to view it, heightened prose (see Bredehoft 2004); some editors also set out Ælfric's texts not as continuous prose but in verse lines. Apart from his early homilies, Ælfric's writings are mostly composed in 'verse' units consisting of alliterating pairs of two-stress half-lines that are strikingly reminiscent of lines of Old English poetry. Ælfric doesn't take over the content or the language of the poetic tradition (indeed he develops an alternative kind of formulaic composition of his own [Magennis 2006] and draws also upon aspects of Latin rhetoric [Corona 2009]) and his metrical patterning is much looser than what we find in the poetry, but it is clear that in a fundamental way he is being guided by his experience of Old English verse. Here is a typical passage from his hagiographic collection *Lives of Saints*, in which he is praising the seventh-century saint Oswald of Northumbria (the passage is presented as set out in the long-serving edition of Skeat, in which the text is divided into verse lines):

> Hwæt þa oswald cyning his cynedom geheold
> hlissfullice for worulde and mid mycelum geleafan.
> and on eallum dædum his drihten arwurðode.
> oð þæt he ofslagen wearð for his folces ware
> on þam nigoðan geare þe he rices geweold.   (ed. Skeat 1881–1900, II, 134)

> [Behold then King Oswald held his kingdom
> gloriously in worldly terms and with great faith,
> and in all his deeds he honoured his Lord,
> until he was slain in defence of his people
> in the ninth year that he ruled the realm.]

One element of the language of Old English verse that Ælfric does take over is his use here, and also widely elsewhere, of *hwæt*, an exclamatory adverb familiar in the poetry.

In the works of Ælfric and to a lesser degree in those of other prose writers we see a creative and highly productive interplay of prose and poetic traditions; these writers thought carefully about what they were doing as they fashioned prose styles suitable to their writerly purposes.

Traditions of Christian poetry

We have noted the multi-faceted interaction of the Old English poetic tradition with other literary traditions in Anglo-Saxon England. As we have seen, Bede praised the beauty of Cædmon's verse and he and Aldhelm may even have composed poetry in the vernacular; Alfred is portrayed by Asser as a lover of Old English poetry; Ælfric, Wulfstan and other homilists adapted aspects of the metre of poetry. What about the Old English poetic tradition itself, however? How did it fare in Christian Anglo-Saxon England, in what was now a textually based culture and one in which the ostensibly worldly values of the poetry would have been viewed as problematic?

Christian teachers were aware of the contradictions between those values and Christian ones – 'What has Hinield to do with Christ?' wrote Alcuin (see above, p. 50), and Ælfric carefully dissociates his Christian heroes from secular heroism – but secular Old English poetry would have continued in oral form throughout the period, and the tradition also acquired a literate dimension, with poems now being preserved and transmitted in manuscripts and also being composed as written literature, as *Beowulf* surely was. As this happened, the poetry became Christianized to varying degrees. References to a single God are introduced and Christian ideas incorporated, to the extent that very few surviving Old English poems lack some Christian point of reference, even though their motivating ideals may remain those of secular heroism, with its cultivation of the themes of revenge, violence and glory. The Christianization can be superficial and even contradictory but a work such as *Beowulf* is deeply imbued with Christian thought. *Widsith*, a composition (mentioned above, p. 43) in which a travelling *scop* catalogues the tribes and leaders of the heroic age and celebrates those who wish to raise up their glory (*dom*) and sustain their heroic standing (*eorlscipe*) in the world (lines 140–1), brings in the Christian idea of providence, with God guiding the good rule of people by their leaders (and it also alludes to the afterlife):

> Thus I have always found it in my travelling,
> that the man is dearest to land-dwellers
> to whom God gives the people's kingdom
> to uphold, while he lives here.   (lines 131–4)

In *Waldere* (trans. Crossley-Holland 1984, pp. 9–11), a fragmentary poem of violent conflict between warriors, the eponymous hero utters a boast against his antagonist before launching himself on him in a fight for treasure, but Waldere also expresses his faith in himself in strikingly Christian terms:

> He who trusts to the Holy One for help,
> to God for aid, will readily find it there.   (fragment II, lines 27–8)

Secular poetry like *Widsith* and *Waldere* continued, but following the conversion to Christianity whole new traditions of religious poetry developed as well, producing some of what have been regarded as the key works of Old English literature. Religious poetry in Old English includes extended narratives based on the Bible and on lives of saints and includes also reflective, devotional and homiletic pieces, and it ranges from straightforward instructional verse to compositions of considerable imagination and artistic complexity. Bede traces the tradition of Christian poetry back to Cædmon, though it is unlikely that the development of religious verse follows a single linear trajectory.

In Christian Anglo-Saxon England the vernacular poetic tradition is adapted and appropriated, then, to give expression to a new subject matter, thus effecting a 'conversion' of the poetry. The Christian message is brought to life for Anglo-Saxon audiences by being expressed in the poetic language they are familiar with. It draws upon the diction, imagery and concepts of that language and transports the characters of Christian story to a Germanic world, thereby presenting its material in a new light. While it is right therefore to speak of an adaptation and appropriation of the Old English poetic tradition for Christian purposes, critics also perceive Christian discourse itself becoming 'Germanic' in vernacular religious poetry, referring to a 'Germanicizing' of the material.

In accordance with this Germanicizing, which is more emphatic in some poems than in others, biblical figures and saints confronting evil are portrayed as warriors going to battle, as in the short hagiographical piece *The Fates of the Apostles* (trans. Bradley 1982, pp. 154–7), which summarizes the missionary travels of the apostles and tells how they died: the apostles are 'bold' (*frame*), for example, and 'brave in battle' (*fyrdhwate*). In this poetry too the relationships of characters are understood in Germanic terms, with reference to the lord's *comitatus* and the ideals that motivate it. Germanic concepts of this kind can be employed effectively in the poetry, and of course the use of military language ties in with martial imagery in St Paul's epistles (see especially Ephesians VI. 7–11) and in the wider tradition of the followers of Christ as Christian soldiers.

The Dream of the Rood (trans. Crossley-Holland 1984, pp. 200–4; for original text, see Marsden 2004, pp. 192–202), a meditative poem on the passion of Christ that is one of the acknowledged masterpieces of Old English literature, takes up the idea of Christ as a brave warrior but subverts it by insisting on his passivity – startling in a Germanic context – in the face of violent attack; *The Dream of the Rood* also has the suggestive notion of the cross as Christ's loving retainer wishing to protect his lord but helpless to prevent his death. Other poems (as indeed *The Dream of the Rood* again) draw creatively on related heroic ideas like that of exile, a powerful theme in the secular tradition, and life in the hall, which in Christian poetry becomes an image of the joys of heaven. The idea of striving for praise (*lof*) through glorious acts is also reconceived in Christian terms, most notably perhaps in *The Seafarer* (trans. Bradley 1982, pp. 329–35; for original text, see Marsden 2004, pp. 221–30), another masterpiece of Old English literature, which, as explained in more detail in a subsequent chapter, presents a complex reflection on human-kind's life on earth. Particularly striking is a dense passage that insistently interweaves secular and religious principles, transforming the desire for worldly reputation into a desire for heaven:

> Therefore for every man the praise (*lof*) of the living,
> of those speaking afterwards, is the best memorial,
> which he can bring about before he has to go on his journey [of death]
> by good actions on earth against the malice of enemies,
> by bold deeds against the devil,
> so that the sons of men may afterwards glorify him
> and his praise may live then with the angels,
> always for ever, the fame of eternal life,
> joy among the hosts (*dream mid dugeþum*).   (lines 72–80a)

The application of heroic language can also be a blunt instrument, however, and can easily look incongruous, as perhaps in the longer saint's life *Andreas* (trans. Bradley 1982, pp. 110–53), in which Andreas (St Andrew) is automat-ically portrayed as a heroic warrior even though some of his actions are distinctly unheroic.

The majority of surviving Old English poems are religious in content – unsurprisingly, as suggested earlier, given the monastic context of much writing in Anglo-Saxon England – though it is interesting that some of the manuscripts in which the religious poems are preserved also contain secular works. Secular poems were evidently thought worthy of being preserved and some compilers did not see a problem in combining them with religious poems in the same book. *Beowulf* is in with a biblical poem (*Judith*) and with Christian wonder-stories in its surviving manuscript, while the manuscript of *The Seafarer* also includes *Widsith* and indeed poems about earthly love. Though there are religious-only manuscripts, the codicological evidence does not suggest a strict segregation of religious and secular poetic traditions, and we have noted that secular poems themselves are 'Christianized' to varying degrees.

In fact, four major poetic manuscripts have come down to us, the Vercelli Book, the Junius Manuscript, the Exeter Book and the *Beowulf* Manuscript, containing between them the bulk of extant Old English poetry. Among other manuscripts containing Old English poetry are those of the verse psalms (psalms 51–150, copied along with the Alfredian prose psalms, 1–50) and the *Metres of Boethius* (part of the translation of Boethius's *Consolation of Philosophy*). Many poems must have been composed that have not survived, the poems of Cædmon for example, but the extant corpus of vernacular poetry consists of only some 30,000 lines. Most poems too exist in only one version, though we can tell from copying errors and other evidence that some of them have complex written transmission histories. Some, like *Waldere*, survive in fragmentary form on scraps of parchment that have turned up fortuitously in the modern period; others, like *The Battle of Maldon*, are preserved in modern transcriptions from manuscripts that have been subsequently destroyed or lost.

The major Old English poetry manuscripts

The Vercelli Book (Vercelli, Biblioteca Capitolare CXVII), a manuscript of the second half of the tenth century containing devotional and homiletic literature in prose and verse, the verse texts being the hagiographical compositions *Andreas*, *The Fates of the Apostles* and *Elene* (about St Helena and the finding of the true cross), and also *The Dream of the Rood*. Its location in northern Italy suggests that it was left behind by an Anglo-Saxon traveller on the way back from Rome, though it is a quite a large book (page-size *c.* 310 × 205 mm) for carrying on a journey.

The Exeter Book (Exeter, Cathedral Library 3501), a substantial (310–20 × 218–25 mm), poetry-only manuscript of the second half of the tenth century, containing a wide range of material both secular and religious, ranging from devotional compositions (including the '*Christ*' poems), saints' lives (*Juliana* and *Guthlac*), 'elegies' (including *The Seafarer* but also secular pieces), *Widsith* and other catalogue poems, other assorted poems offering instruction and lore, and riddles. It is surely to the Exeter Book that the following description from an eleventh-century Exeter book-list refers: *.i. mycel englisc boc be gehwilcum þingum on leoðwisan geworht*, 'one large book in English on various subjects, composed in verse'.

The Junius Manuscript (Oxford, Bodleian Library, Junius 11) (formerly referred to as the 'Cædmon' manuscript), a poetry-only manuscript containing the biblical narrative poems *Genesis*, *Exodus* and *Daniel* and also a biblically inspired work on Christ's triumph over Satan, *Christ and Satan*. The Old Testament pieces were copied *c.* 1000, with *Christ and Satan* being added sometime in the following quarter-century. This large-scale (*c.* 323 × 196 mm) book contains a series, never completed, of line drawings illustrating narrative episodes.

The *Beowulf* Manuscript (London, British Library, Cotton Vitellius A. xv), a modest-sized (*c.* 195 × 115–30 mm) and unspectacular manuscript of the early eleventh century containing *Beowulf*, the biblical narrative poem *Judith* (incomplete) and three prose texts, the *Life of St Christopher* (fragmentary), *The Wonders of the East* (illustrated) and *The Letter of Aristotle*, tales of marvels. The manuscript was damaged by fire in 1731, suffering singeing of the page edges.

Apart from Cædmon (and perhaps Bede) we have the name of only one other Old English poet whose works are still extant, Cynewulf, whose 'signature' in runes is cryptically incorporated into the text of the poems *The Fates of the Apostles* and *Elene* (both in the Vercelli Book) and *Christ II* ('The Ascension')

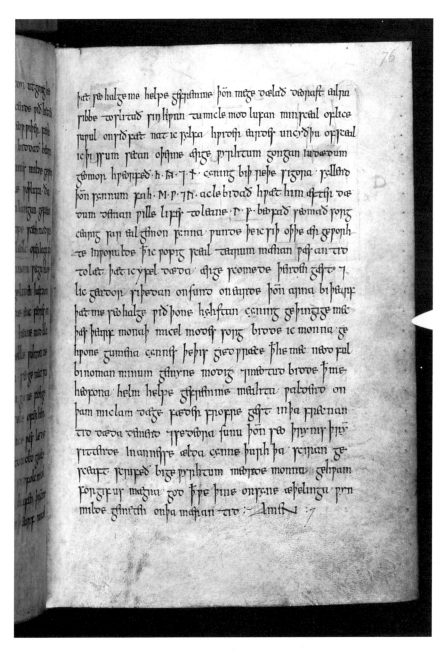

Fig. 2.5 The Exeter Book, f. 76r: the end of *Juliana,* incorporating 'signature' 'CYNEWULF' ('ᛣᛦᚾᛖᚹᚢᛚᚠ'), beginning on the fifth line. Note that the text is written 'continuously' in manuscripts of Old English poetry, not split up into verse lines.

and *Juliana* (both in the Exeter Book. See Figure 2.5). Many religious poems, including those by Cynewulf, are distinguished by their learning and their richness of imagery, combining Christian thought with features derived from Germanic tradition.

Which brings us finally to the issue of the textuality of Old English poetry again. Old English poetry was originally a purely oral medium and even when it acquired a literate dimension with Old English poems being written down and then composed as written texts, it was still very much designed for oral performance, cultivating oral techniques and aural effects and in some cases preserving the fiction of the performer as *scop*. In the oral performance of written texts the texts become available to non-literate as well as literate audiences, enabling them to participate in the textual culture of writing and manuscripts.

Many Old English poetic texts also appeal to the eye, however, having not only aural but also visual effects, which encompass layout, letter forms and illustrations. Such texts are clearly intended to be seen as well as heard. In the Junius Manuscript, for example, the text is illustrated with line-drawings, and I have just mentioned the signatures of Cynewulf, which would not be accessible in oral performance. Not only are the letters of Cynewulf's name worked in to the text of his poems in runic letters in these signatures but in one of them, *The Fates of the Apostles*, the letters of the name (in the variant spelling 'Cynwulf') are jumbled up, appearing in the order F, W, U, L, C, Y, N. Letters, roman as well as runic, are also jumbled and reversed in some of the Old English riddles, adding to the sense of puzzling ingenuity that characterizes these poems. In *The Rune Poem* (though the manuscript is no longer extant) each line begins with a runic letter in alphabetical order, evidently following the Latin abecedarian model, while in the lyrical piece *The Husband's Message* a kind of secret message in runes is incorporated into the text, so enigmatic that critics disagree about its interpretation.

Written Old English verse might lend itself naturally to oral performance, therefore, but manuscript features of many existing poetic texts, along with the learning that they reflect, make it clear that these compositions are deeply implicated in textual ways of thinking and that they would have had a similar readership indeed to that of Latin literature in the period (see further Magennis 2001, pp. 95–8). We have traced differing literary traditions in this chapter but have also noted significant elements of overlap between them. It is appropriate to end with these in mind and in particular to emphasize points of similarity between Latin literature and intellectual vernacular literature.

Postscript: *Riddle 47*: words oral and written

Riddle 47, from the tenth-century Exeter Book, is a scholarly playful six-line poem in which a speaker describes the strange occurrence of a moth/worm eating words:

> A moth ate words; to me that seemed
> a marvellous event when I heard about that wonder,
> that that worm had swallowed up some man's song,
> a thief in darkness had consumed the mighty saying
> and its firm foundation. The thieving stranger was not
> one whit the wiser when he swallowed those words.

In the original Old English (ed. Marsden 2004, p. 316) the poem reads,

> Moððe word fræt. Me þæt þuhte
> wrætlicu wyrd, þa ic þæt wundor gefrægn,
> þæt se wyrm forswealg wera gied sumes,
> þeof in þystro þrymfæstne cwide
> and þæs strangan staþol. Stælgiest ne wæs
> wihte þy gleawra, þe he þam wordum swealg.

The 'scholarly' aspect of *Riddle 47* is borne out by the fact that it is based on a Latin poem by Symphosius. The Latin poem is even shorter than the Old English and reads as follows in translation:

> *Worm*
> Letters have nourished me, but I have no idea what letters are.
> I have lived in books, but am none the more studious for it.
> I have devoured the Muses, but I myself still haven't benefited.

The Latin, which begins by giving the answer to the *enigma*, presents an elegant conceit, applying literally and metaphorically the idea of eating words: scholars are nourished by words, bookworms literally eat books, words and all. The poem situates itself in a context of Latin study, literature and the Muses: it is a literate poem about the world of reading, a world that is sometimes invaded by these annoying pests which eat into books. The implicit message of the poem is a kind of superior self-endorsement of those who can appreciate the higher things in life, like this *enigma*. The poem is clever, but hardly highly wrought; it is a one-idea poem, with the same idea repeated in three variations.

When we turn to the Old English version, we find something that *is* highly wrought. The speaker is no longer the bookworm itself but a fascinated, personalized, observer. And the speaker puts the riddle implicitly, giving clues but not actually asking readers what the subject is, and certainly not telling them the answer. The poem is full of wordplay, including a lot of artful alliteration that isn't taken over in the translation, as in the sequence *word* ('word'), *wrætlicu wyrd* ('marvellous event') and *wyrm* ('worm'), and an image of theft is developed, in *þeof* ('thief') and *stælgiest* ('thieving stranger'). Also the Old English emphasizes the greediness and destructiveness of the bookworm, in contrast with the Latin emphasis on it as going about its business nourishing and sustaining itself. Here it is devouring (*fræt*, suggestive of sharp teeth, as in the modern word 'fret-saw') and swallowing (*forswealg, swealg*).

There is more to the Old English poem than the Latin, and when we look at it closely, it is also telling us something interesting about its moment in history. In an important sense this poem is about the transition from orality to textuality that was taking place in people's experience in the early Middle Ages. In particular, as people entered the Anglo-Saxon schoolroom they moved from a world of traditional orality to one of literacy and grammaticality, with its completely different way of thinking about language. The Latin riddle exists purely in the world of writing, but the Old English one encompasses both traditional oral knowledge *and* writing, in which language becomes a material thing, 'codified'.

In the world of writing the idea of a worm eating words is striking but comprehensible, when it is explained: words are material things in a physical object, a book. In a purely oral world eating words is incomprehensible. And yet our Old English riddle also posits an oral world, in which the speaker has heard (*gefrægn*) about this wonder and in which the moth/worm swallows not writing as such ('letters') but utterances, some man's song (*gied*), a mighty saying (*cwide*).

In a sense, the moth relates to the worm as the oral word relates to the written word: one thing changes into another. The coming of writing can be seen as radically transforming the traditional oral world, and it provokes anxiety as well as wonder on the part of the speaker: the worm is portrayed as a thief 'stealing' words and their firm foundation. The poem has the interesting idea that the words *belonged* to someone – some man's song. When they are written down they can be stolen, which is not possible in the world of pure orality.

The poem itself is written in a manuscript, and therefore presumably not immune from the bookworm. It is written down, but it is composed in the traditional oral style of Old English poetry, appealing to listeners. It is highly aural in its effects, and unlike in the Latin version there is no mention of letters or books, even though the poem exists in a book. We can imagine individuals reading the poem on their own in Anglo-Saxon

England, but the much more common pattern in the early Middle Ages was for poems to be read out, to an audience. A reader sees but an audience 'hears'. The poem exists, therefore, on the border between the oral and the written. Writing, not speech, has become primary in it, superseding utterance: knowledge can now be stored and saved but in the process it also becomes destructible in a way that was inconceivable in the oral age. The firm foundation of a saying is no longer the oral tradition but the physical page, which the worm eats into.

Chapter 3

Varieties of narrative

The literature discussed in this chapter is the literature of secular and Christian narrative and its meaning. It encompasses the tradition of heroic poetry with its 'multitude of stories' (*Beowulf*, lines 869–70), inherited from the pre-Christian past and developed to new uses in the period, and it encompasses too strands that represent Christian-Latin-derived forms of writing, that contrast strikingly with the heroic inheritance but can also interact with it creatively, integrating, as well as opposing, aspects of what we might refer to as the world of Ingeld (on Ingeld, see above, p. 50). In attending to Christian-Latin-derived strands this chapter focuses on three in particular, biblical, historiographical and hagiographical, considering (respectively) treatments of the great events and figures of the Bible, accounts of the course of history and its meaning, especially with reference to Anglo-Saxon England, and writings about the edifying and exemplary exploits of the saints. In discussing varieties of narrative, which represent a substantial and varied proportion of surviving Anglo-Saxon writings, I will focus particularly in each case on one or more representative texts, an approach also to be followed in the next chapter, on non-narrative literature; in most instances these will be writings that are widely perceived as 'major' works of Anglo-Saxon literature.

Heroic poetry

The critical term 'Old English heroic poetry' is used to refer to vernacular Anglo-Saxon verse that portrays the ethos and culture associated with the age of the pre-Christian Germanic tribes of the late Roman and post-Roman world, as imagined in later centuries (see further, Magennis 2010, on which some of the present discussion draws). Old English heroic poetry constitutes a useful critical category and a venerable one in modern scholarship but it is one into which we must be careful not to import romantic associations from times nearer to our own. The critic and clergyman Stopford Brooke, writing at the end of the nineteenth century, is among those who combine the elevation of the heroic life as perceived in Anglo-Saxon literature with a distinctly racial appreciation: he discerns in the poetry 'that steady consistency of national character, that clinging through all difficulty to the aim in view, that unrelenting curiosity, that desire to do better what has been done' (Brooke 1892, I, vii), and he particularly compares Beowulf to Lord Nelson: 'Gentle like Nelson, he had Nelson's iron resolution' (I, 29). Lee Patterson has written recently of the 'ideology of imperial heroism that flourished in Victorian England' and of its links with values associated with the Germanic heroic age. One figure that he focuses on is W. P. Ker, whose influential book *Epic and Romance* was published in 1897; Patterson highlights Ker's celebration of the heroic age and explains that 'he saw the essence of the Middle Ages as residing in the Germanic spirit of the north – a spirit that was gradually corrupted by the dominance of southern, and specifically French, influences' (Patterson 2000, p. 148). Such appropriation tells us more about modern perceptions than about Old English literature itself, and in recent decades commentators such as Martin Camargo (1981), John M. Hill (1995) and Stefan Jurasinski (2004) have sought to extricate the poetry from the romantic associations it acquired in earlier criticism and which still persist in some quarters.

The surviving corpus of Old English texts recognized as heroic poetry is small and consists mostly of narrative verse but includes too the 'catalogue' poem *Widsith* (143 lines), which memorializes individuals and peoples of the 'heroic age' and celebrates the *scop*s and patrons who preserve their glory; and the lyric piece *Deor* (42 lines), which is commonly also classified as an elegy, is usually listed among the heroic poems as well. Other poems too, such as other elegies, have their setting in the heroic world, but are not normally defined as heroic poetry as such. In all, the surviving corpus consists of a handful of shortish poems and fragments – *Widsith, Deor, The Finnsburh Fragment* (47 lines), *Waldere* (62 lines, consisting of two fragments) and *The Battle of Maldon* (325 lines, incomplete at the beginning and end) – along with the 3182-line *Beowulf.* As suggested in an earlier chapter, oral poetry in the heroic tradition would have been composed throughout the Anglo-Saxon period and much written poetry too must have been produced which is now lost. *Beowulf* is unique in its scale and stance but we cannot tell for certain whether other poems like it once existed. It has been argued that the epic grandeur of *Beowulf,* if not its ethos, derives from classical models (Andersson 1997, pp. 138–41). The ancient writers Vergil and Statius were known in Anglo-Saxon England, as were traditions of Latin Christian epic from the late antique period.

Old English heroic poetry presents a tradition-based warrior society in which high-born individuals strive for glory in violent action, retainers fulfilling their obligations of loyalty to their lord in battle, the lord offering them protection and recognition in the *comitatus* which has its social focus in the tribal hall, scene of feasting and gift-giving. It is in battle that through courageous deeds the warrior gains communal esteem; perceived cowardice leads to shame and ignominy, and treachery is a particularly heinous crime. Heroic conflicts are played out in the setting of this uncompromising binary code of behaviour but also in the light of the recognition that failure and betrayal are part of human reality and that suffering is the price of honour. The heroic warrior himself is a fallible figure and is particularly subject to rashness in his embracing of the demands of the code, as seems to be the case, for example, with Byrhtnoth in *The Battle of Maldon,* who fatally gives passageway to the Viking enemy to allow them to engage with his own warriors.

The Battle of Maldon (trans. Crossley-Holland 1984, pp. 11–19; for original text, see Marsden 2004, pp. 251–69) is one of the best-known Old English heroic poems but, unlike most of the heroic poetry composed in Anglo-Saxon England, it is notable as commemorating an event from real, recent, history: a battle that took place in 991. By portraying the battle in emphatically heroic terms the poet of *The Battle of Maldon* magnifies the Anglo-Saxon participants in it and associates them with the great warriors of former times. And one episode in the prose – and otherwise mostly prosaic – *Anglo-Saxon Chronicle,* the 'Cynewulf and Cyneheard' episode, also incorporates aspects of the heroic ethos into its presentation of Anglo-Saxon historical material.

Such application of traditional form and ideas, along with their widespread appropriation in religious verse, testifies to the continuing potency of heroic paradigms for Anglo-Saxon poets and their audiences.

The Battle of Maldon, despite its 'post-heroic' setting, has been viewed as representing a classic expression of Germanic values, with one passage in particular often cited as quintessentially heroic in its sentiment. This is the passage in which the old warrior Byrhtwold urges on his fellows in their doomed fight and willingly goes forward to his own death in his attempt to avenge the killing of his lord (lines 309–19; trans. Crossley-Holland 1984, p. 19):

> Byrhtwold grasped his shield and spoke.
> He was an old companion. He brandished his ash-spear
> and most boldly urged on the warriors:
> 'Mind must be the firmer, heart the more fierce,
> courage the greater, as our strength diminishes.
> Here lies our leader, hewn down,
> an heroic man in the dust.
> He who now longs to escape will lament for ever.
> I am old. I will not go from here,
> but I mean to lie by the side of my lord,
> lie in the dust with the man I loved so dearly.'

In *The Battle of Maldon* the heroic ethos is portrayed as still driving late-Anglo-Saxon fighters. They enunciate and act on its principles, though Christian beliefs are also incorporated into the warriors' outlook and motivation. The leader Byrhtnoth himself as he falls in battle voices a prayer to the Almighty in a startling combination of Christian and worldly values (lines 173–80; trans. Crossley-Holland 1984, pp. 15–16):

> 'O Guardian of the people, let me praise and thank you
> for all the joys I have known in this world.
> Now, gracious Lord, as never before,
> I need Your grace, that my soul may set out
> on its journey to You, O Prince of Angels,
> that my soul may depart into Your power in peace.
> I pray that the devils may never destroy it.'

Action and the hero

Violent action is central to all heroic narrative, and in a society with a strict demarcation of gender roles such action belongs firmly to the sphere of male performance. Females are part of heroic society too but theirs is a supportive role normally acted out in the indoor domestic world. One of the female stereotypes in Old English heroic poetry that have been identified by modern scholars is that of the passive 'sorrowing woman' (*geomoru ides*) (Joyce Hill 1990), though it is also argued that females have a much more active role in the heroic world than this classification suggests. The idea of violent women is a particularly anxiety-provoking one in the poetry, however, with a sense of monstrosity about it, as evidenced most strikingly in the presentation of Grendel's mother in *Beowulf* but suggested too in other references. But then it has also been observed that the male hero too becomes monstrous in the extremity of action.

Women acting in the heroic world: some passages for consideration

1   Widsith's praise of Queen Ealhhild (*Widsith*, lines 99–102):
    The praise [of Ealhhild] extended through many lands,
    when in poetry I had to say
    where I best knew under the skies
    a gold-adorned queen bestowing gifts.
2   Hildegyth urges on the warrior Waldere (*Waldere*, lines 6–11):
    Warrior of Attila, do not at this stage let your courage
    weaken today, nor your noble valour . . .
    The day has come . . .
    that you must simply do one of two things,
    lose your life or gain long-lasting glory
    among men, son of Ælfhere.
3   Hildeburh grieving after violence (*Beowulf*, lines 1076–80a):
    Not without reason did [Hildeburh]
    bewail the decree of fate after morning came,
    when she could see under the skies
    the slaughter of her kinsmen, where she had most possessed
    joy in the world.
4   The imperious Modthryth (*Beowulf*, lines 1933–40):
    No one among the dear companions,
    except the great lord himself, dared bravely to venture
    to look her in the eyes even during the day,
    without expecting an outcome for himself of deadly fetters,
    woven by hand; and, when he had been seized,
    quickly thereafter the sword was the sentence for him,
    that its damascened blade should settle things,
    make known the deadly evil.

But we have to be careful what we mean by 'hero'. The word is often applied by modern readers to Beowulf and to other individuals in Old English heroic poetry but it is worth pointing out that there is no equivalent to our word *hero* in the poetry itself. There are words for warrior and nobleman but no word, at least not in the vernacular, to convey the sense of exceptionality understood in modern and indeed antique usages of *hero* (in Ancient Greek *hērōs* has the sense 'demigod'). The world of Old English heroic poetry is populated by larger-than-life figures but rather than heroes in the super-human sense these are mostly warriors who act uncompromisingly in accord-ance with the code of behaviour outlined above. The definitive qualities of the admirable warrior are identified in the poetry in their actions and speeches, and particularly in gnomic statements and passages of praise. Beowulf himself sums up an important part of the outlook of those who live up to the code when he declares,

> Better it is for each man
> that he avenge his friend than that he mourn much.
> Each one of us must await an end
> of life in the world; let him who can seek
> glory (*dom*) before death. For the noble man
> who has died, that will be the best thing afterwards.   (lines 1384b–9)

There is, however, at least one figure in Old English heroic poetry who displays that element of exceptionality that characterizes the hero in other traditions, Beowulf himself. Beowulf was 'the strongest in might in those days of this life' (lines 196–7); he is on a different level from other humans, capable of superhuman deeds. This again raises the issue of the uniqueness of *Beowulf.* Beowulf has the characteristics of the courageous Germanic warrior living by the heroic code, but is the poet also being influenced by classical ideas about the hero, and/or would comparable figures have existed elsewhere in Old English verse?

A learned Latin-Christian view of heroic poetry and the hero in the early Middle Ages: Isidore of Seville (c. 560–636)

A poem is called heroic (*heroicus*) because the acts and deeds of strong men are recounted in it, for celestial (*aerius*) men, as it were, worthy of the skies because of their wisdom and strength, are called heroes (*heros*) (*Etymologies*, I, 39, 9, trans. Barney *et al.* 2006, p. 65).

In his ferocity, and his exceptionality, Beowulf may also have that suggestion of monstrosity that has been associated with the hero (Dragland 1977). It is interesting, for example, that in *Beowulf* the word *aglæca*, meaning awesome or terrible opponent, is applied both to the monsters Grendel and the dragon and to Beowulf himself.

Beowulf

Beowulf (ed. Klaeber 2008) is the most famous work in all of Old English literature and despite its atypicality in the existing corpus it makes sense to select it as our example of a heroic poem for slightly more detailed consideration. It is steeped in heroic legend and tradition and shows mastery of the art of the *scop*, while at the same time transcending the world that it portrays and bringing a distinctly Christian perspective to its treatment of heroic material.

The reading of *Beowulf* invites us to peel away layer upon layer of the past. This great Old English heroic poem survives in one undistinguished-looking manuscript written at the end of the Anglo-Saxon period, in the early eleventh century (British Library, Cotton Vitellius A. xv). It is not known when the poem itself was composed: the most widely accepted view today would tend to favour the eighth or ninth centuries, but dates ranging from the seventh century to the eleventh have been proposed. The poem may have been recited and passed on over several centuries but, looking back from our modern perspective, we can only be certain that it was being read in the closing years of the Anglo-Saxon age.

Beowulf is itself a poem about the past. It was composed in the Christian era and is pervaded by references to the *Liffrea*, 'Lord of life', and other terms for God and by Christian patterns of thought (Cavill 2004). The events of the poem, however, take place in the past, in that heroic age of the Germanic tribes, long before their conversion to Christianity. The poet looks back on this pagan age from a Christian perspective and tries imaginatively to enter into it. He sees the splendour of it but he is also aware of a painful emptiness in it. One of the abiding images of *Beowulf* is of the brightness and civilization of the great hall of the Danes, Heorot, surrounded by the bleak darkness of the encroaching moors, from which comes the monster Grendel. Other early medieval writers dismissed the pagan past as idolatrous and vicious but the *Beowulf*-poet explores it with sympathetic respect. The virtue and courage of the people in the poem struggling against a hostile nature and caught up in human enmities and discords would have shone through to command the admiration of its original audience. Though the modern reader, at a further remove, may bring other values to bear upon the poem's interpretation, this virtue and courage still shine through.

Beowulf is a large-scale narrative work, telling over the course of its 3182 unhurried and reflective lines of the feats of the Geatish warrior Beowulf both in youth and in old age. Its central events are of a mythic and symbolic nature. In the first part of the poem Beowulf comes as an outsider to the aid of King Hrothgar and the Danes when they are afflicted by the evil of

Grendel. The poet describes his awesome victories over Grendel and over Grendel's fearsome mother, who comes to avenge the death of her son. The second part of the poem takes place years later when in Beowulf's old age his own tribe, the Geats, of which he is now the venerable king, has provoked the anger of a dragon. Beowulf's last great victory comes with the killing of this dragon but he himself is also killed in the fight. In this second part of the poem the characteristic optimism and certainty of the first part give way to a sense of insecurity and elegy which becomes more and more pervasive. The poem begins with a noble funeral, that of the Danish king Scyld, who had come as an unknown child and had initiated a period of glory for the Danes at a time of hardship and uncertainty; and, coming full circle, it ends with Beowulf's own funeral, which bequeaths a time of future uncertainty for the hero's own people after the great success that his reign has brought them.

Interwoven with the main plot of *Beowulf*, which is an archetypally simple one, is a dense mass of legendary material which contributes to the construction of an inter-tribal world of complicated and fluctuating relationships; there are more than a hundred personal names in *Beowulf*, many of which appear fleetingly in the narrative, others being mentioned indeed only in incidental allusion. Beowulf himself seems to be an invented character but these other names are mostly ones that the poet draws from Germanic tradition, a tradition that in *Beowulf* suggests both a sense of shared values and a perception of continuing fragmentation. Beowulf's grand feats punctuate the ceaseless pattern of legendary rivalry and turbulence, standing out as superhuman achievements, but they will soon be engulfed in human strife and change.

This swirl of change, part of the reality of life within which human groups must carve out their existence, is, however, overseen by a providential God, who cares for the people in the poem: in their time of hardship he 'perceived the dire distress' (line 14) of the Danes, and after his death Scyld goes 'into the Lord's protection' (line 27). The predicament of the people of *Beowulf* is that they must live without the Christian revelation that would bring hope and enduring meaning, though even in their unenlightened state the virtuous pagans of the poem discern something of the workings of God in the world and are guided by their sense of them. The poet's presentation of their pre-Christian beliefs, particularly those of Beowulf and Hrothgar, is favourable. As Hrothgar declares in a speech offering advice to Beowulf,

> It is a wonder to say
> how mighty God to mankind
> through his great wisdom gives discernment,
> land and nobility.   (lines 1724b–7a)

At one point in the poem the error of pagan religion is stressed. Oppressed by Grendel, the Danes turn to their pagan gods:

> At times they offered at heathen temples
> sacrifices, asked in their words
> that the soul-slayer might grant them aid
> in the face of their great calamaties. Such was their custom,
> the hope of the heathen.   (lines 175–9a)

Mostly, however, the poet presents the lives of his characters in a good light, with the more uncomfortable facets of paganism generally elided. We get pre-Christian funeral ceremonies (with which we can compare the early seventh-century Sutton Hoo burial: but see Frank 1992) but there is little sign of pagan observance as such.

Beowulf presents to its readers and hearers the most developed image of the heroic age in Old English literature and also the most complex reflection on its nature and meaning. The poem is dominated by the hero Beowulf, who behaves virtuously and engages in great combats against monstrous foes. In accordance with the heroic code, he fights to gain glory. Perhaps he and his world are an image for the Anglo-Saxon audience(s) of the poem of where they came from to arrive at their Christian present (Niles 2007, pp. 13–58). It is a noble but flawed world which the poet looks back to, but it is not the world he knows, any more than it is the world we know today. Beowulf is about the imagined past and about the meaning of the past for those who receive it.

Biblical literature: translations and adaptations in Old English

It is evident that Beowulf, despite its pre-Christian setting, is rich in biblical knowledge. As a profoundly serious work of Christian Anglo-Saxon England it would have been surprising indeed if it did not draw upon the Bible and its message, for the centrality of the Bible to Anglo-Saxon culture, as indeed to medieval culture as a whole, can hardly be overstated. In turning to explicitly Christian strands of narrative literature in our period it is appropriate therefore that we should look first at the Bible and the writings it inspired.

For Anglo-Saxons the Bible provided the essential foundation of religious belief and teaching and it provided the grounding of the church's liturgical observance in worship. In Anglo-Saxon England, as elsewhere, much litera-ture, and indeed art, is based on it directly, and other works, from Beowulf to riddles and from law codes to histories, abound in reference and allusion to it. Academic training was conceived of as leading up to the informed study of the Bible, and major scholars regarded their writings on the Bible as their most important. It is not insignificant, for example, that Bede's list of his books begins with all of his biblical commentaries and then goes on to his miscellaneous other works (*Ecclesiastical History*, V, 24; trans. Colgrave and Mynors 1969, pp. 567–71). Standards of learning among the clergy left much to be desired for long periods in the Anglo-Saxon centuries but a basic knowledge of the Bible was always seen as indispensable to the work of ministry; and religious people of advanced spirituality and learning would as a matter of course be deeply immersed in the sacred text and would know it intimately. The very books that contained the text of the Bible were held in special reverence as holy objects. One of the riddles of the Exeter Book (*Riddle 26*), the solution to which is taken to be 'Bible' or 'Gospel Book', describes its subject as beautifully made and adorned with gold and as bringing honour and prosperity (*tyr ond ead*, line 23) to those who use it. The riddle ends, in words that seem to merge the physical object with its content,

> Inquire what I am called,
> something of advantage to men. My name is glorious,
> beneficial to people, and itself holy.   (lines 26b–8)

The most splendid manuscripts from the early Middle Ages are bibles or part-bibles.

Knowledge of the Bible was considered important for lay people as well as for those in religious orders. A homily for the laity in the 'Blickling' collection of homilies calls upon its audience to have love and faith in their minds 'when we hear God's books explained and read to us, and the gospel declared, and his glories made known to men' (trans. Morris 1874–80, p. 110). In one of his sermons Ælfric tells his (general) audience, 'the words of God are to be considered with so great carefulness, that all his commands, with understanding and effect, be pondered over' (trans. Thorpe 1844–6, II, 281). Elsewhere Ælfric goes so far as to ask, referring to understanding of the Old Testament, 'how can he be accounted a Christian, who will not, according to the capacity of his understanding, search the book-writings, how they refer to Christ?' (trans. Thorpe 1844–6, II, 285).

But of course the medieval Bible was in Latin. The medieval Bible was the 'Vulgate' version, most of which had been produced for ordinary Latin speakers by the great church father Jerome in the late fourth century, based on the original biblical languages. After some initial resistance from proponents of 'Old Latin' versions, the Vulgate established itself as the standard Latin Bible and it remained the (only) 'authorized version', as it were, in western Christendom throughout the Middle Ages. Only the Book of Psalms continued to circulate to any significant degree in different Latin versions.

To have direct access to the Vulgate one needed to be proficient in Latin, however, a qualification that excluded the vast majority of people in Anglo-Saxon England. For most Anglo-Saxons, therefore, the Bible had to be mediated, 'translated' into the vernacular in some way. But how should it be made available in the vernacular? Indeed, was translation of the sacred text legitimate at all? These were real questions for early medieval thinkers, and the range of surviving Old English biblical literature testifies to differing responses to them. This literature comprises close translation, gloss, paraphrase, imaginative adaptation, spiritual interpretation, and reflection on the theory and challenges of transmitting the Bible in English.

Some Old English biblical literature sets out with the aim of making the content of Scripture available at a basic level, but biblical literature also includes works that assume a sophisticated prior knowledge of the Bible and its interpretation on the part of their audiences. Works such as the poems *Exodus* and *The Dream of the Rood*, for example, engage in rich explorations of spiritual meaning and incorporate complex theological interpretation. *Exodus* (trans. Bradley 1982, pp. 49–65) presents an allusive retelling of the story of the passage of the Israelites from Egypt to the Promised Land, focusing particularly on the crossing of the Red Sea. The poem, dense and learned in its treatment, emphasizes – and interweaves – the themes of covenant, victory and journey. The theme of covenant is related to the larger course of biblical history, with reference back to Noah and (especially) Abraham and forward to Christ; the theme of victory, expressed in vivid martial language, is understood symbolically in terms of the Christian message; the poem's understanding of journey, drawing also on images of home and exile, operates at a number of levels, with the idea of the journey of humankind to eternal life being particularly prominent in the closing section (and alluded to also at the very beginning). *Exodus* is based on the biblical Book but moves beyond the narrative to provide sustained reflection on the meaning and significance of that narrative.

The Dream of the Rood was mentioned in a previous chapter as exemplifying the Christian appropriation and transformation of Germanic heroic concepts. This poem draws upon a range of literary traditions, secular and Christian, to present a powerful depiction of the passion of Christ. It is not a literalist treatment of the gospel narrative but a metaphorical reimagining of it and meditation upon it. Cast as a dream in which the narrator experiences a wondrous but disturbing vision of the cross and hears it speak, the poem brings out the theological paradoxes of the crucifixion. It shows the crucifixion to be a cause of both grief and triumph and conveys a sense of Christ's dual nature as man and God and of his dual role as victim and victor. The figure of the dreamer provides a frame for the poem's account of the crucifixion and also a personal dimension, linking the shining world of the vision to the ordinary world of human weakness and imperfection in which this speaker lives. He has a dream of 'the brightest of trees, surrounded by light' but it takes place in the darkness of night and sin: 'in the middle of the night, / when voice-bearers [people] were at rest' (lines 2b–3).

The figure of the speaking cross, which relates the story of the crucifixion and death of Christ from its point of view, is a particularly daring device (strikingly recalling the conventions of the Old English riddles with their inanimate speakers) and one which enables the development of sublime paradox. The cross is simultaneously the follower of Christ, a witness of his passion, and his slayer, and it also functions as a surrogate of the passive suffering Christ, while allowing Christ himself to be portrayed as majestic and active. This portrayal serves to symbolize the willing divine sacrifice that lies at the centre of the theology of Christ's atonement for the sins of humankind. *The Dream of the Rood* is immediate in its impact and urgent in its message for its Christian readers but it is also a highly complex work with, like *Exodus*, an implied audience that already knows the Bible and is theologically informed.

Biblical poetry represents an important strand in the biblical literature of Anglo-Saxon England. The composition of this poetry began early in the period, as Bede's story of Cædmon, for example, and the inscription of verses corresponding to part of *The Dream of the Rood* on the sides of the (seventh- or eighth-century) Ruthwell Cross testify. The tradition continued to be productive right down to later Anglo-Saxon England: the Old Testament poem *Judith*, for example (discussed below), is dated by scholars as coming from the tenth century. And indeed the earlier Old English tradition also influenced Saxon poets on the Continent, as evidenced by the surviving Old Saxon poems *Genesis* (fragmentary) and *The Heliand* (a poem on the life of Christ).

The earliest prose translations of the Bible we have are the version of the first fifty psalms widely attributed to King Alfred and the translated passages from the Old Testament incorporated into Alfredian laws. As mentioned in a previous chapter, Bede is reported to have translated part of St John's Gospel but no trace of this work remains, and indeed the vast majority of surviving prose translations emanate only from the last decade of the tenth century and later, with Ælfric in particular producing a considerable amount of biblical material in Old English prose.

Before I discuss prose translation in slightly more detail, it is relevant to mention one other kind of biblical translation that is well represented in manuscripts from Anglo-Saxon England, the interlinear word-for-word glossing of Latin texts of the psalms and gospels. Nine glossed gospels and fifteen glossed psalters survive. Interlinear glossing comprises the insertion of words in existing Latin manuscripts, as is exemplified most famously in the Lindisfarne Gospels, in which a tenth-century hand has written small Old English words above their Latin equivalents, and also in the production of specially written psalter manuscripts in which a continuous gloss is integral to the layout.

In the Lindisfarne Gospels word-for-word translations are provided for Latin words (though note that in Figure 3.1 *verbum*, 'word', in the second-last line, is glossed *word þ[æt] is godes sunu*, 'word, that is God's son', and *d[eu]m*, 'God', is glossed *god fæder*, 'God the Father', thus adding an explanatory element to the gloss). In the 'integral' psalter glosses the two texts are designed together, with every Latin word, even the simplest, being accompanied by an Old English one written above. Many of the word-glosses provided in such manuscripts are redundant from the practical point of view and must therefore be there to do something more than to aid a stumbling reader of Latin. The glosses have an educative purpose (Brown 1999) but readers don't need to keep being told *et* means *and*, or *est* means *is*. The eleventh-century 'Cambridge Psalter' goes so far as to present a continuous Old English gloss that is the same size as the Latin text and is in red. As Robert Stanton points out, continuous glosses of this kind 'are not readable vernacular versions but word-for-word facsimiles of the Latin' (Stanton 2002, p. 118). A continuous gloss lacks proper syntax and cannot stand on its own. Instead of producing a new version of its original, paradoxically such a gloss draws the reader towards that original, thus also avoiding some of the problematic issues in 'full' biblical translation. In Stanton's persuasive view, 'Word-by-word glossing represents an ideal of fidelity that goes well beyond communication and reaches deep into the mystical divine power of the "original" language' (Stanton 2002, p. 118).

Timeline of Old English biblical translations and adaptations

c. 680	Cædmon's poetry: Cædmon reported by Bede as the first to compose Christian narrative poetry, including biblical, in Old English
735	Death of Bede. His pupil Cuthbert reports that Bede translated part of the Gospel of John into Old English before he died. It has not survived.

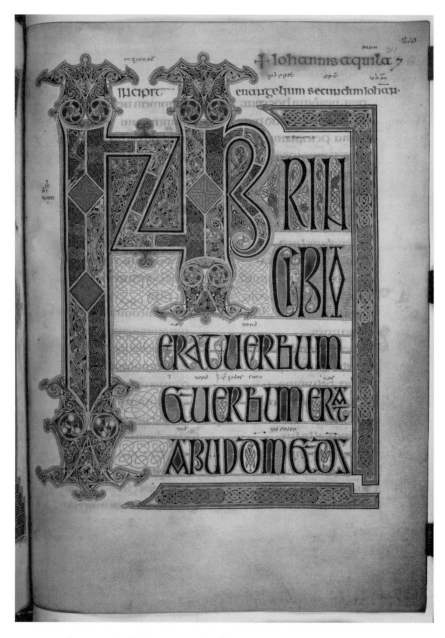

Fig. 3.1 Lindisfarne Gospels: decorative page at the beginning of
St John's Gospel, with interlinear Old English gloss

c. 825	Vespasian Psalter gloss: interlinear gloss added to Latin manuscript
c. 850	Old Saxon poem *The Heliand* ('The Saviour')
c. 895	Translation of Ten Commandments and other portions of Exodus and Deuteronomy into Old English, incorporated into Alfred's Law Code; Old English prose version of Psalms 1–50
c. 950–70	Aldred and Farman write interlinear Old English glosses to Lindisfarne and Rushworth Gospels, respectively
c. 1000	Ælfric translates parts of the Heptateuch into Old English; the remainder of the Heptateuch is translated by other writers Ælfric produces a range of other biblical paraphrases and related works, as well as incorporating a substantial amount of translation of Scripture into his homilies West Saxon Gospels: Old English versions of the four gospels Approximate date of major surviving manuscripts containing Old English biblical poetry (date of composition of the poems not known)

The Old English prose version of the first fifty psalms, attributed by many to King Alfred, is a 'full' translation. It has some very minor additions for the sake of clarification but generally presents as word-for-word a version as possible while (unlike a gloss) conforming to Old English syntax and word order. This version supplies more than a translation, however. Interestingly, the text of each psalm is preceded by a short explanatory introduction (also in Old English), as may be illustrated by quoting the beginning of Psalm 5:

> The fifth psalm is called 'David's Psalm', which he sang about his own experience of consolation and about the praise of all those righteous people who seek their inheritance in the heavenly kingdom with Christ, who is the end of all things. And each person who sings this psalm sings it about his own experience of consolation; and so did Hezekiah when he was released from his infirmity; and so did Christ when he was freed from the Jews.

> (1) Lord, receive my words with your ears, and listen to my voice and my cry, and consider the words of my prayers, (2) because I pray to you in the dawn. But grant that you hear my prayer, Lord ...   (ed. O'Neill 2001, p. 103)

In line with medieval views of biblical interpretation (on which, see further below, pp. 136–7), in the introduction the translator interprets this psalm on four levels, historical (with reference to David), anagogical (with reference to heaven), tropological or moral (with reference to the person saying the psalm) and typological or allegorical (with reference to

Christ, and also mentioning Hezekiah). The introductions are based on an identified Latin source, though scholars have also perceived emphases in them reflective of Alfred's own concerns, and, as Robert Stanton suggests, the translation of the psalms themselves, though literal, provides a version of the psalter 'subtly altered to present a very specific image of the king as wise educator; this image is based on that of King David, whose author-ship of the psalms is affirmed in the Old English introductions' (Stanton 2002, pp. 121–2). Such an image fits well with the Alfredian milieu of the translation, whether or not the Old English psalms are seen as fully the work of the king himself.

The translation of the first fifty psalms survives only in a manuscript of the eleventh century, the 'Paris Psalter', in which the set of 150 psalms has been completed by the inclusion of a verse translation of psalms 51–150. The Old English translations of the psalms were evidently intended to be read independently from the Latin original; it is notable therefore that the Paris Psalter also includes a parallel text of the psalms in Latin, though in a version different from that used for the translations. The compiler of this manuscript wished his (educated) audience to com-pare the Old English and Latin versions, so that one becomes a kind of gloss on the other (thus recalling the glossed manuscripts mentioned above). The Latin text appears in the left-hand column and may therefore be thought of as taking precedence but both versions are otherwise given equal prominence.

About a hundred years after the Alfredian translation of the psalms we arrive at what must be regarded as one of the most remarkable periods of Bible translation in the whole history of English. From the late tenth and early eleventh centuries come a complete translation of the gospels, of unknown authorship, and a translation of the Heptateuch (the first seven books of the Bible: Genesis, Exodus, Leviticus, Numbers, Deuteronomy, Joshua, Judges), some of which was produced by Ælfric but some of which was done by other writers working independently from him. Ælfric him-self was a prolific translator of the Bible, writing a close translation of the Book of Genesis down to the story of Abraham and Isaac and of other parts of the Heptateuch as well as composing looser paraphrases of a wide range of Old Testament material. And if we were to assemble all the passages of the New Testament translated at the beginnings of Ælfric's homilies, this in itself would constitute a substantial body of Bible translation.

Ælfric was a prolific translator of the Bible then, but he was also a reluctant one. He expresses his profound anxieties about making the sacred words available in English most insistently in his *Preface to Genesis*, an accompanying letter sent with his translation of Genesis to the pious layperson Æthelweard, who had commissioned it. Ælfric is acutely conscious of the spiritual depth and subtlety of the biblical text and he fears that by making the 'bare narrative' available to the untrained he will be opening the door to simplistic and wrong interpretation:

> Now it seems to me, beloved one, that the work is very hazardous for me or for any man to undertake, because I fear that if some foolish person reads this book or hears it read, he may suppose that he may live now in the era of the New Law just as our forefathers lived in the era before the Old Law was established, or as men lived under the Law of Moses ... We also declare ahead of time that the book is very difficult to understand spiritually, and that we have written no more than the bare narrative. It will therefore seem to the ignorant that all the meaning is locked in the simple narrative, but that is very far from true.   (trans. Muinzer 1970, pp. 165, 166)

Ælfric goes on in the *Preface* to provide brief illustrative interpretations of the beginning of Genesis and of other parts of the book, bringing out spiritual levels of meaning.

Rather than engaging in the problematic business of translating the 'bare (*nacod*) narrative', Ælfric was happier explaining the Bible, drawing on the sophisticated principles of biblical interpretation developed in Christian tradition to do so. This is what we see him doing in his exegetical homilies and in other writings such as his *Letter to Sigeweard* (*On the Old and New Testament*), the latter being a summary of and brief commentary on all the books of the Bible. Ælfric also writes in his *Preface to Genesis* that he 'dare write no more in English than the Latin has, nor change the arrangement of the words except in those places alone in which the Latin and English usage do not have a common idiom' (trans. Muinzer 1970, p. 166), thus engaging in questions of the 'how' of translation theory. For the Bible, he declares himself bound to stick literally to the original, though it is notable that, even so, he does intervene with the occasional gloss or strategic omission; and many of his versions of Old Testament books are paraphrases in the abbreviating style that we will also see to be typical of his saints' lives. His non-Heptateuch biblical paraphrases include versions of the Books of Esther and Judith (the latter referred to below), and parts of Kings and Maccabees. Biblical translation was something that Ælfric wrestled about, and wrestled with, producing, despite his qualms, the largest body of such translation in English before the Wycliffite Bible of the late fourteenth century.

Judith*: a biblical adaptation in Old English verse*

Most surviving Old English biblical narrative poetry is preserved in the 'Junius Manuscript', an all-poetry compendium containing *Genesis A*, a paraphrase of the biblical book down to the Abraham–Isaac story; *Genesis B*, an account of the Fall of Satan and of Adam and Eve based on an Old Saxon original (and incorporated into *Genesis A*); *Exodus*, on the journey of the Israelites to the Promised Land; and *Daniel*, an adaptation of Daniel I–V, part of which also has an analogue in the Exeter Book poem *Azarias*. This fairly coherent group is followed in the manuscript by *Christ and Satan*, added at a later date and completing the collection in its present form. *Christ and Satan* is biblically inspired but is not a translation or adaptation as such.

Judith (ed. Griffith 1997; ed. and trans. Hamer 1970, pp. 135–57), by contrast, is to be found in the *Beowulf* manuscript, along with *Beowulf* itself and three prose texts in which wondrous and monstrous people figure centrally. The manuscript has been read by critics as a themed 'book of monsters' or a collection on 'pride and prodigies' (Orchard 1995), with the pride and monstrosity in *Judith* being supplied by the evil Holofernes, according to this view. Certainly, *Beowulf* in particular provides an interesting context for reading *Judith*, since both poems have heroic saviour figures who act alone to preserve communities from oppression perpetrated by seemingly invincible enemies, killing those enemies with their own hands. Except that in *Judith* the saviour is a woman.

The Book of Judith tells the story of the siege of Bethulia, a border city of Israel, by an Assyrian army under Holofernes, and of the deliverance of the city from the clutches of the enemy thanks to the widow Judith, who braves the Assyrian camp and there seduces and then beheads Holofernes. The discovery of this calamity leads to panic and despair among Holofernes's followers, who flee from Israel, while Judith is glorified as the saviour of her people. The opening of the version of the story in Old English verse is missing, as the text begins in the middle of a sentence corresponding to a point about two-thirds the way through the narrative as presented in the Old Testament book; the rest of the poem is complete. Scholars disagree as to whether the deficiency at the beginning means that the majority of *Judith* is missing or whether the Old English poet might have concentrated only on the climax of the story (as the poet of *Exodus* did, for example, in treating the journey of the Israelites out of Egypt), omitting much of the biblical book or reducing it to a summary – in which case perhaps only a small proportion of the text may be lacking. The original Book of Judith consists of sixteen chapters, but the 350 lines of *Judith* cover only from near the end of chapter IX to the first verse of chapter XVI, and even then the treatment is highly selective.

Judith presents a vigorous adaptation of the biblical book which focuses on the faith and courage of its protagonist and on the depravity of Holofernes. Complicating narrative detail is cut out and the original cast of characters much reduced, with the result that the conflict between Judith and Holofernes dominates the poem. Unlike in the Book of Judith itself, and in contrast too to Ælfric's Old English paraphrase (ed. Assmann 1889, pp. 102–16), there is no sign in *Judith* of sub-plots or networks of relationship, and the bigger picture of the threat against Israel posed by the Assyrian advance is pointedly left out of consideration. *Judith* is a poem about the attack on Bethulia and about how Judith saved the city by confronting and destroying the godless oppression personified in Holofernes. The pattern of opposition is insistently brought out in a manner that we will see later to be similar to that typical of saints' lives (see, for example, Belanoff 1993).

Critics have also drawn attention to the parallels between the situation described in the Judith story and that in Anglo-Saxon England at the time the poem was likely composed (in the tenth century), when the country was hard pressed by pagan Viking attack (see, for example, Pringle 1975). Indeed, referring in a later work to his own abbreviated paraphrase of the Book of Judith, Ælfric specifically makes this parallel, saying that he put this book into English 'as an example to you our people, to defend your land with weapons against the invading army' (*Letter to Sigeweard*, trans. Magennis 2004, p. 224). Some Anglo-Saxon audiences might well have read Ælfric's version and the Old English poem as rallying calls against the Danes but, despite Ælfric's later comment, there is nothing in either Old English version which explicitly urges such a reading. At the end of his paraphrase, indeed, Ælfric appends a brief commentary on the story in which he interprets Judith not as an example against the Danes but as spiritually signifying the Christian church and chastity and as giving inspiration in particular to religious women. And the poem *Judith* plays down the national dimension of the story, which seems to work against the rallying-call reading; rather than offering a clear political message, or indeed an obvious allegorical meaning, *Judith* focuses on the achievement of the heroine, and it develops its theme of opposition very much on a personal level.

The sexually alluring Judith of the original was, however, clearly a problematic figure for the Old English poet (as she was also for Ælfric: see Clayton 1994), and so she is transformed from the seductive widow who uses her female wiles to entrap her enemy, to become a virtuous Germanic noblewoman, who, driven by necessity, takes on the role of heroic slayer of the enemy. Judith executes this violent deed with impressive bravery even though she is unsuited to it in terms of her physical attributes; it is notable, for example, that she needs two attempts to cut off the head of the unconscious Holofernes, and she is full of fear as she prepares to do the deed. The *Judith* poet is aware that the idea of a female acting violently provokes great anxiety in an Anglo-Saxon cultural context and works, by highlighting her courage despite her womanly frailty, to make Judith an admirable figure. A seductive Judith could never provide an acceptable female role model in this cultural context, however, which leads the poet to excise the temptress theme completely, a big ask given the specifics of the inherited story.

Holofernes, Judith's opponent, is portrayed as a Germanic chieftain or rather as a parody of such a figure, one who is completely lacking in the self-control and strength of spirit of a successful leader; ironically these are qualities that Judith herself displays. Holofernes inspires fear rather than loyalty among his *comitatus* and sets them a bad example in his self-indulgence, as epitomized by the drunken feast with which the existing text opens. In contrast to the stately banquets of *Beowulf*, for example, this feast is an occasion for riotousness:

> So the evil one for a full day
> drowned his retainers with wine,
> the violent-minded distributor of treasure, until they lay unconscious,
> his whole troop completely drunk, as if they were slain in death,
> drained of every good thing.   (lines 28–32a)

The biblical book describes how Judith plies Holofernes with alcohol at the feast, getting him to drink more than he is used to, so that she can incapacitate him. In the Old English poem on the other hand Judith is not even present at the feast and Holofernes, a habitual drunkard, is wholly responsible for his own downfall. And rather than being seduced by Judith Holofernes is portrayed as aggressively lustful, ordering Judith to be brought to his tent under military escort so that he can do his worst: 'he intended to defile the bright lady with impurity and sin' (lines 58b–9a). Fortunately for Judith he passes out before he can harm her.

Judith is creative in its use of Germanic heroic tradition, presenting Germanic values in a broadly positive light. It even includes a battle scene, replete with the theme of the 'beasts of battle' familiar from secular poetry, according to which the wolf, the raven and the eagle gather in anticipation of slaughter (on the beasts of battle, see especially Griffith 1993). In this battle, which has no counterpart in the original, the Bethulians, inspired by Judith's killing of Holofernes, rout the invaders.

The poem makes use of heroic tradition but also complicates that tradition by taking account of problematic gender issues and by deploying elements that have been described as mock-heroic and even comic (Heinemann 1970, Herbison 2010); and it also appropriates features of the saint's life, as is most strikingly evident in its oppositional approach. *Judith* is alert in recasting its biblical material, ensuring in the process that the virtue of its protagonist is in no way brought into question. Judith, whose state of widowhood and hence sexual experience are not mentioned (at least not in the surviving text), is a figure of chastity, threatened, like the virgin saint of hagiographical tradition, by a raging pagan. In resisting and triumphing she shows herself to be a heroic woman.

The past and its meaning: writing history

The most important history book for the Middle Ages was the Bible. In accordance with the scheme of the 'six ages' of the world, as elaborated particularly by the great patristic writer Augustine, the Bible constituted a history of God's people from the creation down to the early decades of the sixth age, the age which was instituted by the momentous event of the coming of Christ and will last until doomsday at some unknown time in the future; as Ælfric writes in his *Letter to Sigeweard*, echoing the teaching of Augustine, 'The sixth age of this world stretches from Christ right to dooms-day, the time of which is unknown to all men, though the Saviour knows it' (trans. Magennis 2004, p. 233). The course of history has providential meaning, shape and structure; it has a beginning, a mid-point and an end-point. The Bible also taught medieval Christians that God shows favour or anger towards his people in accordance with their actions, a theme that we have already seen brought out in Anglo-Saxon writings.

These ideas arising from biblical interpretation inform medieval Christian conceptions of history and are widely reflected in Anglo-Saxon England, as is an appreciation of Augustine's biblically grounded general theory of history, as laid out in his *City of God* (trans. Bettenson 1972). According to Augustine's paradigm-setting theory, history enacts a conflict between the spiritual City of God and the temporal City of Man, a conflict in which the City of God is destined, despite the vicissitudes that it encounters, to triumph in the end. For Augustine the City of God is to be understood in spiritual terms as 'the supernatural reality' (Knowles 1972, p. xviii) of those predestined to reign with God in heaven, though at one point he identifies the City of God with the Christian church (Book XIII, 16) and it is easy to see how in the Middle Ages it could be associated with the church. For early medieval historians, churchmen themselves, the history of the church as the overarching divinely authorized institution of Christian society provides a definitive ideological framework.

Augustine wrote his *City of God* in the aftermath of the sacking of Rome by the Goths in 410, which some Romans argued had come about because the state had abandoned the old religion and adopted Christianity. Augustine refuted this view, pointing to the calamities that had also taken place in the pre-Christian era. His follower Orosius took up this theme in his *History against the Pagans*, showing in detail that there have always been disasters in human history. Orosius's *History against the Pagans* is a 'universal history', intertwining biblical and classical material in its opening chapters but going on to concentrate on Roman history, cataloguing in the process the calamities that have overtaken humankind down to the fall of Rome.

As we saw in an earlier chapter, Orosius's *History* was adapted into Old English as part of King Alfred's programme of translating 'the books most needful for all people to know'. The Old English *Orosius* is a significant work of Anglo-Saxon historiography, which freely edits and rewrites its source in a way that shifts the emphasis away from the focal year 410 and places it instead on the incarnation of Christ. This reworking has the effect of taking the *History* out of its original fifth-century context and making it more obviously a work of broad relevance to early medieval readers, a work which more clearly than the original expresses the theological understanding of history in which the decisive event is the coming of Christ. As Janet Bately writes of the Old English version, 'through careful selection and rearrangement of the material provided by [Orosius's original *History*] special emphasis is given to Christ's birth as the dividing point, separating a past of unrelieved misery from a present characterized by universal manifestations of mercy and peace and an undeniable improvement in man's lot' (Bately 1980, p. xciv). The Old English *Orosius* broadens the message of the original while at the same time, through the inclusion of the 'Ohthere and Wulfstan' material (see above, pp. 60–1), it relates the text to Anglo-Saxon England and the court of King Alfred.

For early medieval observers God's providence over humankind is manifest in the larger course of history with its divinely ordained structure, but is also to be seen in the miracles that he has caused to take place both in the Bible and in later history. Miracles – occurrences above, contrary to or outside the normal workings of nature – are not part of modern historiography but can have a place in the theologically based historiography of the Middle Ages. Ælfric, following Augustine in Book XXII of the *City of God*, preaches that the age of miracles is over now that Christianity is firmly established:

> These wonders were needful at the beginning of Christianity, for by these signs was the heathen folk inclined to faith. The man who plants trees or herbs, waters them so long until they have taken root; when they are growing he ceases from watering: so also the Almighty God so long showed his miracles to the heathen folk, until they were believing: when faith had sprung up over all the world, then miracles ceased. (*Catholic Homilies*, trans. Thorpe, I, 305)

Ælfric goes on to say that the church continues to perform 'spiritual' (*gastlice*) miracles through the sacraments.

Miracles occurred in earlier history, therefore, particularly in contexts of conversion and it is understood to be proper for writers of history – and of saints' lives – to chronicle them; Bede, for one, includes miracle stories in his *Ecclesiastical History of the English People*. It should be added that while acknowledging that the age of miracles is over both Augustine and Ælfric tell of miracles that have taken place in their own times: the age of miracles may be over but miracles can still occur. It is only in the very end of the course of human history, says Ælfric, that miracles will cease altogether: 'in the time of Antichrist miracles will cease and the devil will then perform miracles through his sorcery with false delusions to lead astray the faithful' (*Passion of Saints Chrysanthus and Daria*, trans. Upchurch 2007, p. 99; cf. Matthew XXIV. 24).

As the present discussion will continue to demonstrate, the importance of Christian ideology as the basis of medieval historiographical thinking cannot be overstated. It must also be noted, however, that as well as being guided by the theological underpinnings of the works of Augustine, Orosius, Isidore and other Christian writers, medieval historians were also indebted to antique literary traditions. The influence of Roman biography, for instance, is apparent (via Einhard's *Life of Charlemagne*) in Asser's *Life of King Alfred*. More generally, ancient traditions of rhetoric were transmitted to medieval historians by Christian writers of the late Roman period. And, crucially, medieval historiography inherited the classical principle, found in Cicero for example, that history furnishes moral lessons. As Bede puts it at the beginning of his *Ecclesiastical History*, 'Should history tell of good men and their good estate, the thoughtful listener is spurred on to imitate the good; should it record the evil ends of wicked men, no less effectually the devout and earnest listener is kindled to eschew what is harmful and perverse, and himself with greater care pursue those things which he has learned to be good and pleasing in the sight of God' (Preface; trans. Colgrave and Mynors 1969, p. 3).

Bede, the 'father of English history', as he has often been called, is of course the major figure in Anglo-Saxon historiography. Steeped in the *City of God*, he was also an original and highly influential thinker on the subject of history in his own right. He was the author not only of the monumental *Ecclesiastical History* but also of the *Lives of the Abbots of Wearmouth and Jarrow*, which is a detailed biographical work (trans. Farmer 1983), and of two treatises dealing with chronology, each of which incorporates a mass of historical material in the form of a 'universal chronicle'. These treatises on what would later become known as '*computus*' are the short *On Times* (*De temporibus*) and, a master-work on the subject, the compendious *The Reckoning of Time* (*De temporum ratione*) (trans. Wallis 1999). *Computus* was about the measurement of time and the establishment of a Christian calendar based on the cycles of nature; it charted the divisions of day, month and year but its key function, an essential one for ecclesiastical purposes, was to calculate the changing date of Easter over the years. The dating of Easter, the feast around which the whole Christian year is constructed, is based on an elaborate calculation that takes account of both the solar and lunar calendars. In *The Reckoning of Time* Bede provided a comprehensive and clear exposition of *computus* that was to be recognized as the standard textbook on the subject for many centuries.

In *On Times* and *The Reckoning of Time* one of the striking ways in which Bede broke new ground was by integrating into his account of the measurement of time a universal chronicle, thereby producing what Kathleen Davis refers to in her recent discussion of *The Reckoning of Time* as a 'political theology of time' (Davis 2008, p. 105). As Davis explains (p. 105), 'Organized as a comprehensive, exegetical treatment of cyclic and linear time on a universal scale, *De temporum ratione* explicates time as a regulated and regulating system that is integrated with and propelled by the histories of peoples and kings.'

The chronicle in *On Times* (known as the *Lesser Chronicle*) and that in *The Reckoning of Time* (known as the *Greater Chronicle*) trace the history of the world through its six ages from the beginning down to Bede's own day, with particular reference to biblical and Roman history; there is also a significant amount of attention to Britain. These universal chronicles take the form of an unbroken sequence of dates of rulers, accompanied by mention of contemporaneous occurrences and developments that Bede considers notable. Less discursive and less overtly polemical than histories of Orosius's kind, Bede's universal chronicles consist mainly of brief annotations based on a wide range of sources.

In the chronicles the dates are given '*anno mundi*' – starting at the beginning of the world – in a scheme in which Bede recalculates the date of the creation as occurring in 3952 BC. The *anno mundi* system serves to integrate the strands of history into a single unified sequence, reflective of God's all-encompassing providential scheme. In Orosius's *History* many dates are given in the course of the narrative but they don't serve a structural function, as they do in the universal chronicles, and they are based on Roman dating systems, making the perspective Rome-centred rather than pointing to 'theological' history: events in Orosius are dated from the foundation of the city of Rome and by reference to Roman consulships (each of which normally lasted for one year). As Davis points out, a consequence of Bede's recalculation of the date of the creation is that the ages of the world are worked out to be of unequal length (not, as certain previous schemes had it, of uniform periods of 1000 years). For Bede, the first five ages had lasted 1656, 292, 942, 473 and 589 years, respectively. The unequal length of the ages in turn confirms the indeterminacy of time and the unknowability therefore, as Augustine also had insisted, of the date of the end-point of history. This circumstance ensures that human action is not to be viewed as meaningless in the face of providential history: it is 'the indeterminacy of time itself that guarantees meaningful human history' (Davis 2008, p. 108).

Bede also includes a timeline of important events at the end of the *Ecclesiastical History* but that one focuses only on the history of Britain, of course, while the dates in the universal chronicles refer to the whole world. The dating system in the *Ecclesiastical History* goes one step further in theological terms, however, than that of Bede's universal chronicles. In the *Ecclesiastical History*, which was written after *The Reckoning of Time*, Bede adopts the *anno Domini* system, making the year of Christ's birth the reference point for everything in history, before or since. Bede was the first writer to use this system for a work of history, thereby instituting a practice that soon became the norm and that has remained so ever since. The *anno Domini* system is used mostly unreflectively today (though the religiously neutral label 'Common Era' is often preferred for it) but it is worth remembering that the system derives from a theological understanding of history, just as the *anno mundi* system does.

The first date given by Bede in the *Greater Chronicle* is 130, the year in which Adam begot Seth (cf. Genesis V. 3). Jesus Christ was born in 3952 and he died in 3984: 'In the eighteenth year of the reign of Tiberius the Lord redeemed the world by his Passion, and the Apostles, preparing to preach throughout the regions of Judea, ordained James the brother of the Lord to be bishop of Jerusalem' (trans. Wallis, p. 196). Bede's timeline goes down to 4680 (= AD 717), the date of the accession of the Byzantine emperor Leo (III); at this time, says Bede, the Saracens besieged Constantinople and engaged in other wars, and, introducing a detail of more personal interest, he notes that just before this his own former abbot Ceolfrith died while travelling on a pilgrimage to Rome (= AD 716) (trans. Wallis 1999, p. 236).

This mention of Rome also serves to illustrate for us that, while Bede used theological, not secular-Roman, dating systems as the framework for his historiographical works, Rome loomed very large for him both historically and geographically, as it did for Anglo-Saxon thinkers more generally. Rome the imperial superpower had been swept aside (one consequence of which, in Bede's view, was to open the way for the divinely sanctioned conquest of Britain by the Anglo-Saxons), but the city had been reborn as the see of St Peter and his successors as pope down to the Anglo-Saxon present. The continued centrality of Rome to Anglo-Saxons is brought out nicely in the title of one of Nicholas Howe's incisive articles, 'Rome: Capital of Anglo-Saxon England'. In that article Howe argues with reference to Bede, 'within the abstract cosmology of the universal church, Jerusalem was the center of the world for Bede; within the political and conversion history of the Anglo-Saxons, Rome was the capital of England' (Howe 2004, p. 156). It was also the capital of the western world more generally, of course.

In writing his universal chronicles the erudite Bede was adapting an existing Christian tradition in which the seminal figure had been Eusebius of Caesarea (*c.* 262–*c.* 339), whose *Chronicon* was known in the West through the Latin translation of the second of its two books, by Jerome. It should be added that, as well as providing a source for Bede's chronicles, Eusebius was also a key influence on the *Ecclesiastical History* through another of his works. Eusebius's *History of the Church*, translated into Latin by Jerome's contemporary Rufinus, was the first 'ecclesiastical history' and provided a model for Bede and other Christian historians. As well as providing a model in terms of its form, Eusebius's *History* is animated by thematic concerns, such as tracing the lines of succession of bishops and championing religious orthodoxy, that appear again in Bede's *Ecclesiastical History.* And though Eusebius wrote in a pre-/non-Augustinian tradition, he too as a Christian historian portrayed history as providential.

Moving on from this overview of senses of history inherited into and developed in the early Middle Ages, the rest of the present section will focus on the two historiographical works from Anglo-Saxon England generally considered to be by far the most significant, Bede's *Ecclesiastical History* and the *Anglo-Saxon Chronicle*. It is hoped that the discussion so far will have provided a general orientation for approaching these texts in their period, but of course other political and cultural contexts and agendas also need to be taken account of in approaching them. Works of history always explain the past in terms of the beliefs, values and circumstances of the present. It is the present that furnishes the setting in which the historian constructs an image of the past and in which existing historical writings are interpreted. While each present will have individual distinctive features, I have been concerned here to bring out some general ideas about history operative in Christian Anglo-Saxon England, the basis of which was biblical and theological.

Before I move to the *Ecclesiastical History* and the *Chronicle*, however, it is relevant to mention briefly one other historiographical work from the period widely read today, Asser's *Life of King Alfred* (trans. Keynes and Lapidge 1983, pp. 65–110). The *Life* is a laudatory biography of the king down to the time of writing, which is given as 893; the work seems to be incomplete and has nothing to say about the closing years of Alfred's life even though Asser outlived the king by nearly a decade. The literary model that the *Life* follows is that of Einhard's *Life of Charlemagne* (which, however, includes the death of its subject) and its major source of information about Alfred and other contemporary figures and events is the *Anglo-Saxon Chronicle*, though its use of the *Chronicle* ceases at 887 for some reason. The writer also frequently refers to his personal knowledge of the king, which has supplied him with a wealth of information.

Asser's *Life of King Alfred* is an important document for historians – it is the only source for many details of the king's life – but it is also a literary work which goes out of its way to idealize Alfred in every possible respect and needs to be approached critically as a historical source. In its glowing treatment of its protagonist, who emerges as saintly, heroic, devoted to learning and wise in his judgements, the *Life* is often viewed indeed as part of the propaganda machine associated with the king. Alfred is portrayed embracing the chronic illness with which he was afflicted and as being like Solomon, who achieved 'both wisdom and renown in this world' (ch. 76; trans. Keynes and Lapidge 1983, p. 92).

Unlike other Alfredian works, however, the *Life of King Alfred* seems to place itself in a Welsh textual community rather than an Anglo-Saxon one and to have the aim of selling King Alfred to his Welsh subjects. If this is right, the *Life* is only tangentially, if at all, an Anglo-Latin work. Interestingly, it is not noticed in surviving Anglo-Saxon writings until the end of the tenth century, which is also the approximate date for the one manuscript in which it was transmitted to the modern period (the manuscript was destroyed in the Cotton fire of 1731 but the *Life of King Alfred* had been previously transcribed). Indeed, it has been argued that it is really in this later period that the *Life* was written: in the view of Alfred Smyth it is a forgery by Byrhtferth of Ramsey or an associate, who sought to magnify the memory of Alfred, constructing him at the turn of the millennium as 'his ideal West Saxon king' (Smyth 2002, p. 204). Smyth's theory has received little if any support but it is true that the later period provides a significant reception context for the *Life of King Alfred*. The *Life* was surely written in 893 and presents what Richard Abels characterizes as 'a ninth-century ideal of Christian kingship' (Abels 1998, p. 326), but it was picked up by Byrhtferth and others about a hundred years later as a source for propagandizing Alfred as an inspirational model of kingship for the present, the troublesome time of King Æthelred.

Alfred the ideal Christian king

He was also in the invariable habit of listening daily to divine services and Mass, and of participating in certain psalms and prayers and in the day-time and night-time offices, and, at night-time, as I have said, of going (without his household knowing) to various churches in order to pray. He similarly applied himself attentively to charity and distribution of alms to the native population and to foreign visitors of all races, showing immense and incomparable kindness and generosity to all men, as well as to the investigation of things unknown. Wherefore many Franks, Frisians, Gauls, Vikings, Welshmen, Irishmen and Bretons subjected themselves willingly to his lordship, nobles and commoners alike; and, as befitted his royal status, he ruled, loved, honoured and enriched them all with wealth and authority, just as he did his own people. He was also in the habit of listening eagerly and attentively to Holy Scripture being read out by his own countrymen, or even, if the situation should somehow arise, of listening to these lessons in the company of foreigners. With wonderful affection he cherished his bishops and the entire clergy, his ealdormen and nobles, his officials as well as all his associates. Nor, in the midst of other affairs, did he cease from personally giving, by day and night, instruction in all virtuous behaviour and tutelage in literacy to their sons, who were being brought up in the royal household and whom he loved no less than his own children.
(Asser, *Life of King Alfred*, ch. 76; trans. Keynes and Lapidge, p. 91)

Bede's Ecclesiastical History of the English People

Bede's *Ecclesiastical History of the English People* is widely acknowledged to be the most significant history written in Britain throughout the entire Middle Ages, and of all literary works produced in Britain it is the one which has been continuously read and studied for the longest period (by far). From the Middle Ages alone more than 150 manuscripts of it survive, exponentially more than for any other Anglo-Saxon work discussed in this book, and printed editions of it have appeared regularly from the sixteenth century on. In the most recent overview of Bede's writings it can credibly be argued that the *Ecclesiastical History* 'shaped historiography not only of England but also of the Western world' (Brown 2009, p. 101).

I will have something to say briefly about the 'afterlife' of the *Ecclesiastical History* in my concluding chapter but in approaching it in its original Anglo-Saxon historical context, a key initial point to make is that it strikingly exemplifies the understanding of history as providential as outlined in the introductory part of this section – history as overseen and guided by God. In the *Ecclesiastical History* history is providential not only in a general universal sense but also specifically with respect to Bede's own people. In Bede's version of providential history, the Anglo-Saxons – the *Angli*, as he insistently calls them – are the rightful inheritors of the land of Britain, having usurped it from its undeserving existing inhabitants, the Britons, who themselves, Bede notes, had been immigrants many centuries earlier.

Directed at an elite and learned readership in eighth-century Northumbria and further afield, the *Ecclesiastical History* tells the story of the progress of the Anglo-Saxons in Britain down to the time of Bede's completion of this, his last great work, in or around 731. It tells the story of the Anglo-Saxons and in particular of their development as a Christian people, narrated in the context of larger salvation history (as reflected in Bede's use of the *anno Domini* dating system) and always with reference to Rome, whose influence is restored in Britain by the Anglo-Saxons when they embrace Roman Christianity. But, as Nicholas Howe points out, the *History* also tells the story of the other peoples of Britain, the Britons, Picts and Irish (Scots), who take their place in an Anglo-Saxon order willed by God (Howe 1989, pp. 50–2), an order that fulfils a kind of 'manifest destiny'. The central focus of Bede's narrative is the institutional church, which provides a foundation for the construction of an English ethnic identity but also participates in the community of the Rome-centred universal church.

Britain in 731

(from the very end of the *Ecclesiastical History*)
   The Picts now have a treaty of peace with the English and rejoice to share in the catholic peace and truth of the church universal. The Irish who live in Britain are content with their own territories and devise no plots or treachery against the

English. Though, for the most part, the Britons oppose the English through their inbred hatred, and the whole state of the catholic church by their incorrect Easter and their evil customs, yet being opposed by the power of God and man alike, they cannot obtain what they want in either respect. For although they are partly their own masters, yet they have also been brought partly under the rule of the English.

In these favourable times of peace and prosperity, many of the Northumbrian race, both noble and simple, have laid aside their weapons, preferring that they and their children should take monastic vows rather than train themselves in the art of war.

(V, 23; trans. Colgrave and Mynors 1969, p. 561)

Over the course of its five books (five being a number that Bede and his readers would associate with that first history of God's people, the Penta-teuch), the *Ecclesiastical History* presents a detailed, though partial and carefully selective narrative. After a geographic and ethnographic description of the island, Book I gives an account of the history of Roman Britain and of the unhappy period after Roman rule when the Britons were afflicted by internal division and external attack and were led astray by heresy. It is in this period that the Anglo-Saxons arrive and begin to conquer the land. Bede gives a precise date for their arrival (449), thus suggesting that the settlement of the colonists was a single event rather than a less organized continuing process (Michelet 2006, p. 258). He writes of the Britons with great hostility, seeing them as unworthy possessors of the land. He notes with particular disapproval that though they were Christians they never attempted to convert the pagan Anglo-Saxon settlers: 'To other unspeakable crimes, which Gildas their own historian describes in doleful words, was added this crime, that they never preached to the Saxons or Angles who inhabited Britain with them' (I, 22; trans. Colgrave and Mynors 1969, p. 69). Bede tells us that when Christian missionaries first came to the Anglo-Saxons they came from Rome, sent under the leadership of Augustine by the saintly Pope Gregory to begin their preaching in Kent (in 597). The remainder of Book I covers the early years of this mission, reproducing in its account of it a number of letters of advice and guidance sent by Gregory.

Book II begins with the death of Gregory and gives a glowing account of the life of this 'apostle' of the English, as Bede describes him. The book goes on to tell of the early bishops of Anglo-Saxon England and of the continu-ation of the activities of the Roman missionaries, focusing in particular on the conversion of the virtuous King Edwin of Northumbria by Paulinus. In describing the spread of Christianity in this book, as throughout the *Ecclesi-astical History*, Bede's attention is entirely on royal and aristocratic society, presenting conversion very much as a 'top-down' process.

Book III deals with the reconversion of Northumbria after, as Bede puts it, 'King Edwin's next successors betrayed the faith of their race' (III, chapter headings; trans. Colgrave and Mynors 1969, p. 209). In explaining the context of this process, Bede refers to the conflict and dynastic rivalry between the two kingdoms that make up Northumbria – Deira and Bernicia – and paints a picture of wars between Northumbria and British and Anglo-Saxon neighbours. The reconversion to Christianity is carried out by Irish – not Roman – missionaries, under Aidan, and is actively sponsored by King Oswald, who had spent a period in exile among the Irish. The book also chronicles the process of conversion in other kingdoms, Wessex, East Anglia, Essex and Mercia, mentioning a number of leading bishops and kings, and it develops the theme of disagreement and contention between Roman and Celtic Christianity. Bede treads carefully in covering this topic; though regarding the Celtic church as misguided in key practices, he shows admiration for Irish (though not British) tradition, and particularly for Aidan, who, with Oswald, stands out as the most impressive figure in Book III. The ecclesiastical controversy is settled at the Synod of Whitby (664) with agreement that Roman practices, notably concerning the date of Easter and the monastic tonsure, should be accepted throughout England. Bede gives a detailed account of the passionate debate at Whitby between the 'Roman' Bishop Wilfrid and the Irish Bishop Colman, with King Oswiu of Northumbria in the chair. The outcome is victory for Wilfrid, after which those who had followed the Celtic way 'gave up their imperfect rules, and readily accepted in their place those which they recognized to be better' (III, 25; trans. Colgrave and Mynors 1969, p. 309).

At the beginning of Book IV the learned Theodore of Tarsus is consecrated archbishop of Canterbury (seventh after Augustine), 'the first of the archbishops whom the whole English church consented to obey' (IV, 2; trans. Colgrave and Mynors 1969, p. 333). Under Theodore's firm guidance Christianity is seen to flourish and spread further throughout the country. The period covered in this book and the next one is presented by Bede as a time of settled Christianity among the Anglo-Saxons, as reflected in the profusion of miracle stories that are included here and the accounts of English people of exemplary holiness. In Book IV Bede tells of the holy women Etheldreda and Hild, the poet Cædmon and the exemplary bishop Cuthbert, who, along with Gregory, is his greatest hero. Bede had already written prose and metrical lives of Cuthbert, bringing out, as he does here in the *Ecclesiastical History*, his 'Gregorian' features as monk and reluctant but effective bishop. Bede presents Cuthbert as one who combined the virtues of Celtic spirituality with a firm acceptance of orthodoxy and (again recalling Gregory) an exemplary humility.

The final book of the *Ecclesiastical History* includes approving coverage of the beginning of Anglo-Saxon missionary work on the Continent, in areas from which the Anglo-Saxons originally came, and of the extension of Roman practices among the Irish and Pictish peoples; Bede quotes a long and eloquent letter from Abbot Ceolfrith of Wearmouth-Jarrow to King Nechtan of the Picts chiefly on the correct dating of Easter. Meanwhile the piety of Anglo-Saxon kings is praised, some of whom indeed give up their royal power to devote themselves to the religious life. The death of Theodore is recorded, as is that of another of the major churchmen who bestride the *History*, Wilfrid, a turbulent and divisive figure according to other testimony but presented by Bede as a champion of orthodoxy and a zealous missionary and, as N. J. Higham argues (Higham 2006, p. 69), as much 'a focus of apostolic humility' as Bede can make him. The book ends with a survey of the Anglo-Saxon world as Bede sees it around him at the time of writing. The Britons persist in their 'evil customs' but generally the picture that Bede leaves his readers with is one of stability and right rule, in both the church and the secular world: 'these favourable times of peace and prosperity' (V, 23; trans. Colgrave and Mynors 1969, p. 561).

The *Ecclesiastical History* is accompanied by a preface (written after the work had been first released) addressed to King Ceolwulf of Northumbria, and it ends with a recapitulation in the form of a brief chronicle giving the dates of important events mentioned in the *History*, followed by an autobiographical note and a list of Bede's books. In the preface Bede gives a detailed account of his sources, referring to many written documents and naming many inform- ants. The list of trustworthy oral as well as written sources imparts a sense of authority and authentication. He has availed himself of reliable witnesses, Bede insists, but asks readers who may find anything other than the truth in what he has written not to blame him, for 'in accordance with the principles of true history (*uera lex historiae*, literally 'true law of history'), I have simply sought to commit to writing what I have collected from common report, for the instruction of posterity' (Preface; trans. Colgrave and Mynors 1969, p. 7); *lex uera historiae* has been convincingly explained as referring to 'that which would be generally acceptable (e.g. by religious communities) from whatever kind of source', Wallace-Hadrill 1988, p. 5).

Bede has done much more, of course, than simply to commit to writing what people have told him. He has chosen and marshalled his sources to produce not, as earlier generations of commentators had accepted, a straightforward version of history by a disinterested monk removed from all worldly concerns but something more calculated. Bede has emerged for more recent critics very much as a writer with a political agenda, manipulating his material (Goffart 1988; Howe 1989), rewriting his characters in order to promote particular models of leadership (Higham 2006), and presenting 'the facts' in a highly rhetorical fashion (Gunn 2009). It has been pointed out that Bede focuses almost exclusively on the eastern part of the country, including nothing for example on western Mercia or western Wessex, let alone the non-Anglo-Saxon areas, and it has been suggested that his blanket condemnation of the British church may conceal a more complex reality – and even indeed the possibility of continuity and community between British and Anglo-Saxon Christianity (Brooks 2006). There is much about the period he covers that Bede does not know about, or chooses to pass over in silence.

Scholars disagree about Bede's narrower agenda in early eighth-century Northumbria but, following groundbreaking studies by Goffart (1988), Howe (1989) and others, recognition of Bede's own situatedness and of the essentially political nature of his approach to history has become central to current research on the *Ecclesiastical History*. Bede, the Northumbrian and the committed monk in the Roman Christian tradition, constructs the Anglo-Saxons as a single ethnic group, united by their divinely guided experience, by their language (which is a single language, one of five, including Latin, spoken in Britain) and by the ecclesiastical order that they embrace. The pivotal figure of their history is Gregory the Great, who brings the Christian faith to this special people and renews the bond between Britain and Rome, a bond that Bede portrays as having become increasingly firmer throughout the period that his narrative covers.

In elaborating his grand narrative Bede applies his formidable knowledge of literary models and rhetorical technique and draws upon the range of his own powers as a writer. Critics praise the imagination, stylistic elegance and intelligence of the *Ecclesiastical History*, in which a gallery of memorable characters and a succession of key episodes and descriptions provide moral lessons for the reader – a primary aim of history for Bede – and give vivid expression to the overall understanding of Anglo-Saxon history that the work seeks to convey. I have mentioned Gregory, Edwin, Oswald, Aidan, Hild, Cuthbert and Wilfrid as major figures in the *History* and the list could certainly be extended considerably. Among episodes and descriptions that stand out are those on the Synod of Whitby, referred to above, and the poet Cædmon, which was discussed right at the beginning of this book. One episode that was particularly influential for Bede's readers in Anglo-Saxon England and later is the story of Gregory and the English slave boys at the

Forum in Rome in which Gregory puns that their name 'Angles' (*Angli*) is fitting since they have the faces of angels (*angeli*) and resolves that their race should be converted to Christianity (III, 1). A story that modern readers have been especially drawn to is that of the conversion of King Edwin by Paulinus, especially the part in which one of the king's counsellors makes an eloquent speech recommending that they accept the new religion (II, 13); the counsellor compares human life to the flight of a sparrow inside a warm hall in winter, in one door and out the other in the briefest of moments. Tellingly, Bede comments in his account that the desire of these pagans to accept Christianity is 'divinely prompted': God is guiding them. This vignette, which echoes themes seen also in *Beowulf,* thus highlights the working of divine providence. It also shows its readers the yearning emptiness of paganism, the sensibleness of the early English, the attractiveness of the Christian message and the zeal of Roman missionaries like Paulinus.

The brilliance of Bede's writing is everywhere to be seen in the *Ecclesiastical History.* It is marshalled to deliver a particular view of Anglo-Saxon history and a particular image of Anglo-Saxon England, a view and an image that generations down the centuries have taken to be the unvarnished truth. What Bede presented was a partial and ideologically inspired picture, however, composed to a specific purpose in a specific historical context. It was also a self-fulfilling version of past and present, foundational in its construction of the English as an imagined community and in its elaboration of a myth of origins that persisted in Anglo-Saxon imagination to the end of the period (Howe 1989, pp. 8–32). The *Ecclesiastical History* was an important source for Ælfric, who is drawn to Bede's English saints and particularly to Gregory (Lees 2009); and of course (as Ælfric also knew) the *History* was translated into Old English at the end of the ninth century in a version that takes up the themes of conversion and Englishness, while reducing the Northumbrian emphasis and cutting out much of the non-English material. In its likely context of Alfredian Wessex and of the king's project of promoting literature in English, Bede's *History* is appropriated in the translation for a new vernacular readership, living in different circumstances from those of Bede's original (pre-Viking) audience but deemed receptive to what Bede could tell them about themselves.

The conversion of King Edwin: a counsellor advises

Another of the king's chief men ... added, 'This is how the present life of man on earth, King, appears to me in comparison with that time which is unknown to us. You are sitting feasting with your ealdormen and thegns in winter time;

the fire is burning on the hearth in the middle of the hall and all inside is warm, while outside the wintry storms of rain and snow are raging; and a sparrow flies swiftly through the hall. It enters at one door and quickly flies out through the other. For the few moments that it is inside, the storm and wintry tempest cannot touch it, but after the briefest moment of calm, it flits from your sight, out of the wintry storm and into it again. So this life of man appears but for a moment; what follows or indeed what went before, we know not at all. If this new doctrine brings us more certain information, it seems right that we should accept it.' Other elders and counsellors of the king continued in the same manner, being divinely prompted to do so.

(II, 13; trans. Colgrave and Mynors 1969, pp. 183–5)

The Anglo-Saxon Chronicle

The production of Old English versions of Orosius's *History against the Pagans* and Bede's *Ecclesiastical History* in the late ninth century represents a remarkable development in historiography. The normal language for writing history in the medieval West was Latin but here, for the first time, was history in the vernacular. These works, which are surely to be associated with King Alfred's initiative of translating the books 'most needful for all people to know', rendered history available to a new audience, and in doing so they also made a statement about the status of the English language, legitimizing it as a worthy medium for the learned discourse of history, a radical step indeed. Even more extraordinary in terms of language politics and perception, however, is another historiographical production emanating originally from the same period as these translations, the *Anglo-Saxon Chronicle* (trans. Swanton 2000). Though basing its early entries on Latin sources, the *Anglo-Saxon Chronicle* was composed directly in Old English; it is written in the vernacular language of the people whose history it records. That history is recorded, on the model of Latin chronicles, in the form of annals, giving information about things that happened in particular years. Often the annals are extremely brief but in some sequences, notably those dealing with King Alfred's time and other times of crisis and conflict, a considerable amount of narrative detail is provided (see Figure 3.2).

The *Anglo-Saxon Chronicle* is also extraordinary for the period over which its composition stretched. It was begun in the early 890s but was regularly updated thereafter by generations of writers in different parts of the country right up to the end of the Anglo-Saxon period and indeed well beyond it: in one version, the 'Peterborough Chronicle', it continues on

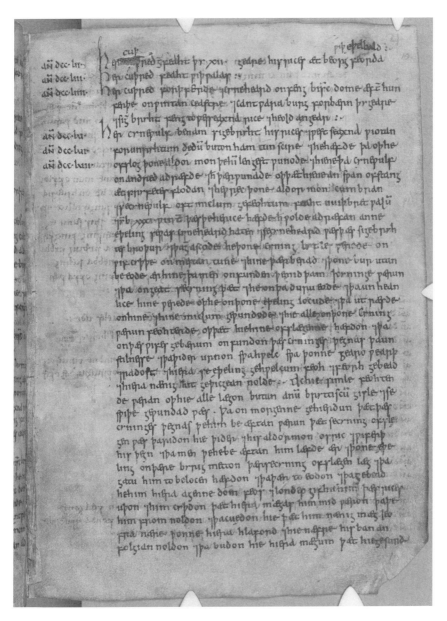

Fig. 3.2 A page from the *Anglo-Saxon Chronicle* (Parker Manuscript): dates (*anno Domini*) in left column

down to 1154. The *Chronicle* is an invaluable source for studying Anglo-Saxon history and politics, therefore, though (like Bede) it has to be read critically. And it strikingly exemplifies changes in prose and verse writing over the period of its composition (the *Chronicle* is written in prose but incorporates a number of specially written poems). Notably, while preserving some conservative stylistic traits, the narrative mode of the *Chronicle* evolves over time, becoming more literary and rhetorical, as Cecily Clark demonstrated in a classic study (Clark 1971). For long stretches, especially in the earlier centuries, the *Chronicle* entries consist of single declarative sentences or short strings of such sentences covering events that may or may not be related to each other. The entries get fuller in the ninth century, where we find mini-narratives with more developed information about people and places. The style remains plain and unemotive, however, giving the impression of objective and straightforward reporting of events worthy of note. The selection of those events is in itself significant, of course, and the selection of what to say about events can guide the reader to a particular view. It is in the tenth century that the tone becomes more emotive, first glorifying the successors of King Alfred and then at the end of the century and in the early eleventh century developing a register of moral fervency in the face of perceived treachery and failure of leadership in England.

Particularly notable for the fervour of their glorification of West Saxon kings are the *Chronicle* poems, especially (the most accomplished of them) *The Battle of Brunanburh*, which uses traditional poetic language and motifs to eulogize King Athelstan and his bother Edmund, who have comprehensively defeated an alliance of Norse and Celts at a place called Brunanburh (unidentified). The poem focuses on the two leading figures and on the opposing commanders, who are humiliated in the battle. In an earlier chapter I quoted the end of the poem (see above, p. 19), which declares that no greater slaughter had taken place in the history of Anglo-Saxon England. The beginning of it (ed. Marsden 2004, p. 88), employing a series of familiar formulas, establishes the tone of triumphal celebration:

> King Athelstan, lord of men (*eorla dryhten*),
> ring-giver to warriors (*beorna beafgifa*), and his brother also,
> Prince Edmund, won life-long glory
> in battle with the edges of swords (*sweorda ecgum*)
> at Brunanburh.   (lines 1–5a)

As well as being a key source for historians and literary scholars, the *Chronicle* is also an invaluable resource for studying linguistic change, as we see its language moving from Early West Saxon to Standard Old English and eventually, in the very latest entries, morphing into Early Middle English. The English language had been changing throughout the late Anglo-Saxon period (for example, influenced by the Norse of Scandinavian settlers) but those changes are masked in texts from the period due to the dominance of Standard Old English; they become visible when the cultural structures that had sustained Standard Old English are no longer in place. And, since the latest *Chronicle* entries were written, at Peterborough, in a centre far removed from the influence of the new Norman-French order, we can see the language changing not under external pressure but, as Seth Lerer puts it, 'on its own' (Lerer 2007, p. 39).

The *Anglo-Saxon Chronicle* consists of annals recording significant events in the past and then as they occurred year by year. The project was begun in Wessex in the time of King Alfred. A product of clerical learning but with a close eye on political issues, the first part was written in one sweep and covers the period from the birth of Christ and the Roman conquest of Britain to the year 891. For earlier centuries this first part uses as its main source Bede's *Ecclesiastical History* and the chronicle at the end of it, supplementing these by drawing on lists of kings and bishops, and relying on a range of other sources (including oral) for the post-Bede period. The *Chronicle*, which follows Bede in using the *anno Domini* dating system, may have been conceived as a continuation of Bede's chronicle but it emerges from the different context of late-ninth-century Wessex and is concerned with the Anglo-Saxons first as conquerors – as Michelet points out (2006, p. 256), this is a theme that Bede plays down – and then as defenders in a series of campaigns against heathen Vikings, campaigns in which West Saxon kings, and especially Alfred, are portrayed as playing the leading role. Alfred himself is presented in a particularly favourable light, to the extent that the *Chronicle* has commonly been viewed by scholars as Alfredian propaganda. As one recent commentator writes, 'A clear theme emerges from the *Chronicle*'s account of political and military developments among the "English" peoples in the British Isles, that Alfred's reign was the culmination of English history' (Abels 1998, p. 17).

The *Chronicle* shows great interest in the reigns and succession of King Alfred's predecessors as king of Wessex. The oldest manuscript, the 'A' version, begins with a detailed genealogy of Alfred, tracing him back, via Cynegils, 'the first of the West Saxons' kings to receive baptism' (trans. Swanton 2000, p. 2), and Cerdic, the first king of the West Saxons, to Woden himself. There is much about the wars that the early kings engaged in against the Britons but the latter remain shadowy and largely absent from the narrative; nothing is said about the religion of the Britons.

Throughout the Anglo-Saxon Christian period, on the other hand, ecclesiastical accessions and deaths are steadily recorded and relatively frequent reference is made to links with Rome, providing a reassuring religious framework for the secular events and natural phenomena that the *Chronicle* also records.

After 891 the *Chronicle* was continued in several versions in different parts of the country, with the first part, the 'common stock', forming a shared foundation upon which the later chroniclers built. In a previous chapter I also mentioned a Latin prose translation of the *Chronicle* by Ælfric's lay patron Æthelweard (see above, p. 53). In these distinct but overlapping versions the *Anglo-Saxon Chronicle* presents a unique picture of Anglo-Saxon history, cultural values and self-perception. It is a Christian picture, of course, based on the incarnational understanding of history, and the Anglo-Saxons are seen as having a special place within this larger history. The very opening words of the 'common stock' of the *Chronicle* are, 'Sixty years before the Incarnation of Christ, Julius Caesar, the first emperor of the Romans, sought out the land of Britain' (trans. Swanton 2000, p. 4), a formulation that brings together the Incarnation, the island of Britain and the Roman world, the identity-defining elements that will be embraced by the Anglo-Saxons. By covering the various Anglo-Saxon kingdoms but not the other parts of Britain the 'common stock' follows Bede in constructing the English as a single entity, and this construction is very much carried through in the later era of the 'kingdom of England', though there we get an increasing sense of the individual character of the *Chronicle* versions and, along with this, an increasing sense of political complication and of differing interests and viewpoints.

'Cynewulf and Cyneheard': death and vengeance in eighth-century Wessex

The best-known entry of all in the *Anglo-Saxon Chronicle* is that for 755, the 'Cynewulf and Cyneheard' episode, which takes the form of a fully developed narrative telling a bloody story of dynastic rivalry within the royal house of Wessex (the first two-thirds or so of this entry appear in the manuscript facsimile on p. 111, above). This entry does not confine itself to a single year but, uniquely, relates a complete story, the stages of which stretch over a period of thirty-one years. It is a story of usurpation, killing and revenge that in its content sounds more like something out of a heroic poem than a piece of real history. It is different from anything else in the *Chronicle* and has been the most fascinating section for modern readers.

The episode begins with the deposition of King Sigeberht of Wessex by Cynewulf and the killing of the ousted king some time afterwards. Then thirty-one years later Sigeberht's brother Cyneheard seizes an opportunity to kill Cynewulf, before he too is caught up with and killed by Cynewulf's men. Both Cynewulf's and Cyneheard's men go down fighting to avenge their lord rather than submitting to his enemy; as the *Chronicle* account tantalizingly puts it in the case of the slaughter of Cynewulf's men, 'they all lay dead except for one British hostage, and he was very wounded' (trans. Swanton 2000, p. 48). There is no other mention of British hostages in this allusive narrative, nor indeed elsewhere in the *Chronicle*.

The 'Cynewulf and Cyneheard' episode is full of high drama and has the immediacy of an eye-witness account, though it is written in the unadorned and apparently dispassionate style characteristic of much of the *Chronicle*. The action seems unmediated and there is no analysis of the characters' motivations. The story is outlined in a series of declarative statements of the type *then . . . and then . . . and then*, without causal or other kinds of qualification. This annal is far less simple than it might look at first sight, however, and through its careful handling of information subtly endorses a particular (pro-Cynewulf) interpretation of events. A sense of the narrative mode of the episode can be suggested by quoting the opening sentences, which seem very unforthcoming in terms of explanation but reward careful reading:

755 Here Cynewulf and the councillors of Wessex deprived King Sigeberht of his kingdom because of unlawful actions – except for Hampshire; and he had that until he killed the ealdorman who stayed with him longest. And Cynewulf then drove him away to the Weald, and he stayed there until a herdsman stabbed him by the stream at Privett – and he thus avenged the ealdorman Cumbra. (trans. Swanton, p. 46 ['A' Version])

Every detail in these sentences is significant for understanding the issues, which are extremely serious ones to do with kingship, loyalty, civil order and governance.

The events of the 'Cynewulf and Cyneheard' annal are set in the eighth century and are based on an unknown source, perhaps oral. The *Chronicle* account of them comes from more than a hundred years later, in King Alfred's Wessex. One of the intriguing issues connected with the story is, if the *Chronicle* is to be connected with Alfred, what would he have made of this tale of apparently legitimate usurpation and the killing of a king? Interestingly Asser's *Life of King Alfred* records, in a horrified tone, a more recent attempt to overthrow a king of Wessex (not mentioned in the *Anglo-Saxon Chronicle*): in 856 while King Æthelwulf was in Rome 'his son Æthelbald, with all his councillors – or rather co-conspirators – attempted to perpetrate a terrible crime: expelling the king from his own kingdom' (trans. Keynes and Lapidge 1983, p. 70).

The 'Cynewulf and Cyneheard' episode ends with snippets of information that at first sight might seem inconsequential: 'And that Cynewulf ruled for thirty-one years, and his body lies at Winchester, and the ætheling's [Cyneheard's] at Axminster; and their direct paternal ancestry goes back to Cerdic' (trans. Swanton, p. 48). The last clause adds a seemingly throwaway detail, but it is one that in fact retrospectively provides the whole basis of the conflict at the centre of the story.

Christian heroes: writing about the saints

Saints' lives are one of the definitive literary genres of the Middle Ages. Across western Europe and in the Christian East many thousands of them were written over the medieval centuries, embodying the values and ideologies of the communities that produced them and providing edification, and wonder, for readerships and audiences of diverse kinds. Saints' lives are richly represented, not least in the literature of Anglo-Saxon England, from which we have a wide range of hagiographical texts in Latin and Old English and, in both languages, in prose and verse. The Old English lives constitute the earliest body of such writings in a western vernacular language.

Ælfric, the most prolific writer of Old English saints' lives, writes that the greatness of God is manifested in the wonders of his saints: 'Christ reveals to men through his saints that he is almighty God who performs such miracles' (*Passion of St Edmund*, trans. Crossley-Holland 1984, p. 233). Elsewhere Ælfric declares that the stories of saints are recorded and celebrated because they give example and bring intercession for the faithful: the saints, who are in heaven, 'do not need our praise while we are living, but that which we say about them benefits us, first as an example that we might be the better and then for intercession when we need it' (*Passion of Saints Chrysanthus and Daria*, trans. Upchurch 2007, p. 99). Saints are powerful and glorious. Veneration of them brings spiritual benefits, and the stories of their lives of heroic faith and holiness and of the miracles associated with them provide example and sustenance for those who read them or hear them.

Because of its conventionality and its ceaseless celebration of miracles the saints' lives genre was long despised in post-medieval critical circles but is recognized today not only as reflecting illuminatingly medieval perceptions, beliefs and anxieties but also as having produced writings of remarkable power and imagination. It is notable that some of the most important Anglo-Saxon writers, including Aldhelm, Bede, Alcuin and of course Ælfric, wrote about saints. The subject matter of hagiography is of profound seriousness and spiritual significance, and, as demonstrated below, the literary characteristics of this kind of writing have been shown to be of considerable critical interest, when it is approached in its own terms.

An extensive corpus of hagiographical writings was inherited by the Anglo-Saxons from the earlier Christian church, consisting of accounts of the lives (and deaths) of the apostles after the Ascension of Christ, the martyrdoms of men and women executed during the Roman persecutions, the strivings of the desert saints, who withdrew from the world to live in solitude and self-mortification, and biographies of famous 'confessors', church leaders whose lives displayed extraordinary sanctity. This inherited material, written in Latin (some of it having been translated from Greek), formed the core of the Anglo-Saxon hagiographical canon and provided the sources and the models for the saints' lives that the Anglo-Saxons themselves produced. Latin saints' lives could range in length from a thousand words or so to many thousands of words, and as well as circulating in the early Middle Ages as separate books they were typically transmitted also in large collections, 'legendaries', or reading-books, intended for use in religious houses, such books often containing well over a hundred individual items. And, in addition to saints' lives as such, the broad category of hagiography also includes calendars, listing the dates of saints' feast days, and martyrologies, collections which present brief notices or résumés of saints rather than developed narratives.

The surviving hagiographical literature from Anglo-Saxon England itself comprises the following:

> Lives in Latin: early anonymous lives (*Gregory, Cuthbert*), summaries by Aldhelm (*De virginitate*), lives by Bede (*Cuthbert*; Bede also incorporates hagiographical material into his *Ecclesiastical History*), Stephen of Ripon (*Wilfrid*), Felix of Crowland (*Guthlac*), and others; later lives, including by the continental writer Abbo of Fleury (*Edmund*), Lantfred, also continental (*Swithun*), Wulfstan of Winchester (*Æthelwold*), and a number of anonymous lives (including *Dunstan*).
>
> A small number of verse texts in Old English (many more must have been produced): *Andreas, The Fates of the Apostles, Elene, Guthlac A, Guthlac B, Juliana.*
>
> 'Martyrologies' (calendars of commemorative festivals of martyrs and other saints, giving brief digests of their lives and deaths), of which two important examples were produced in Anglo-Saxon England, one in Latin, the other in Old English: Bede wrote a martyrology in Latin (trans. Lifshitz 2001), containing about 125 commemorations; the *Old English Martyrology* (trans. Herzfeld 1900) is a ninth-century collection of some 230 brief accounts (and it is incomplete).
>
> Over fifty Old English prose hagiographical texts by Ælfric, in his *Catholic Homilies* and *Lives of Saints*; Ælfric also produced in Latin an abbreviated version of the *Life of St Æthelwold*, based on Wulfstan's version.
>
> Thirty-six anonymous prose Old English saints' lives, thought to have been produced mostly in the tenth century or later.

As mentioned above, critics now approach Anglo-Saxon saints' lives, and saints' lives in general, more sympathetically than used to be the case. Students of Old English verse saints' lives have been struck in particular by the creative ways in which poets explore the nature of the heroism of their subjects, drawing upon the resources of the secular poetic tradition to do so. More generally, in its attachment to the wondrous, hagiography has been linked to romance. It is evident that the earliest narratives of the saints, in Greek, were influenced in their style and story patterns by the traditions of ancient romance, both directly and via the example of the Acts of the Apostles in the Bible. At a deeper level, certain structural and compositional features, such as characterization, the theme of trial and tribulation success-fully overcome, the victory of good over evil, and the lack of interest in social and economic specificity, ally hagiography generically with romance (see T. D. Hill 1996).

As medieval hagiography developed, including in early England, its inher-ent structural romance features remained but the treatment of saints and their stories tended to become more stylized and starker than previously. Early saints' lives had sought to entertain as well as to edify in their stories and treatment, for example displaying a concern for the human feelings of their idealized protagonists that again makes us think of romance. The 'human' and entertaining qualities of the tradition were embraced in some quarters in the early medieval period, but the more characteristic impulse reflected in surviving lives from Anglo-Saxon England was to present saints as increasingly superhuman, rarefied figures beyond ordinary earthly limita-tion, who, rather than exhibiting evidence of fallibility and struggle, appear already serenely to reflect the perfection of heaven in their lives. Saints imitate Christ and in doing so they transcend normal human capacities.

In Anglo-Saxon England this rarefied kind of hagiography, though by no means universal, is widely found and is exemplified particularly in the writings of Ælfric. In its presentation of the serenity and impassivity of the saint in the face of persecution and vicissitude this hagiography calls to mind stylistic qualities associated not with romance but with early medieval art, as inherited from Byzantine and other early Christian tradition. In this tradition the holy figure is an image of stasis and contemplative spirituality, not at all one of action or struggle. Visual depictions of saints in Anglo-Saxon England exhibit similar qualities and thus provide telling parallels to what we find in literary tradition.

One famous example (among many) of the representation of sanctity in Anglo-Saxon art is the picture of St Etheldreda in the Benedictional of St Æthelwold (see Figure 3.3), the sumptuous service book made for the

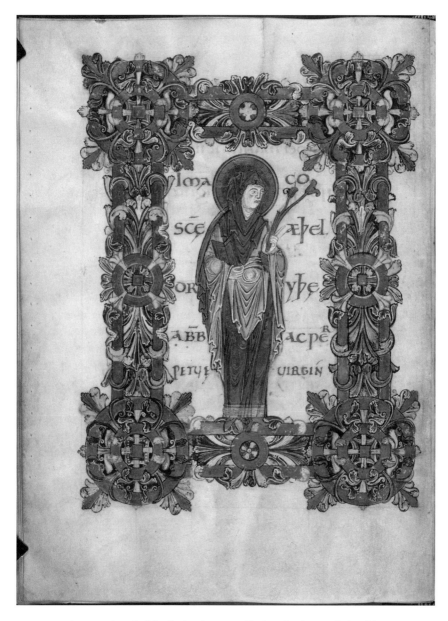

Fig. 3.3 St Etheldreda in the Benedictional of St Æthelwold

Benedictine-reform leader, and teacher of Ælfric, Bishop Æthelwold of Winchester. The image of Etheldreda is one of holy stasis, in which the impassive and austere figure of the saint, with a gold halo and holding the flower that is the symbol of her virginity, stands motionless in an eternal sacred space looking across at God in his omnipotence on the facing page; her feet rest on the frame of the enclosed space, symbolizing the merging together of earthly and heavenly realms in the person of the saint.

The same approach to the portrayal of sanctity is characteristic of much early medieval hagiography. One influential commentator writes of the 'motionless moment' of the saints' life, declaring, 'We read a text that obviously does not belong to temporality, it takes place in a sort of small eternity' (Boyer 1981, p. 29). Rather than engaging them in the human interest and excitement of its stories, this hagiography causes its audiences to wonder at the differentness of the saints from ordinary experience, presenting them 'iconographically' (Earl 1978) as representing a Christ-like perfected sanctity on earth. Their narrative becomes a celebration, incorporating veneration and in some ways suggestive of the register of ritual.

This incorporation of veneration and suggestion of ritual in hagiographical narrative accords with the context in which this literature was produced and received. Hagiographical literature did its work in Anglo-Saxon England, as elsewhere, within the institution of the church, confirming the church's message of salvation and providing comfort and inspiration for those in religious life and, when translated into the vernacular, for people in lay society too. In doing so, saints' lives endorsed the authority and structures of the church and helped its members relate to these. The institutional dimension of hagiography is reflected in the fact that most saints' lives continued to be written first in Latin; it is notable also that the vast majority of surviving Old English hagiographical texts are based directly on specific Latin sources. Cults of individual saints might have arisen spontaneously among lay people but writing about saints was done in the first instance by those with clerical and/or monastic training, and the first audiences of saints' lives in Anglo-Saxon England were people in this same textual community.

There is tension within the genre of saints' lives, however, as not only did some saints succumb to temptation before redeeming themselves but in real life holy people could be awkward customers, not easily biddable, and unconventional in their behaviour. Though there is considerable heterogeneity in saints' lives, many hagiographers are concerned to manage their saints, therefore, and to write them as unproblematic institutional representatives, especially when they are writing for lay audiences (religious audiences were evidently deemed more able to cope with controversial material). Etheldreda (Æthelthryth in Ælfric), for example, was an Anglo-Saxon saint famous for being married twice but refusing to consummate either marriage. Both Bede and Ælfric, but especially the latter (writing in Old English), have to tread carefully in writing about this holy woman (see Jackson 2000), since her stance contradicts the recognized purpose of Christian marriage, and disobedient wives are not acceptable role models in Anglo-Saxon society. Ælfric, for one, was also nervous about extreme forms of monasticism; it is interesting that he mostly steers clear of hermit saints and that when he deals with Cuthbert (an English saint too important to ignore), who spent part of his life in solitude on an uninhabited island, he plays down the aspect of the saint's self-mortification, emphasizing instead Cuthbert's pastoral work in society (Clayton 1996).

Old English hagiographers are particularly careful to excise from their versions elements occurring in their Latin sources that might be seen as compromising the perfection of their saints in any way. As Gordon Whatley notes, 'Particularly vulnerable to the censor's pen, apparently, are the delicate area of relations between ecclesiastical and secular roles and powers, and the equally delicate and controversial area of propriety in clerical conduct, including sexuality' (Whatley 1997, p. 207). But even lesser weaknesses are characteristically edited out. The Old English poet of the verse saint's life *Andreas* (trans. Bradley, pp. 110–53), for example, inherits from his Latin source a fallible protagonist who learns things the hard way (Herbison 2000), and the vernacular poet struggles (unconvincingly in my view) to repackage him as a heroic figure. The anonymous prose adapter of the Latin *Legend of the Seven Sleepers* (ed. and trans. Skeat 1881–1900, I, 488–541), on the other hand, who also inherits a fallible protagonist, is exceptional in taking a different approach. Rather than transforming his protagonist into the perfect saint, this writer brings out the human interest of the story in a very unÆlfrician way, finding comedy as well as edification in the experience of his hapless hero and his companions. The subjects of this legend are seven nervous Christian youths in pagan Ephesus whom God protects from execution by miraculously putting them into a three-hundred-and-seventy-two-year sleep in the cave to which they have fled. They wake from this sleep in what is now a Christian city, thinking they have been asleep for only one night. Far from presenting his saints iconographically, the Old English writer relishes the comic possibilities of their situation, fashioning an astute narrative of misunderstanding and incongruity, leading up to a rhapsodic scene in which the youths finally undergo heavenly transfiguration.

One could add to the areas identified by Whatley as susceptible to the censor's pen that relating to the whole question of the role and power of women. Ælfric in particular has concerns on this front; I have mentioned his unease about Æthelthryth. Ælfric's female saints tend to be young virgins, fearless in standing up to their pagan oppressors but not threatening to the

Christian world in which their stories circulated. Ælfric's hagiography does not celebrate wives (except those with unconsummated marriages) or female authority figures, even though women had played significant leadership roles in the earlier Anglo-Saxon church: Hild of Whitby, for example, whom we met in the first chapter in connection with Cædmon, was the abbess of a double-monastery of monks and nuns, a position of high responsibility and one held by a number of other powerful women in earlier Anglo-Saxon England; Tetta at Wimbourne was another such figure, and Tetta's pupil Leoba, who 'through the combination of her reading with her quick intelligence, by natural gifts and hard work, became extremely learned' (*Life of St Leoba*, ed. Talbot 1954, p. 215), was an admired participant with Boniface in the process of establishing Christian life in Germany in the eighth century. In their learning and institutional standing Leoba and her peers were considerable figures, respected for their sanctity and also for their abilities as leaders (Hollis 1992).

We know of no comparable figures in Ælfric's time, and Ælfric himself was not interested in promoting such models of female sanctity. Ælfric's St Eugenia, we learn, did play an active role in converting the women of Rome in the period of paganism, but only under the direction of the Christian bishop Cornelius; earlier Eugenia, unwilling to be given in marriage, had taken the daring step of disguising herself as a man and joining a male monastery, but she did so again on the advice and with the secret support of another bishop, Helenus (Ælfric, *Life of St Eugenia*, ed. and trans. Skeat 1881–1900, I, 24–51).

Not all Old English hagiographers are as strict as Ælfric in policing gender boundaries. The anonymous *Life of St Euphrosyne* (ed. and trans. Skeat 1881–1900, II, 334–55), for example, deals with another transvestite young virgin who flees to a monastery, but Euphrosyne acts independently, without male authorization. And interestingly the short account of Eugenia in the *Old English Martyrology* (ed. and trans. Herzfeld 1900, pp. 4–7 [translation quoted below, textbox, p. 126]; also ed. Marsden 2004, pp. 178–80) makes no mention of episcopal endorsement of the saint's action.

A saint who would have appeared particularly troubling to someone like Ælfric is Mary of Egypt, a hermit, a spiritual teacher to the monk Zosimus, a woman with a lurid sexual history, and someone who acts autonomously outside the realm of male authority. It is hardly surprising that Ælfric passes over St Mary of Egypt in silence, even though her life occurred in the Latin legendary that was his principal hagiographical source. The life was translated (fairly faithfully) into Old English, however (ed. and trans. Magennis 2002; this trans. also in Black *et al.*, eds., 2009, pp. 135–48), and, as noted above

(p. 63), it ended up being transmitted along with saints' lives by Ælfric. It was added to the main extant manuscript of Ælfric's *Lives of Saints*, as indeed were three other non-Ælfrician lives, including two mentioned in the present section, the *Legend of the Seven Sleepers* and the *Life of St Euphrosyne*. Ælfric himself would not have approved. The production and transmission of these saints' lives is an indication of the heterogeneity in hagiographical literature alluded to above, though it is also the case that among surviving Anglo-Saxon texts they represent the exception rather than the rule.

A virgin martyr: Juliana

Among the small number of surviving Old English hagiographical poems (as listed above) is *Juliana*, a retelling, based on a Latin prose original, of the story of the martyrdom of a young woman during the time of the Roman persecution of Christians. Juliana's legend is set in the reign of the emperor Maximian (286–305) in Nicomedia, in what is now Turkey, though, as is characteristic of saints' lives, versions of the story are entirely lacking in local detail or historical specificity. A short account of St Juliana also appears in Bede's *Martyrology* (trans. Lifshitz 2001, pp. 181–2). In *Juliana* the narrative is transferred to a distinctly Germanic version of the Roman world, with chieftains, strongholds and a *comitatus*. The Old English writer abbreviates his source somewhat, excising references to Roman gods for example, and heightening the theme of opposition between the saint and her enemies.

Juliana (trans. Bradley 1982, pp. 301–20) is one of the four 'signed' poems of Cynewulf, those Old English poems in which the name Cynewulf is spelled out in runes and worked into a personal passage at the end of the text. It is preserved uniquely in the Exeter Book and consists of just over 700 lines, with two substantial textual gaps, however, due to missing folios, amounting to the loss of perhaps seventy lines. The other signed poems of Cynewulf are two further hagiographical pieces, *The Fates of the Apostles* and *Elene* (the latter being about St Helena, mother of the first Christian Roman emperor Constantine, a formidable female saint of a different kind from Juliana), and the homiletic *Christ II*, or *The Ascension* (like *Juliana*, preserved in the Exeter Book).

The story narrated in *Juliana* conforms closely to the classic pattern of the *passio*, 'passion, suffering', of the virgin martyr. Juliana is a nobly born and beautiful Christian in the era of paganism who is determined to preserve her virginity because of her love of Christ, but she is desired as a wife by the heathen city-governor Heliseus and promised to him by her father Affricanus. Juliana finds herself faced with a powerful alliance of male power-figures and provokes their fury by refusing to agree to their demands. Affricanus threatens her that she must give up her faith and marry Heliseus or suffer death, and after having her flogged and beaten he hands her over to Heliseus to be put on trial as a Christian. At her trial Juliana steadfastly refuses to renounce her faith. She stands up contemptuously to the frenzied threats of her prosecutor, answering his verbal attacks with fierce eloquence, and she unflinchingly undergoes a series of cruel tortures at his command. In a break between these Juliana is housed in a prison cell, where in a lengthy scene a devil appears to her and tries to tempt her; under cross-examining by her, however, he is defeated and humiliated (this scene parallels and inverts Juliana's own trial scene). When her tortures resume she is miraculously protected from their effects, to the fury of Heliseus, who finally has her executed by the sword. Juliana shows serenity and composure as she goes to her death. Later the wicked Heliseus and his band of warriors are drowned at sea, their souls going straight to hell; the body of Juliana, on the other hand, is reverently brought inside the city ramparts to be honourably buried with songs of praise.

Like other hagiographical poems in Old English, *Juliana* exploits the resources of the secular poetic tradition, but rather than associating its saint with Germanic heroic values, as other verse saints' lives do, presenting their protagonists as brave warriors going to battle against the devil or against wicked human enemies, this poem sets its heroine in opposition to the heroic world, which is a symbol of worldliness and is inextricably linked with paganism. In the intensely oppositional approach of *Juliana* it is Juliana's irrational suitor who represents the secular heroic outlook: he rules over strongholds, possesses lordly treasure-hoards, puts great store in the code of honour ('Your daughter has shown me great disrespect,' he complains to Affricanus, line 68), and is followed by retainers, who enjoy with him life in the hall. The retainers, drowned with Heliseus at the end of the narrative, gain no benefit or protection from their lord:

> For his thegns in that dark home [of hell],
> his band of retainers in that deep pit,
> there was no point in looking to their leader
> for their allotted riches, that in the wine-hall
> they might receive treasures at the beer-bench,
> shining gold.   (lines 683–8a)

Juliana rejects worldly values and defies worldly power, standing alone against her oppressors, including her father, who looks to Heliseus as his lord and is unable to comprehend the senseless position adopted by his daughter:

In foolishness
through your opposition you have taken,
against the judgement of sensible people, a futile course.   (lines 96b–8)

Cynewulf's handling of his material sharpens the sense of opposition between Juliana and the hostile world in which she finds herself, as compared to the treatment of the Latin original (for the Latin source, in a version closely similar to that used by Cynewulf, see Allen and Calder, trans., 1976, pp. 122–32); for example, the Old English version excises the potentially complicating figure of the saint's good-hearted mother, who makes an appearance at the beginning of the Latin; similarly, the pious widow who takes care of Juliana's body at the end is not there in Cynewulf's poem. The treatment of Juliana herself in the Old English is very much consistent with the desire to present the saint as beyond any conceivable reproach which I have suggested to be widely reflected elsewhere in Anglo-Saxon hagiography, with Cynewulf striving to fashion Juliana as an entirely faultless example of the virgin martyr. Thus he makes it clear that she is not taken in by the devil when he appears to her in her prison cell disguised as an angel; in the Latin source she is deceived by him at first. And Cynewulf omits the episode found in the Latin in which Juliana, apparently disingenuously, tells her suitor that she will marry him if he attains the rank of senator.

The Old English poem goes further than the Latin source in specifying that Juliana intends from the beginning to preserve her virginity perpetually; in the Latin, marriage seems not to be out of the question for her. This change leads Cynewulf into inconsistency at one stage, however, when he has the saint declare that she will marry Heliseus if he becomes a Christian (lines 108–16), thus contradicting her categorical stance against marriage. Cynewulf has imported this declaration from the Latin, having his eye too closely on the detail of a dramatic scene in the source in which it occurs. As a result, Juliana the potential converter momentarily displaces Juliana the perpetual virgin.

Juliana is hardly complex in its depiction of sanctity but in it Cynewulf builds up a series of scenes of dramatic confrontation enlivened by extensive use of highly rhetorical direct discourse and exploiting paradox; in these scenes the saint faces her father, her suitor/prosecutor and the devil. The scenario is that of apparent weakness against apparent overwhelming power, with Juliana's triumph reflecting the glory of God and Juliana emerging as the real figure of power in the story.

This impressive figure is also someone the narrator can look to for intercession in the 'personal' coda at the end of the poem, the tone of which is completely different from that of the narrative part. Here, in a section that links the saint's life to the real world of human imperfection, Cynewulf presents himself as a humble and sinful soul in need of prayer and divine mercy, who looks to the sublime Juliana as the time of his death approaches: 'I have great need that the saint will give help to me' (lines 696b–7).

Two virgin martyrs in the *Old English Martyrology*

St Eugenia (25 December)

On the first day is the festival of the noble virgin St Eugenia; she lived in the time of the emperor Commodus and loved Christ before she was baptised. She was the daughter of a very distinguished man, Philippus by name; and he was prefect of the great town called Alexandria, and all the people of Egypt obeyed him. When the maiden was fifteen years old, her father wanted to give her in wedlock to a certain nobleman. At night she cut off her hair as men do, and took men's garments and left her father's province with two servants. Then she went into a monastery of men where no woman came before, and she received baptism and served God and lived with them, so that nobody could find out that she was a woman. Within three years she became abbot of this monastery, and was so powerful with God that she restored the eyesight of blind men and cured the insane. After many years she was recognised by her father and her brothers, and afterwards she lived with women in their fashion; after her father's death she went to Rome with her mother, and there she suffered martyrdom for Christ. Necittius, the town-reeve of Rome, urged her to renounce Christ and believe in his idols. As she refused this, a stone was fastened to her neck by his command, and she was thrown into the river Tiber; then the stone burst, and she floated to the land across the water. Then he ordered her to be thrown into a burning oven, and it cooled down at once. Then he commanded her to be put into prison, and she was there ten days and nights without food. The Lord appeared to her on the night when he was born, and said to her: 'I shall take you away, Eugenia; I am he whom you loved. I ascended to heaven on the same day on which I came on earth.' On the same day she gave up her ghost to God, and her body rests near Rome on the road called Latina.

St Agnes (21 January)

On the twenty-first day is the passion of the holy virgin St Agnes; she suffered martyrdom for Christ when she was thirteen years old. Symphronius, prefect of the town of Rome, tried to compel the virgin by threats to become his son's wife. When she refused this, he commanded her to be led naked to a brothel, where God's angel brought her such an apparel as no fuller, that is no weaver, ever could make on earth. The son of the town-prefect was about to assault and ravish her in the brothel, but he died torn by devils. Thereupon the Romans said that she was an enchantress and a sorceress, and a sword was thrust into her throat. Thus she yielded up her ghost to God, and her body rests near the town of Rome on the road called Numentana. Not long after her martyrdom she appeared to her parents at midnight as they were watching at her grave, and she said to them: 'Do not weep as if I were dead, but be as joyful as I am, for I am joined in heaven to Christ whom I formerly loved on earth.'

(trans. Herzfeld 1900, pp. 5–7, 27–9, modified)

An English saint: Ælfric's Passion of St Edmund

Unlike *Juliana*, Ælfric's *Passion of St Edmund* is about an Anglo-Saxon saint. *Juliana* adapts an inherited (sixth-century?) Latin life of a universally acknowledged early martyr, whereas Ælfric's *Passion of St Edmund* tells the story of an Anglo-Saxon king from the fairly recent past (d. 869), and is based on a Latin source written only ten or fifteen years before Ælfric's version.

Ælfric's *Passion of St Edmund*, an abbreviated adaptation of Abbo of Fleury's *Passio Sancti Eadmundi*, occurs in his *Lives of Saints*, which also contains the stories of a number of other English saints, Swithun, Oswald and Æthelthryth (as well as the 'pre-English' Saint Alban, a third-century Romano-Briton). In including these figures in his collection Ælfric is consciously promoting them among his readers as worthy English members of the canon of the saints. At the end of his *Passion of St Edmund* he declares, 'The English people is not lacking in the Lord's saints when there lie in England such holy men as this holy king ... There are also many other saints in the English nation who perform many miracles, as is widely known, to the praise of the Almighty in whom they believed' (trans. Crossley-Holland 1984, p. 233). The existence of English saints might be 'widely known' but most of the writings that we have about them are in Latin; the only reasonably substantial body of non-Ælfrician vernacular hagiography dealing with an English saint is the *Guthlac* texts, two poems and a prose translation. Thus in promoting English saints for vernacular audiences Ælfric seems to be breaking new ground to a considerable extent. His example would not set a trend but his own lives of English saints became an integral part of the corpus of late Old English hagiography and continued to be copied, alongside other saints' lives by Ælfric and others, down to the twelfth century.

In his *Catholic Homilies* Ælfric had already given an account of St Cuthbert and had also included St Gregory, emphasizing the latter's role as converter of the English; and, honouring his own mentor, he would go on to produce an abbreviated version (in Latin) of Wulfstan of Winchester's *Life of St Æthelwold*. The English dimension of Ælfric's hagiography is thus apparent, and may be viewed as an aspect of his larger commitment to the idea of a national English church. It is also interesting that Ælfric's English saints happen to represent different parts of the country.

Since in his *Passion of St Edmund* he is promoting a saint not universally acknowledged, Ælfric (as Abbo had done) feels obliged to provide more by way of authenticating detail than is normally the case with hagiographical texts. At the very beginning of the *Passion* he traces the line of transmission of his own account of Edmund back, via several unimpeachable intermediaries, to the testimony of an eye-witness who was close to Edmund himself:

> A very learned monk came from the south over the sea from the place of St Benedict [Fleury], in the days of King Ethelred, to Archbishop Dunstan, three years before his death, and the monk's name was Abbo. Then they fell into conversation, until Dunstan related the story of St Edmund, as Edmund's sword-bearer had related it to King Athelstan, when Dunstan was a young man and the sword-bearer was an old man. Then the monk set all the narrative in one book, and later, when the book came to us, within a few years, then we translated it into English, as follows.   (trans. Crossley-Holland 1984, p. 228)

Ælfric is highly specific here, but once he turns to his actual narrative the audience immediately finds itself in the timeless and unspecific world of hagiography. After a eulogizing introduction to Edmund, the story begins with 'Then it happened', without any contextualizing reference to when the 'then' was.

The *Passion of St Edmund* is written in Ælfric's distinctive rhythmical prose (on this, see above, pp. 65–6), a heightened form of discourse using alliteration and emotive language. The *Passion* tells the story of King Edmund of the East Angles, whose people are ruthlessly attacked by a formidable army of Vikings under the heathen Dane Ivar. Ivar sends a message to Edmund commanding him to accept him as overlord or else forfeit his life, to which Edmund gives a defiant reply. He refuses to submit to a pagan but at the same time he offers no resistance: 'I was never accustomed to flee, but I would rather die, if I have to, for my own land, and the almighty God knows that I will not swerve from his worship ever nor from his true love, whether I live or die' (trans. Crossley-Holland 1984, p. 229). Ivar then comes and seizes Edmund in his hall. The king allows himself to be taken, throwing down his weapon, thus, it is stated, following the example of Christ, who forbade St Peter to defend him when he was arrested. Here is an Anglo-Saxon king who chooses not to fight.

Edmund is beaten, shot with arrows, 'like St Sebastian', and finally beheaded, with the name of Christ on his lips. Afterwards the Vikings dispose of his head in the countryside so that it may not be buried, but in a miraculous occurrence the head is recovered and protected by a wolf, and when local people come to search for it, shouting out as they do so, the head replies to them, 'Here, here, here', until they find it and are thus able to bury the whole body.

Many years later the body is moved to a new resting place inside a church and is discovered to be uncorrupt, with no sign of the wounds that it had suffered and only a thin red line on the neck to indicate the beheading. Ælfric relates several miracles associated with Edmund's uncorrupt body, viewing its wondrous preservation as proof of the doctrine of the resurrection of the body: 'By this holy man and by other such men it is evident that almighty God, who will preserve Edmund uncorrupt in body until the great day although he has been buried, can resurrect man on doomsday unblemished from the earth' (p. 233).

Ælfric has inherited all the details of his narrative from Abbo, thus going against the (non-hagiographical) account of Edmund's death given in the *Anglo-Saxon Chronicle*, where we read in the entry for 870 (= 869), 'and that winter King Edmund fought against [the invading army], and the Danish took the victory and killed the king and conquered all that land' (trans. Swanton 1993, p. 70). Though inheriting the details of the narrative from Abbo, through his abbreviating and simplifying approach and his emotive style Ælfric enhances the dramatic impact of the scenes of Edmund's oppression, as he heroically accepts martyrdom at the hands of savage heathens; as in *Juliana*, the theme of opposition between the saint and pagan enemies comes out strongly. The starkness of Edmund's choice – submit or die – is emphasized, as is the extent of his courage in facing a cruel death.

The stance of the king is heroic but this is a version of the heroic very different from that of the Germanic world. Rather than being expressed through violence and boasting – behaviours associated with the Vikings in the *Passio* – Edmund's heroism is, like Christ's, non-violent; it is the apparently passive heroism of endurance to the point of death, and, also like Christ's, endurance that involves ostensible humiliation. The contrast with traditional Germanic heroic values, according to which humiliation would be unacceptable, is brought out strikingly by the circumstance that Edmund allows himself to be attacked in his hall and by his declared willingness to surrender overlordship of his land to Ivar if he becomes a Christian. In another speech, having been called upon by the Vikings to surrender, Edmund exclaims, 'I desire and wish with my heart that I alone should not remain after my dear thegns, who have been murdered suddenly in their beds with their children and wives by these pirates' (p. 229). This might seem to recall in some ways Tacitus's account of Germanic warriors dying in battle after their lord has been killed, but here it is the other way round, with the lord dying after the warriors; and Edmund's thegns have died in their beds, not in battle.

Edmund behaves very differently indeed from the heroes of Germanic literature. He is constructed by Ælfric, following Abbo, as a type of the holy martyr familiar from hagiographical tradition. It is the paradigm of the martyr that directs his portrayal and provides his essential qualities of defiance, acceptance of suffering and death in the face of pagan persecution, and non-violence. He doesn't fit the paradigm of the martyr in an entirely comfortable way, however, as he has not actually been required to renounce his faith. Also his non-violent stance appears not to be absolute, since his declaration to the Vikings, 'I was never accustomed to flee', implies experience of battle. Does this mean that he would have resisted the Vikings if he had the resources to do so? But at one point he also says that he will not defile his hands with Viking blood since he follows the example of Christ (p. 229).

Ælfric works hard, as had Abbo, to construct his protagonist as a holy martyr. It could be pointed out that Edmund does not emerge from the story as a successful king in any practical sense and that his heroism is effectively worse than futile since the East Angles end up being ruled not by Edmund with Danish permission but directly by the fierce Danes themselves. But the story is not presented as being about a king acting in the real world of power and politics but rather as being about a holy person in the absolute world of hagiography. One of Edmund's bishops counsels pragmatism and negotiation with the Danes but the king will not hear of it. That is not how saints behave in the oppositional arena of hagiography. Bishops may be pragmatic, and good rulers have to be pragmatic, but that is not the way of the saint.

Postscript: gained in translation

Much of the Old English literature discussed in this chapter and some of that in the next one is in some sense translated literature. Most of it was appreciated as such in the period, though the Anglo-Saxon understanding of translation was more inclusive than the ordinary modern one as given in dictionary definitions today. For the Anglo-Saxons, to translate was to 'turn' (*cierran* or *(a)wendan*), in a range of possible ways. The Old English word for translator, which is a 'native' word, not a calque or copy of a Latin word, is *wealhstod*, the first element of which means 'foreign' while the second seems to be based ultimately on the idea of shining a light on something, a familiar metaphor of cognition in many societies (Hough 2004).

Some Old English texts, particularly biblical, are what modern readers would categorize as close translations of Latin originals, others would be classed as free translations, others again as adaptations, recreations or appropriations; some would be seen as mixtures of some or all of these. Ælfric repeatedly refers to his homilies and saints' lives as translations although he happily dips in and out of his (often multiple) sources, freely expands them and combines them with passages of original composition, as do some of the

Alfredian translators, for example. Translation from Latin into Old English is of many kinds, then, and it should also be noted that as well as from Latin into Old English there was translation in the other direction, as with Bede's Latin version of Cædmon's *Hymn* and Asser's and Æthelweard's appropriations of the *Anglo-Saxon Chronicle*.

Speaking more broadly, many *types* of vernacular literature are versions of Latin types: genres as well as individual works are 'turned' into Old English – for example, the chronicle genre. And indeed, as explained by Robert Stanton (2002), Anglo-Saxon Christian culture in general can be thought of as a culture of translation, in which Latin tradition is expressed in a new language, becoming transformed in the process, as we see most obviously perhaps in Old English Christian poetry, and in which, reciprocally, non-Christian culture gets 'turned' to become Christian, as in the conversion of existing 'heathen' words such as *god, Easter, bless* and *holy* to new Christian meanings. St Gregory himself, as described by Bede, had sanctioned a policy of cultural translation in Anglo-Saxon England when he authorized that churches be set up in buildings that had previously been pagan temples (*Ecclesiastical History*, I, 30). 'Acculturation' in Christian Anglo-Saxon England, and in the Germanic world more generally, is increasingly being seen as a two-way process (see especially Russell 1994).

Anglo-Saxon writers reflected self-consciously on the processes and methodologies of translation, and on its limitations. Writing of his translation of Cædmon's *Hymn*, Bede declares that he 'gives the sense but not the order of Cædmon's words' and that 'it is not possible to translate verse, however well composed, literally from one language to another without some loss of beauty and dignity' (*Ecclesiastical History*, IV, 24; trans. Colgrave and Mynors 1969, p. 417). In his *Preface* to the *Pastoral Care* King Alfred writes of the stages of translation as learning and understanding, interpreting, and then turning: 'And when I had learned [the *Pastoral Care*] as I could best understand it, and as I could most clearly interpret it, I translated (*awende*) it into English' (trans. Crossley-Holland 1984, p. 220); this sequence may remind us of Bede's account of how Cædmon 'learned' passages of Scripture instructed by scholars and then 'turned' them into poetry in English (*Ecclesiastical History*, IV, 24). In his *Preface* Alfred also mentions that he has translated 'sometimes word by word, and sometimes according to the sense' (trans. Crossley-Holland 1984, p. 220), thereby taking up a traditional distinction in translation theory (see Venuti 2004, pp. 13–16). Ælfric alludes to that same distinction in his *Preface to Genesis*, insisting in the special case of Bible translation on the word-for-word approach (while taking account of differences in idiom between Latin and English): 'we dare write no more in English than the Latin has, nor change the arrangement of the words except in those places alone in which Latin and English usage do not have a common idiom' (trans. Muinzer 1970, p. 166). As we have seen, Ælfric remains extremely nervous indeed about attempting to translate the sacred text: word-for-word translation is exegetically unmediated, a dangerous circumstance for those untrained in interpretation, while at the same time, linguistically, even this kind of translation *does* mediate Scripture by putting it in different words in different order, which is even more dangerous given the holiness of the very words of the Latin Bible. As Ælfric writes, 'He who makes a translation from Latin into English, or who turns Latin into English in his teaching must always so arrange the wording that the English is set forth in its own idiom' (*Preface to Genesis*, trans. Muinzer 1970, p. 166).

The translation culture of Anglo-Saxon England has been studied most fully by Robert Stanton in his indispensable book of 2002. Meanwhile other scholars continue to focus illuminatingly on the translation strategies of individual writers and groups of writers (for example, Discenza 2005, Gretsch 2009). Anglo-Saxon translators, working in a language that originally possessed no learned register, had to invent techniques and tools of translation, developing an adequate vocabulary and syntax for the task and evolving styles to fit the content and at the same time appeal to audiences. These translators transformed the vernacular and made it a worthy partner of Latin in the bilingual world of Anglo-Saxon England. In doing so they also changed what they translated, of course. All translation by definition changes, and translation into Old English tends to conform very much to the 'domesticating', as opposed to 'foreignizing', mode in terms of translation theory (see especially Venuti 1995, 1998): it accommodates the source material to the experience of the target audience. The works which are turned – translated, adapted, recreated, reimagined, paraphrased – into Old English become distinctively Anglo-Saxon.

Chapter 4

Belief, knowledge, experience: some non-narrative strands

Like the types of literature highlighted in the preceding chapter the three strands examined in this one – homilies, writings of wisdom and lore, and elegies – now figure centrally in the study of Anglo-Saxon literature and culture, though in the past some of them (specifically, homilies and some varieties of wisdom and lore) were largely neglected. Our three strands are an ostensibly disparate group but we will see that they overlap interestingly in some ways, as well as relating to traditions focused on in Chapter 3. There is naturally a clear relation between our first strand, Old English homilies, and biblical literature but other intertextual connections will also emerge in the discussion below.

Old English homilies

Homilies are edifying religious discourses intended primarily for public delivery in oral performance. Written in prose with varying degrees of rhetorical elaboration, they are preaching texts, explicitly instructional in mode. In strict usage the designation 'homily' refers specifically to explanatory expositions of passages from the Bible – exercises in scriptural exegesis – though in practice modern scholars use the term synonymously with 'sermon'. Old English homilies, understanding homily in the broader sense referred to above, are among the most widely preserved types of literature from Anglo-Saxon England, and indeed homilies in the narrower – exegetical – sense figure prominently within this large corpus. Scholars tend to view saints' lives as a separate category from homilies, though saints' lives are typically incorporated into collections of homilies and versions of saints' lives were regarded in the period as (to repeat my earlier formulation) religious discourses intended primarily for public delivery in oral performance.

Preaching would have gone on to some extent throughout the Anglo-Saxon age from the time of the conversion onwards but most of the surviving evidence about Old English homilies comes from only the tenth century and later, when, particularly under the influence of the Benedictine reform, there were concerted attempts to provide instructional material for the faithful. We hear of earlier ecclesiastical figures, such as bishops Aidan, Chad, Wilfrid and others, preaching to the people but these may have been extemporized compositions or oral recollections of material in Latin; at least, no written Old English homilies are extant from the earlier centuries. The existing, later, Old English homilies are for the most part carefully crafted, with formal expression, considerable cultivation of aural effects and widespread use of verbal patterning.

The major homily writer in later Anglo-Saxon England, as with other aspects of religious writing in the period, is Ælfric, producer of some 125 individual homilies in his two series of *Catholic Homilies* and in other writings; some of his saints' lives and biblical writings also incorporate homiletic teaching. His later homilies are composed in his distinctive rhythmical prose but most of the items in *Catholic Homilies* are in 'ordinary' prose, of considerable lucidity and fluency.

Ælfric's homilies formed the core and the bulk of preaching materials used in the late Anglo-Saxon and post-Conquest periods, but as well as the homilies of Ælfric, and those of his associate Wulfstan of York (which number some two dozen), about 135 anonymous Old English homilies also survive, many of which circulated with and were combined with Ælfric's writings. This homiletic corpus, along with other religious material such as service books and penitentials (which specified the penance to be imposed by a priest for particular sins), would have served the needs of clerics working in the secular world.

The most substantial surviving anonymous collections are two later-tenth-century books of homilies (the individual homilies may be older than the books), the *Blickling Homilies*, which contains fourteen homilies, along with four prose saints' lives in homiletic format (beginning 'My dearest people'), and the *Vercelli Book*, which contains a number of poems as well as twenty-one homilies and two homiletic saints' lives. In the *Blickling Homilies* the homilies and saints' lives are set out chronologically following the course of the Sundays and feast days of the church year, as is the case too (on a larger scale) with Ælfric's two series of *Catholic Homilies*, while those in the Vercelli Book do not appear to be in any particular order. The Blickling and Vercelli collections have received little critical attention in comparison with the homilies of Ælfric and to a lesser extent Wulfstan, but recent work on them brings them out of the shadows and draws attention to their literary qualities as well as their historical significance (see especially Toswell 2007, Zacher 2009).

The beginning of two homilies from *Blickling Homilies*

Dearest people, this Easter festival presents to us a manifest symbol of the eternal life, as we may now hear related, so that none need doubt that the event shall happen at this present season, when the Creator will sit upon his judgement seat, and before him shall be present all the race of angels and the human race, and also accursed spirits; and there each person's deeds shall be scrutinized. And he who is now humble, and with all his heart mindful of Christ's passion and of his resurrection, shall receive a heavenly reward. And he who neglects to observe God's commands, or to bear at all in mind our Lord's meekness, shall hear a severe sentence and afterwards shall dwell in eternal torments, of which there shall be never any end.

(VII, 'Easter Day', trans. Morris 1874–80, p. 82 [modified])

Dearest people, we may now, in some few words, tell you of the significance of this holy season, and of this holy day, that we at this present time are now celebrating. It was on this day that our Lord and Saviour Christ exalted above all the hosts of angels the humanity that he took upon his divine nature, when he went to the abode of his Father, from which, by reason of his eternal Godhead he has never departed. We have also, previously, at this holy season, heard tell of our Lord's holy passion, and also of his marvellous resurrection, which took place afterwards on the third day.

(XI, 'Ascension Day', trans, Morris 1874–80, pp. 114–16 [modified])

From earlier Anglo-Saxon England come a range of homilies in Latin aimed at an academically sophisticated monastic and clerical readership. Biblical homilies by Bede and Alcuin were widely transmitted in England and beyond in the early Middle Ages, along with homilies by the other authoritative fathers of the church. In Carolingian Europe such homilies were collected and supplemented in large homiliaries (the ninth-century homiliary of Paul the Deacon, for example, contains nearly 250 homilies), which in turn would function as sources for vernacular homilists in later Anglo-Saxon England. Acknowledging his dependence on earlier patristic homiletic writing, Ælfric speaks indeed of having 'translated' his homilies from the works of Latin writers. Ælfric's referring to his homilies as translation scarcely does justice to his careful adaptation, combination, abridgement, expansion and recasting of his source materials but it does serve to bring out his view of his role as being that of transmitter rather than originator of Christian teaching. Most Old English exegetical homilies, whether by Ælfric or by other writers, are adaptations of Latin writings, as is the case also with doctrinal and moral homilies, though some of the latter, including Wulfstan's *Sermon of the Wolf to the English*, are not based on specific pre-existing material. Ælfric was very particular about what sources he used for his homilies and other writings, being zealous in ensuring purity of doctrinal teaching, but, as we saw in an earlier chapter (see above, p. 61), he did not have a high opinion of other religious material available in Old English: 'I have seen and heard of much error in many English books, which unlearned men, through their simplicity, have esteemed as great wisdom.' Critics have suggested that homilies in the Blickling and Vercelli collections are among the vernacular texts that he would have had problems with.

Old English homilies are mostly targeted at unlearned lay audiences, though Ælfric seems in some of his to address a mixed audience of lay people and religious. Perhaps these homilies were originally intended to be delivered in a monastic church at services attended also by the local people (Clayton 1985). Ælfric clearly also had a wider audience in mind for his homilies, however, as comes out in his prefaces to *Catholic Homilies*, in which, dedicating his productions to Sigeric, archbishop of Canterbury, he says that he writes for the edification of people (in general) who do not read Latin and that he seeks to benefit the 'ordinary people of our race'. In his prefaces to his *Catholic Homilies* Ælfric also confirms several times that his homilies are intended to be heard, though he writes at one point that he wishes to 'reach the hearts of those reading or listening', which indicates that, as well as intending them as public sermons, he saw them as providing pious reading for literate individuals. Indeed, many of Ælfric's expositions are so detailed and multi-faceted that they would have lent themselves to careful study – as well as making a strong impression in performance.

Before turning to specific examples of Old English homilies, I should point out that early medieval scriptural interpretation, as reflected in Anglo-Latin and Old English exegetical homilies, stressed both literal and spiritual – non-literal – levels of meaning of the sacred text. In Latin exegesis, spiritual interpretation can be highly sophisticated and elaborate; in Old English, the treatment is normally somewhat simplified by comparison, though complex patterns of meaning are also 'led out' (the literal meaning of the Greek word *exegesis* is 'leading out') in some vernacular expositions, particularly in the writings of Ælfric. Spiritual levels of meaning, more than one of which may be discerned in any particular passage, comprise three manners of interpretation: the 'allegorical' sense, according to which meaning is associated particularly with Christ and Christian teaching; the 'tropological' or 'moral' sense, which draws moral lessons from the biblical passage; and the 'anagogical' or 'eschatological' sense, in which interpretation is in terms of the 'last things' and eternity. The allegorical sense includes 'typological' correspondences between the Old Testament and the New.

A medieval Latin tag on levels of biblical interpretation

Litera gesta docet, allegoria quod credas,
moralia quod agas, quo tendas anagogica.
   [The literal teaches what happened, the allegorical what you should believe, the
   moral what you should do, the anagogical where you should be going.]

Explaining scripture: Ælfric on the Innocents

Scriptural exegesis is the mode of much sermon writing in the early Middle Ages, and, among vernacular writers, the characteristics of such exegesis are represented pre-eminently in the homilies of Ælfric. To exemplify the range and manner of the tradition of homiletic exposition as practised by Ælfric, we will look at his treatment in his First Series of *Catholic Homilies* of the story of the 'Holy Innocents' – the infants of two years old and less put to death by Herod in his attempt to find and kill the baby Jesus, who was perceived by Herod as a threat to his own rule. Ælfric treats this episode in two items in the First Series, both written in 'ordinary' prose: he discusses it in his homily for the Feast of the Innocents, 28 December (*Catholic Homilies* I, V; ed. Clemoes 1997, pp. 217–23; trans. Thorpe 1844–6, I, 77–91), basing his account of it on Matthew II. 1–23, which alone of the gospels contains this episode; and he comes back to it in the next homily but one in the same series, the homily for 6 January, the Feast of the Epiphany (*Catholic Homilies* I, VII, ed. Clemoes 1997, pp. 232–40; trans. Thorpe 1844–6, I, 105–21), this being the day on which the Matthew passage is the gospel text designated by the church for reading at Mass. Ælfric's two series of *Catholic Homilies* complement each other, and so not unexpectedly there is no homily for the

Feast of the Innocents in the Second Series, though there is an alternative homily for the Epiphany in the Second Series, as is the case also with a small number of other days in the church year.

Ælfric's detailed exposition of the gospel passage comes in the homily for the Epiphany, the feast with which it is liturgically associated. It is interesting to compare his exegetical approach in the Epiphany homily with what we might refer to as his hagiographical approach in the Innocents homily, in which he is setting out not to bring out the non-literal meaning of Scripture but to honour his subjects as saints slaughtered by an evil tyrant. The homily for 28 December begins with a close translation from Latin into English of verses 1–18 of the gospel text, which tell of the coming of the magi or 'wise men' guided by a star, their questioning by Herod and their worship of the new-born Jesus; it goes on to relate the flight of Joseph, Mary and the child to Egypt and the execution on Herod's orders of all of the male children of two years and under living in the area of Bethlehem. The scriptural narrative is briefly interrupted only by a seven-line comment accounting for why it took Herod two years to get round to killing the children: following his Latin sources, Ælfric explains that Herod had been called back to Rome by the emperor to answer a charge of misconduct but managed to clear himself, and so it was only after his return to the Jewish kingdom that he was able to carry out his cruel plan. The translation of this part of the gospel text takes up about seventy of the 189 lines of the homily (in Clemoes's edition).

Ælfric's interpretation of this passage in the body of the homily emphasizes the contrast between the wickedness of Herod and the innocence of the slaughtered children, whom he praises rhapsodically, presenting them as martyrs for Christ and insisting too that the children's suffering mothers became partakers in the eternal reward since 'the sword that pierced their children's limbs entered the hearts of the mothers' (trans. Thorpe 1844–6, I, 85). He contrasts the eternal reward of these glorious martyrs with the terrible end that Herod was to endure. Drawing on a wide range of patristic sources, including Rufinus's Latin version of Eusebius's *History of the Church* and a homily by the Carolingian writer Haymo, he explains in graphic detail that a horrible disease came upon Herod and that tormented with agony he ended up committing suicide. Then in the closing lines of the homily Ælfric returns to the gospel narrative, translating verses 18–23 (eleven lines in the Old English), relating how with Herod now dead Joseph brought Mary and Jesus back from Egypt to live – in fulfilment of an Old Testament prophecy – at Nazareth. Ælfric ends with further praise for the innocents and prays for their intercession on behalf of the homily's audience, as they stand before the throne of God in the white garments of their sinlessness.

Ælfric's insistent concentration on the historical context and aftermath of the gospel episode is striking and is also somewhat at odds with his usual exegetical practice, which stresses the spiritual meaning rather than the literal. His focus on the saints and on their glorification in heaven is highly appropriate for this feast day but, as Ælfric himself is perfectly aware, it does constitute a full exposition of the Matthew passage. To explain the spiritual significance of the passage, he returns to it (specifically Matthew II. 1–12) in his homily for the Epiphany. Rather than translating the Latin text again, he begins the latter, and longer (it is 210 lines in Clemoes's edition, even without the gospel translation), homily by referring his audience back to the earlier item:

> Most beloved people, a few days ago, we read over this gospel passage before you, which belongs to the service of this day, for the interpretation of the gospel narrative; but we did not touch on the exposition further than belonged to the dignity of that day: we will now again run over the same gospel narrative and expound it with regard to the present festival.   (trans. Thorpe [modified], p. 105)

In his interpretation of the Matthew passage Ælfric focuses in this homily not on the innocents but on the magi, to whom Christ manifested himself at the Epiphany. Basing his exposition on an array of specific patristic sources – chiefly a homily by Gregory the Great but also expositions by Haymo, Smaragdus and others – he explains that 'epiphany' means showing forth, manifestation, and that it was on this same day in later years that Christ was manifested to the world at his baptism (Christ's manifestation at his baptism is the subject of the Epiphany homily in the Second Series of *Catholic Homilies*) and again on the occasion of his first miracle, the changing of water into wine (treated by Ælfric in his homily for the Second Sunday after Epiphany in the Second Series). Developing the theme of manifestation he also links the magi to the shepherds who came to Bethlehem immediately after the nativity: Christ was made known to the shepherds and the magi at the same time but it took the magi, who were more remote geographically, twelve days to journey to him. Spiritually, the shepherds signify those discerning Jews who knew God's law, while the magi signify the heathens. But while the magi acknowledged Christ as a man (they asked, 'Where is he born?'), as king (they called him 'king of the Jews') and as true God (they said, 'We come that we may adore him'), only the impious Jews, asserts Ælfric, resorting to the routine anti-semitism widespread in medieval Christianity – which in this case he has inherited from Gregory – would not accept him. He adds, however, 'They were not all equally unbelieving, but of their race there were both prophets and apostles, and many thousands of believing men' (trans. Thorpe 1844–6, I, 109). Herod, who wished to deceive the magi, signifies the devil. Such 'leading out' of hidden meaning is typical of the spiritual understanding of the sacred text that Ælfric seeks to convey to his audience, following the fathers of the church. The fact that the wise men were astrologers prompts him to an extended excursus (eighty-five lines) on the heretical idea of astrological destiny; giving examples from the Bible, he insists on the truth of the doctrine of free will, while acknowledging the mystery of God's foreknowledge of all human actions. In this excursus Ælfric is not appropriating any specific identifiable source, though the doctrines put forward have been described as 'Augustinian in the main' (Godden 2000, p. 54). Then in the closing part of the homily he returns again to the gospel narrative and in particular to the significance of the three gifts brought by the magi, which again teach lessons about the nature of Christ, contradicting the claims of those who would insist that, though a king, he was not divine, or was not human: 'The gold betokened that he is a true king, the frankincense that he is a true God; the myrrh that he was then mortal; but he now continues immortal to eternity' (trans. Thorpe 1844–6, I, 117). As well as having this allegorical meaning, applying to Christ, the three gifts also have a moral sense for the homily audience to consider: as diligent reading of the Bible indicates, says Ælfric, gold signifies wisdom, frankincense prayer and myrrh mortality. And, referring to the journey of the magi back to their own country by a different route, Ælfric in a short peroration (recalling sentiments of *The Seafarer*) draws out an anagogical message concerning the journey of the members of the Christian community back to their own 'homeland' (*eðel*), 'to which we cannot return by the way we came':

> We should, by obedience, and continence, and humility, unanimously proceed to our home, and with holy virtues attain the country, which we lost through sins ... [Christ] is to be sought with a true heart, and steadfast mind, who liveth and ruleth with the Father and the Holy Ghost, for ever and ever.   (trans. Thorpe 1844–6, I, 119–21 [modified])

Moral exhortation: Wulfstan's Sermon of the Wolf to the English

Ælfric sought to present what to him were the eternal truths of orthodox Christian doctrine to his vernacular audiences in a manner that they could comprehend and apply to their lives. As a product of the Benedictine reform, he was also intensely interested in things going on in the world outside the monastery and in the place of the church in that world, and he commented on current events and issues, notably the state of national leadership in England and ethical questions arising from the conflict with the Danes (see, for example, Clayton 1999, 2000). Ælfric's tone in such interventions is restrained and his manner cautious, and this forms a striking contrast with what we find in the best-known work of his contemporary Wulfstan of York (d. 1023), the *Sermon of the Wolf to the English* (ed. Marsden 2004, pp. 209–20; trans. Swanton 1993, pp. 178–84), to which I wish to turn in concluding our look at Old English homilies. Wulfstan, a bishop and arch-bishop and a proponent of reform ideology, pulls no punches in his castiga-tion of the immorality he sees around him at the time of the sermon's composition.

Wulfstan is the author of at least twenty-two surviving homilies in Old English and four in Latin and also of law codes, the socio-political treatise *Institutes of Polity* and a number of other works. As well as the uniquely thunderous *Sermon of the Wolf* (the title incorporates the pen-name *Lupus*, 'Wolf', favoured by Wulfstan), his homilies include treatments of the 'last things', instruction for the laity in the fundamentals of the faith and sermons relating to his duties as archbishop. His writings are distinguished by their rhetorical verve, a quality that is reflected pre-eminently in the *Sermon of the Wolf*. Wulfstan's rhetoric is the rhetoric of cumulation, variation, heightened diction and directness of address, and is firmly rooted in the strongly aural medium of his distinctive rhythmical prose. Composed basically of two-stress phrasal units, often alliterating, adapted from the half-line metrical structure of Old English poetry, Wulfstan's prose is a powerful vehicle for stimulating emotional involvement in a listening audience. In its cultivation of recurrent phrasing and thematic patterns it not only recalls formulaic aspects of Old English poetry but also resembles other preaching traditions that make use of features of oral/oral-derived composition. In particular, Andy Orchard has drawn attention to parallels between the techniques of Wulfstan and those of modern African-American preachers, as represented most famously in the speeches of Martin Luther King (Orchard 1997). The *Sermon of the Wolf*, like the speeches of King, is compelling in the sustained surge of its rhetoric but more specifically, as King does in his speeches, Wulfstan uses in the *Sermon* and his other homilies techniques of oral as well as written literature in a manner calculated to achieve immediacy of impact in performance.

The *Sermon of the Wolf to the English* is an urgent call for the people of the English nation – the English nation is now clearly understood to be both a political and a conceptual entity – to repent their sinful ways in what is a time of social and spiritual crisis. The *Sermon* is not, like most of Ælfric's homilies, a sermon for a particular church occasion but is a 'general' sermon that arises from Wulfstan's perception of the distressing state of England at a time of disorder and lawlessness. It exists in three identifiable versions, one of which specifies that it was preached in 1014, the year of the exile of King Æthelred II, 'when the Danes persecuted [the English] most', but its sentiments would have applied throughout the final years of Æthelred's reign and beyond, a time of political uncertainty and military failure for the English; and indeed the homily continued to be copied over the following century, one of a number of sermons on the theme of repentance that were in circulation. In Wulfstan's graphic portrayal the final years of Æthelred's reign have been witness to an apocalyptic severing of the bonds of society, with God's laws being held in contempt, offences being committed against the church, and the traditional secular ideals of kinship, honour and loyalty being repudiated in the grossest acts of treachery and betrayal.

Over the course of its 167 lines (in Marsden's edition) the *Sermon of the Wolf* moves from an opening that fulminates that things are bad in England and will get even worse with the approaching end of the world and the coming of the Antichrist; to a series of images of the breakdown of society, including vivid catalogue-passages listing the sins of the English, interwoven with repeated reference to God's anger against the sinful nation, an anger that has permitted the Vikings to humiliate them; working towards the climactic voicing of a warning from history when Wulfstan compares the plight of the English at this present time of crisis to that of the Britons who, as related by Gildas, were overcome and destroyed because of God's anger at their sinfulness (and, says Wulfstan, the acts of the English are worse than those of the Britons ever were); and ending, in a sustained peroration that incorporates the restatement of key religious obligations and social values highlighted earlier in the homily, with an appeal to the people to repent and to think upon the final judgement that awaits them. Throughout, Wulfstan is the preacher admonishing his audience but in doing so he consistently uses the homiletic first-person-plural pronoun, thereby avoiding the impression of his dissociation from that audience or rejection of them but instead asserting a sense of community in which he too participates.

Wulfstan, like Ælfric, was concerned to promote in his writings the Benedictine-reform ideal of a Christian society in which the 'three orders', the (monastically inspired) church, the warrior-class or nobility and the working people (on the 'three orders' see Powell 1994), were led by a good king guided by right-minded ecclesiastical leaders, but the *Sermon of the Wolf* shows a world in which such an ideal is very far from being achieved. Wulfstan would see his desired social order based on firm hierarchical structures being fostered only in the period of peace under the Danish king Cnut, whom he was to serve. At the end of the *Sermon of the Wolf to the English* he calls upon the people to repent and to think upon the last judgement to which they will be called. It is interesting, and a mark perhaps of the poor state of civil structures of order, that, as is the case also with other late Old English homilists, Wulfstan does not invoke earthly sanctions that those who commit crimes should fear (see further K. Greenfield 1981).

Wulfstan in full flow

In a passage in the *Sermon of the Wolf*, incorporating parallelism, word-pairing, alliteration, rhyme, formulaic phrases and other rhetorical effects, Wulfstan catalogues evils that have come upon the English:

Ne dohte hit nu lange inne ne ute ac wæs here and hunger, bryne and blodgyte, on gewelhwylcan ende oft and gelome. And us stalu and cwalu, stric and steorfa, orfcwealm and uncoþu, hol and hete, and rypera reaflac derede swyþe þearle; and us ungylda swyðe gedrehtan and us unwedera foroft weoldan unwæstma. Forþam on þysan earde wæs, swa hit þincan mæg, nu fela geara unrihta fela and tealte getrywða æghwær mid mannum. (ed. Marsden 2004, p. 214)

[For long now, nothing has prospered here or elsewhere, but in every region there has been devastation and famine, burning and bloodshed over and again. And stealing and slaughter, plague and pestilence, murrain and disease, slander and hatred, and the plundering of robbers have damaged us very severely; and excessive taxes have greatly oppressed us, and bad weather has very often caused us crop-failures. Wherefore for many years now, so it seems, there have been in this country many injustices and unsteady loyalties among men everywhere. (trans. Swanton 1993, p. 180)]

Wisdom and lore

If the homilies introduced in the preceding paragraphs represent the literature of religious knowledge and instruction, the writings considered in the present section represent the literature of knowledge and instruction in broader senses, and they combine the religious with the secular. The types of literature that I wish to pick up on here are something of a mixed bag but they have it in common that they reflect the widely evident enthusiasm of Anglo-Saxon writers in transmitting various kinds of wisdom and lore, producing compositions that offer instruction, advice and knowledge ranging from the proverbial and commonplace to the obscure, and from the folk-based to the learned. The texts under consideration here bear striking witness to the fondness of writers in the period for the cataloguing of information and wise sayings and to a fascination with what people today might call the weird and the wonderful. Some of the wisdom and lore that this literature contains is utilitarian enough but much of it also seems to have a broader cultural role, confirming inherited understandings of the workings of the world and of society, offering ways to accommodate to existing paradigms that which is strange, and expressing wonder at God's creation while at the same time reflecting strategies for categorizing that creation in its remarkable variety.

And going along with this interest in wisdom and lore is an appreciation and cultivation of cleverness, puzzle and paradox. The poet of the short poem *The Ruin*, for example, is delighted by the ingenuity of ancient builders whose work he observes – 'ingenious in ring-design (*hwætred in hringas*)' (line 19) – and that of *Riddle 47* (see above, pp. 73–5) relishes the 'wondrous event' of a moth eating words and is witty in describing it. Indeed, literary riddling itself, which is richly represented both in Anglo-Latin and in Old English strains, is a product of the Anglo-Saxon love of verbal cleverness and play, as is the composition of acrostics, abecedarian and rune poems, and surely also the attachment to hermeneutic Latin, all of which forms show delight in the display and manipulation of knowledge. The Old English riddles also incorporate elements of popular tradition, transforming them, however, in artful ways.

Though an extensive corpus of writings of wisdom and lore has survived from Anglo-Saxon England, most of this literature has received relatively little attention in modern scholarship, partly, no doubt, due to the fact that it doesn't conform very well to modern literary expectations and preconceptions. Such writings were clearly of great interest to Anglo-Saxons, however, and they reveal a lot about their outlook and worldview. Best known among them, with the exception of the riddles, are the Old English poems expressing sententious wisdom and advice, but even these have languished in the shadow of texts more immediate in their appeal to modern taste. T. A. Shippey points to a distinguishing characteristic of the 'poems of wisdom and learning', as he calls them, as being their immediacy and ambitiousness: 'They do not hesitate to make the most sweeping generalizations about men, God, nations, the state of the world, even the nature of the universe' (Shippey 1976, p. 1). These are not characteristics valued in most modern criticism; and the poems are also perceived as lacking in obvious principles of structure.

The poems that make up this 'sententious wisdom' group include collections of observations concerning the world and human experience, discourses giving social, moral and religious guidance, and demonstrations of obscure knowledge. Two surviving poems, *Maxims I* and *II*, consist entirely of short sententious generalizations of the kind that also occur individually throughout Old English poetry, as when (to give just one example) Beowulf exclaims as a truth, 'Better it is for each man that he avenge his friend than that he mourn much' (*Beowulf*, lines 1384b–85). Such utterances have a normative quality, assuming acceptance in the minds of right-thinking people. The 67-line *Maxims II* has the following sequence (lines 26b–33a), which may be seen as typifying this kind of verse:

> A dragon must dwell in its barrow,
> old and proud with its treasures. A fish must in the water
> bring forth offspring. A king must in the hall
> give out rings. A bear must dwell on the heath,
> old and fearsome. A river must flow downhill,
> grey as the sea. An army must remain firm together,
> a troop thinking on glory. There must be loyalty in a nobleman,
> wisdom in a man.

The maxim poems, like most of the Anglo-Saxon literature of wisdom and lore, integrate secular wisdom into a Christian worldview. At the beginning of *Maxims I* it is insisted that 'God is to be praised first' (line 4), while *Maxims II* intertwines statements about nature and culture with acknowledgement of God's power and knowledge. As Paul Cavill has recently put it, *Maxims* 'outline, and in the process construct, an Anglo-Saxon understanding of reality, quite deliberately focusing on the everyday, the typical, the social, the natural, in order to build up a framework which potentially comprehends all human and natural phenomena and sets the whole construct under the omniscience of God' (Cavill 1999, p. 183).

A recent survey of Old English *prose* of 'secular learning' (Hollis and Wright 1992) identifies pragmatically five broad divisions, comprising 'proverbs', including translations from Latin learned traditions as well as native proverbial lore; 'dialogues', notably those of *Solomon and Saturn*, in which the wise Solomon provides answers on points of obscure knowledge; 'romance' (here I would prefer a designation like 'writings about faraway places'), including *Alexander's Letter to Aristotle* and *Wonders of the East*; 'Byrhtferth of Ramsey and *computus*', the latter consisting chiefly of calculations pertaining to the liturgical calendar; and the vast area of 'magico-medical literature' (again the label is problematic, however: see below), comprising herbal remedies and other treatments and information, including charms, the purpose of which is to ward off particular illnesses and misfortunes.

There is overlap between Old English and Latin texts, and indeed the *Enchiridion* (*Manual*) of the Benedictine-reform scholar Byrhtferth, a compendium (with diagrams) of astronomical and calendrical information, is written partly in Latin and partly in English, and there is overlap too between prose and verse: dialogues (including those of Solomon and Saturn), charms and proverbs, for example, exist in both forms. Verse literature of wisdom and lore would have been in existence before the coming of writing, and in its oral and written forms verse may be seen as having a mnemonic function, using metrical features to render content more memorizable, as would have been the case with the catalogue poem *Widsith*, for example, which lists peoples and leaders from the heroic age, or with the verse charms, the rhythmical forms and repetitive phrasing of which (often mixing Old English and Latin and incorporating unintelligible words) lend themselves to memorized incantation.

As is the case with Anglo-Saxon writings generally, the bulk of the literature of lore and learning survives in manuscripts from the tenth century and later. This literature would have been produced mostly in religious centres, where it would have provided texts of interest to scholarly monastic readers but also, as we saw to be the case with homilies, material for use in the secular world – notably, perhaps, under this heading, medical remedies. Among the material of interest to monastic readers would be learned handbooks from Latin-Christian tradition, including works on such topics as the natural world, chronology, rhetoric, poetics (Bede, for example, had written on all of these subjects) and geography, under which heading we can place the writings about faraway places mentioned above.

Writings about faraway places express perceptions about centre and margin and about otherness, complicated in the case of Anglo-Saxon England by the teachings inherited from classical geography that put what we still refer to as the 'medi-terranean' lands at the centre of the known world and Britain itself at the outer edge (see Figure 4.1). In an earlier chapter we saw the West Saxon account of the voyages of Ohthere and Wulfstan negotiating such categories and they continued to be of concern to Anglo-Saxon thinkers (see Lavezzo 2006).

Anglo-Saxon knowledge about distant countries was largely second- and third-hand, relying on accounts of some travellers (the eighth-century saint Willibald visited the Holy Land, for example) but deriving in the main from classical tradition as transmitted by authorities such as Orosius and Isidore and developed in accounts of monstrous races dwelling in the exotic east. Among the latter are the Latin *Liber monstrorum* ('Book of Monsters'), thought to be an Anglo-Saxon compilation of the period 650–750, and the

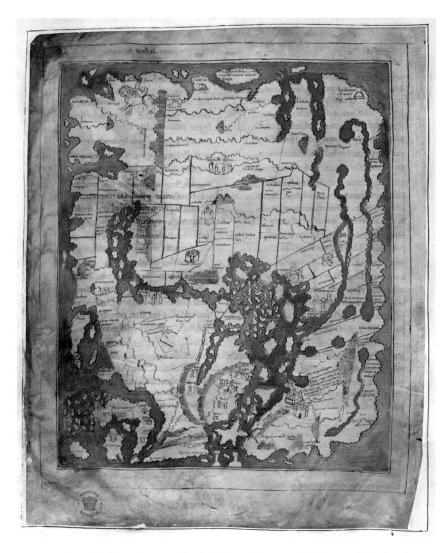

Fig. 4.1 The 'Cotton Map' (British Library MS Cotton Tiberius B. v [*c.* 1050]), showing Britain and Ireland in the bottom-left corner

Old English version of the *Wonders of the East,* preserved in two eleventh-century manuscripts (one of which is the *Beowulf* manuscript, the other being the manuscript that also contains the 'Cotton Map', an Anglo-Saxon *mappa-mundi*). A brief quotation from the *Wonders of the East* (trans. Swanton 1993, p. 230) may serve to illustrate the kind of lore transmitted in this tradition:

16. Then there is another island south of the [river] Bryxontis on which men are born without heads, who have their eyes and mouth in their chests. They are eight feet tall and eight feet broad.

17. Dragons are born there which are in length one-hundred-and-fifty-feet long, and are as thick as great stone columns. Because of the size of the dragons, nobody can travel easily in that country.

18. From this place to another kingdom on the south side of the ocean, is measured three-hundred-and-twenty-three of the lesser *stadia* miles, and two-hundred-and-fifty-six of the greater called *leagues*. And *Homodubii*, that is 'doubtfully men', are born there. They have a human form down to the navel, and from there on the form of an ass. They have long legs like birds and a gentle voice. If they notice or see any man in those lands, then they go far off and flee.

The fascination with monstrous races and strange customs in distant lands persisted right to the end of the Middle Ages, of course, and beyond.

As alluded to above, among the wisdom and lore that would have been of use in the secular world as well as in the monastery are medical remedies and related writings in the vernacular. As explained by Karen Jolly, vernacular medical manuscripts reflect an effort on the part of textual communities to meet popular needs: 'Just as penitentials, liturgical manuscripts and homilies functioned as aids to the clergy, so too the medical books served as manuals of instruction and transmission of Anglo-Saxon religious folklore concerned with alleviating people's physical and spiritual ills. The overlap between physical and spiritual well-being is obvious in these texts; the development of Christian remedies was therefore very much part of the effort to create an Anglo-Saxon Christian tradition that met the needs of the populace' (Jolly 1996, p. 131).

The literature that has been categorized as 'magico-medical' is a particularly interesting, though little-studied, textual grouping, within which we find classical medical lore combined in an integrated manner with pre-Christian ritualistic practices and a Christian worldview. An essential component of this literature are the charms that combat ailments caused by demons, elves, dwarfs and other mysterious inhabitants of the natural world. A substantial number of these charms survive, including eleven in verse or having passages of verse included in them. As pointed out by Jolly (1996, p. 100), modern commentators, whether writing from a scientific progressivist standpoint or romantic-ally searching for the pagan Germanic roots of Anglo-Saxon culture, have tended to regard such material as largely magical in character (hence the designation 'magico-medical') but Anglo-Saxons would have viewed it as based on experience of God's natural world as they understood it and as part of popular religion rather than being magical. Unease about the way charms amalgamate ideas from folk culture with references to Christ and his saints and to liturgical symbols and practices comes from the perspective of modern rationalism rather than from observers in the period itself.

Two metrical charms

(trans. Glosecki 2009, p. 41)

The Old English Bee Charm

Against a swarm of bees take earth, cast it with your right hand under your right foot, and say:

I seize it under foot: I've found it now.
Lo! earth has might   over all creatures
and against malice   and over mindlessness
and over the mighty man   with his mighty tongue.

And thereupon, when they swarm, throw gravel over them and say:

Victory-wives! sit: sink to earth now!
Never to the woodland   wild may you fly!
Be as mindful   of my fortune
as folks all are   of food and home.

Against a Dwarf

Against a dwarf take seven little wafers like those one offers [at Mass], and write these names on each wafer: Maximianus, Malchus, Johannes, Martinianus, Dionisius, Constantinus, Serafion [the names of the saints known as the Seven Sleepers of Ephesus]. Then one should sing the charm that follows here, first in the left ear, then in the right ear, then over the person's crown. And then have a virgin go in and hang it around his neck; and so do for three days, and he will soon be well.

Spider creature   came right in here –
had his harness in hand: you're his horse, he claimed!
and to your neck tied reins!   Then they began to rise from the land.
As they left the land   their limbs grew cool.
Then in she dashed –   the dwarf's sister!
Then she ended it all   and oaths she swore:
no hurt would come   to harm the sick,
nor whoever gets the lore   and learns this charm
and knows how to chant   this charm as well.
Amen, Fiat [So be it].

The riddles of the Exeter Book

The Exeter Book contains some one hundred riddles, one of them in Latin, the remainder in Old English (ed. ASPR III [the numbering of the ASPR edition is adopted here]; also ed. Williamson 1977). These riddles are poems which vary in length from one line to more than a hundred, with the majority of them being less than twenty lines long (the Latin one, *Riddle 90*, has five lines). The riddles are clever pieces of writing for clever readers, who must decipher the teasing puzzle of what is being cryptically described.

The Old English riddles are highly allusive and metaphorical in their treatment of a subject matter that encompasses the sublime and the ridiculous and that ranges from descriptions of down-to-earth objects to topics of abstruse learning. They clearly were designed for the appreciation of discerning Anglo-Saxon readers, who would have been puzzled, entertained, edified and, in the case of the riddles with sexual content, shocked by what they read. Though the riddles might have been read out as well as read privately, their ideal audience would be readers who have the text visually in front of them. They are composed in the oral-derived style of Old English verse, with its rich word-hoard and inheritance of evocative poetic images, particularly from the heroic world, but these are texts that also appeal to the eye through their use of runic letters and other features of visual presentation.

In the modern period the Old English riddles have fascinated scholars and exercised their ingenuity for approaching two hundred years, and interest in them continues to be as lively as ever, with exciting new work on them individually and as a group being produced by today's scholars. Much of the academic work on the riddles has been concerned with 'solving' them, responding to the invitation in the text which is often directly expressed by a personified speaker as 'Say what I am', 'What am I called?', and so on. For, unlike in the Latin *enigmata* discussed earlier in the book, these riddles don't come with answers. Scholars have long been engaged in the task of providing convincing solutions that account for the clues laid out in the riddles, clues that are often straightforward enough but can also be paradoxical, contradictory, far-fetched and deliberately obfuscating. In many cases the scholars have succeeded but there are still plenty of examples that continue to baffle or that have been given rival solutions that are hard to adjudicate between. Cracking the code of individual riddles requires knowledge of a wide range of medieval learning, literary convention and social practice, and some key factors for solution may never be recoverable. Researchers persist with their efforts, however, throwing new light on old problems and occasionally producing satisfying original solutions to apparently intractable puzzles.

But current approaches to the Old English riddles are interested in something more than doing detective work on individual poems. The questions of what kind of literature this is, what traditions inform it and what it was doing in its period are very much to the fore, as is a concern with the aesthetic appreciation and critical understanding of the riddles as poetry. Thus, for example, attention has recently been drawn to the literary techniques of the riddle poets and specifically their playfulness and use of metaphorical language (Niles 2006); the indebtedness of the riddles to the conventions of Latin *enigmata* has been stressed (Bitterli 2009); and their interrelationship with oral folk tradition has been argued (Murphy forthcoming), the latter view presenting a compelling challenge to an orthodoxy that insisted on the entirely bookish character of the Old English riddles. The riddles are indeed bookish, according to this persuasive new reading, but they draw upon oral as well as learned tradition, transforming that oral tradition in a self-conscious and artful manner.

As alluded to above, often the object of the riddle is personified and takes the role of speaker, telling the reader about itself and its experiences, as is the case with *Riddle 5*, which begins,

> I'm by nature solitary, scarred by spear
> And wounded by sword, weary of battle.
> I frequently see the face of war, and fight
> hateful enemies; yet I hold no hope
> of help being brought to me in battle,
> before I'm eventually done to death.
>
> (lines 1–6; trans. Crossley-Holland 1979, p. 27)

In *Riddle 9* another speaker relates its life story:

> In former days my mother and father
> forsook me for dead, for the fullness of life
> was not within me. But another woman
> graciously fitted me out in soft garments
> as kind to me as to her own children,
> tended and took me under her wing.
>
> (lines 1–6; trans. Crossley-Holland 1979, p. 31)

Elsewhere the speaker is not the object itself but an observer who 'saw a strange creature' or 'heard' about something; earlier (see above, pp. 73–5) we looked at the 'bookworm' riddle, *Riddle 47*, which begins,

> A moth ate words; to me that seemed
> a marvellous event when I heard about that wonder.

The answer to a particular riddle may be an everyday object, like a plough or a key, or it may be a domestic or wild animal or bird, or an aspect of nature, like wind or water, or a topic from the world of religion or learning. 'Creation' itself is the subject of two of the riddles, one which is the mighty

Riddle 40, a poem of 107 lines, and it is incomplete. The second 'creation' riddle (*Riddle 66*) is a much shorter poem, which ends with the conventional challenge to the reader:

> I fill far and wide all the corners of the earth
>   and the ocean streams. Say what my name is.
>
> (lines 8b–10; trans. Crossley-Holland 1979, p. 86)

The range of subject matter is heterogeneous indeed and the riddles overall may be seen as reflecting a perception of the richness and variety of God's creation and of the delight-giving interconnectedness of things. As Craig Williamson puts it, the riddles constitute 'a profound statement about the categories of human perception and the power of human imagination' (Williamson 1977, p. 27). Through imagination, wonder is revealed and the ordinary is shown to be extraordinary.

This is all very edifying, but a good number of the Exeter Book riddles have obvious sexual double meanings, which they elaborate with evident relish. As shown by Patrick Murphy, 'sex riddles' are widely found in later folk tradition but are developed with particular knowing artistry in the Old English collection. One example is *Riddle 25*, quoted here in Crossley-Holland's lively and alert translation, though inevitably translation fails to capture all the play and possibilities of the original and some lines could be taken differently:

> I'm a strange creature, for I satisfy women,
> a service to the neighbours! No one suffers
> at my hands except for my slayer.
> I grow very tall, erect in a bed,
> I'm hairy underneath. From time to time
> a beautiful girl, the brave daughter
> of some churl dares to hold me,
> grips my russet skin, robs me of my head
> and puts me in the pantry. At once that girl
> with plaited hair who has confined me
> remembers our meeting. Her eye moistens.
>
> (trans. Crossley-Holland 1979, p. 46)

The agreed answer to this riddle is 'onion', though there is a game going on in it of leading the reader up the garden path, so to speak, to a different solution. Interestingly, in the manuscript *Riddle 25* is immediately followed by a riddle on a very religious topic, 'Bible'. Murphy explains the presence of riddles like *Riddle 25* in a monastic manuscript by arguing that they make sexual activity look ridiculous and therefore bring out the superiority of religious life (Murphy forthcoming). There is a tone of delight rather than censoriousness in the sex riddles, however, which indicates an appreciation of the earthy humour of folk tradition and an awareness, perhaps, that sex may be ridiculous but is an appropriate topic therefore for a type of literature that, as suggested above, encompasses the sublime and the ridiculous.

These double-meaning riddles continue to raise eyebrows, as they must have been designed to do in their own period, but it should be emphasized in concluding this too brief introduction to them that they are among the cleverest in the collection and the densest in their use of metaphor – poems like the 'onion' riddle have (one might say) rich layers of meaning that we can work to peel away in close analysis. They are highly crafted poems in what is a highly crafted genre, as continuing study of it serves to confirm ever more strongly.

By the way, the accepted solutions to *Riddles 5* and *9* are 'shield' and 'cuckoo', respectively.

Old English elegies

The term 'elegy' has been applied by scholars to a number of Old English poems found, uniquely (like the riddles), in the Exeter Book. The 'elegies' do not occur together in the manuscript but are spread out among other poems; it is their sentiment and content rather than their location that have drawn scholars to view them as a generically related group. And as well as the 'elegies' as a specific group of poems, critics also refer to an 'elegiac mood' more widely in Old English verse, which has been seen as reflecting a pervasive thematic interest of the poetry.

An influential definition of Old English elegy was provided by Stanley B. Greenfield in 1966:

> a relatively short reflective or dramatic poem embodying a contrasting pattern of loss and consolation, ostensibly based upon a specific personal experience or observation, and expressing an attitude towards that experience.   (S. B. Greenfield, 1966, p. 143)

More recently, Anne L. Klinck, the editor of what is now the standard collected edition of the 'elegies', has written,

> [T]he concept of 'elegy' in an Anglo-Saxon context provides us with a convenient locus for particular themes: exile, loss of loved ones, scenes of desolation, the transience of worldly joys. The elegiac themes are presented in a lyrical-reflective mode with characteristic features such as monologue, personal introduction, gnomic or homiletic conclusion, and refrain or rhyme. These structural features, like the

> scenic elements, are not peculiar to elegy, and no elegy contains all of them, but the conjunction of several of them in the same poem is distinctive.   (Klinck 1992, p. 11)

The idea of an elegy genre is viewed with some scepticism in current scholarship, as reflected even in our quotation from Klinck, which presents the grouping as convenient rather than one based on firm compositional principles. We referred above to nineteenth-century understandings of heroic literature; similarly, we need to recognize here that the category of elegy is, historically, a construction of the nineteenth century, fulfilling desires about poetry as personal expression that developed as part of the romantic aesthetic. As has recently been written, 'Elegy as a compositional class is a projection of the sensibilities of the Romantic Age back onto the early Middle Ages ... Victorians of a romantic disposition saw mirrored in these works their own tendency to melancholy introversion with a Keatsian awareness of mutability' (Fulk and Cain 2003, p. 180). This kind of poetry corresponded satisfyingly to the values of the romantic aesthetic and soon achieved privileged objectified status in the canon as an important genre. Objectifying the idea of Old English elegiac poetry brings significant dangers, however, including that of skewing perception of Old English literature as a whole.

The poems generally viewed as making up the perceived group are also a disparate lot in many ways, not least in the fact that some of them are purely secular while some are religious, and there is disagreement about exactly which poems should be included in the group. Nonetheless, characteristics of the kind identified above have been seen as giving reasonable pragmatic justification for the 'elegy' label and it will be helpful to employ it here, on the understanding that it does not represent a sharply delineated category but, in Klinck's words, a 'convenient locus'.

Poems commonly classified as elegies

(in the order of their appearance in the Exeter Book):
The Wanderer (115 lines), describing personal experience and observation and leading to a conclusion that recognizes earthly transience and looks for security with the Father in heaven.
The Seafarer (124 lines), which is strongly homiletic in its response to experience in the world and urges that we should strive to attain eternal blessedness.
The Riming Poem (87 lines), contrasting the speaker's former happiness to present sorrow, with a homiletic conclusion, rejecting worldliness and looking to heavenly joy.
Deor (42 lines), referring to stories of sorrow overcome in the legendary past and looking for (earthly) consolation in the future.

Wulf and Eadwacer (19 lines), in which a female speaker expresses sickness of heart at her separation from 'Wulf'.

The Wife's Lament (53 lines), also spoken by a female and expressing sorrow and bitterness in a situation of separation from a loved one.

Resignation (118 lines), combining a meditative opening section with the image of a voyage in the second part; some critics regard the two parts as two separate poems.

The Husband's Message (54 lines), in which a male figure sends a message to the wife from whom he is separated, telling her that he has overcome his troubles and asking her to join him in his new life; some scholars would combine *The Husband's Message* with the poem immediately preceding it, *Riddle 60*; others link in with *The Wife's Lament*.

The Ruin (49 lines), in which the speaker observes the effects of time on a ruined building and imagines the splendid life of those who once inhabited it.

There is variety in the voices heard in the elegies and a variety of attitudes displayed. *The Wife's Lament* and *Wulf and Eadwacer* are distinctive in taking the form of highly emotional utterances by female speakers living in the heroic world, who refer to their personal experience in love-relationships and who express the overwhelming feelings of pain arising from that experience. Other 'elegies' are more restrained in their expression of emotion, as is the case with *The Husband's Message*, with which *The Wife's Lament* is sometimes associated, or *The Ruin*, in which the speaker is an impersonal figure, observing the relentless effects of time in the world rather than undergoing personal suffering himself. Other poems express consolation, as is seen in *Deor*, which, referring to distressing experience both in past legend and in the speaker's own life, has the refrain-line, 'þæs ofereode; þisses swa mæg', 'That passed away; so can this'. *Deor* also has a mention of the 'wise Lord' as the bringer-about of change in the world, thus introducing a Christian note. Other poems again, notably *The Wanderer* and *The Seafarer*, are thoroughly Christian in the message they derive from personal experience and from the observation of earthly transience. In this respect they contrast radically with the stance of *The Wife's Lament*, *The Husband's Message* and *Wulf and Eadwacer*, in which religion plays no part.

Such variation reflects the looseness of 'elegy' as a category, and although all the poems in the perceived group display a selection of the themes referred to by Klinck, it should be borne in mind again that elegiac themes in Old English poetry are not confined to our Exeter Book poems but are also represented elsewhere. Beyond the elegies group, critics point to the 'elegiac mood' in the poetry, in which sentiments and ideas similar to those of the elegies are given expression. Elegiac passages, expressing sorrow, loss, regret, the experience of exile and the awareness of transience, occur notably in *Beowulf*, in which two passages in particular are often highlighted in this regard, the 'song of the "last survivor"' (lines 2247–66) and the 'father's lament for his dead son' (lines 2444–62). A short extract from the latter passage may serve to suggest the kind of feelings to which it powerfully gives voice:

> Sorrowful he sees in his son's dwelling place
> the wine-hall deserted, the sleeping-place wind-swept,
> devoid of joy, – the horsemen sleep,
> the warriors in the grave; there is no music of the harp,
> delight in the courtyards, as once there were.   (lines 2455–9)

Traditional formulaic language, both in the 'elegies' and in such passages in *Beowulf* and elsewhere, contributes to expression of elegiac themes.

Two secular elegies: Wulf and Eadwacer *and* The Wife's Lament

The 'women's songs' *Wulf and Eadwacer* and *The Wife's Lament* (trans. Crossley-Holland 1984, pp. 59 and 56–7; for original texts, see Marsden 2004, pp. 335–44) have fascinated readers since the Victorian period and continue to be the object of much interest in recent criticism. *Wulf and Eadwacer* is remarkable for the allusiveness of its expression and for the obscurity of its treatment of narrative. The earliest modern readers found the poem to be so cryptic that they could make no sense of it or thought that it must be one of the Old English riddles, a sequence of which comes immediately after it in the Exeter Book. The poem is in fact a dramatic monologue, expressing the feelings of its female speaker in a situation of personal distress. Emotion rather than a sense of narrative coherence dominates the utterance. A narrative is implied but that narrative is not spelled out in logical terms, so that basic questions about the poem, concerning the nature of the relationship(s) alluded to in it, the number of people involved, their relative location, and the presence or not of proper names, continue to be debated.

Wulf and Eadwacer

> It's like a gift given my people:
> they'll take care of him if he comes to them:
> it's different with us!
> Wulf's on an isle, I on another.
> That island's secure, guarded by fens.
> Deadly-fierce men dwell on that isle:
> they'll take care of him if he comes to them;

it's different with us!
For my Wulf's far-journeyings I waited with hope.
When weather was rainy and I wept,
when the battle-bold man embraced me,
I took some pleasure, but it pained me too.
Wulf, my Wulf, wanting you,
your rare arrivals, have made me ill –
a sorrowing heart, not hunger for food.
Do you hear 'Eadwacer'? Our poor whelp
Wulf bears to the woods.
It's easy to sever what never was seamed:
our song together. (trans. Greenfield 1986)

The most widely accepted interpretation of *Wulf and Eadwacer* is as a poem of love, in which the female speaker expresses her longing for the absent Wulf, who is separated from her by the enmity of the people with whom she lives. She is on one fenland island, he on another. It is generally accepted that the speaker is, unhappily, with a second man, Eadwacer, her husband, and that she has a child, of whom Eadwacer is understood to be the father. The large majority of critics find this general scenario to be the most likely and the most convincing one, though others have been put forward, including that of a mother–son relationship. It has also been argued that there is only one man in the poem, 'Wulf', and that *eadwacer* is not a proper name but an adjective applied to Wulf, meaning 'watchful of property/prosperity'. Like all Old English poems, *Wulf and Eadwacer* is untitled in the original manuscript and would therefore have been approached by Anglo-Saxon readers of the Exeter Book without the interpretative guidance that the modern title supplies – or imposes.

Wulf and Eadwacer is one of the shortest Old English poems but one of the most striking. Many modern readers are happy to relate to it in its own enigmatic terms, though some scholars have argued that this lyric utterance must be based on specific narrative material and have sought to identify the people and the story lying behind it. The occurrence of 'Eadwacer' has suggested to some that the poem may relate to legends concerning the Germanic hero Odoacer, and notable correspondences to the story of Signy in *Volsunga saga* have also been pointed out.

While not quite as cryptic as *Wulf and Eadwacer*, *The Wife's Lament* is also highly allusive in its treatment of narrative. The speaker is a woman and she is separated from her male loved-one, but the details of the story lying behind this separation are uncertain. The terms the speaker uses, however, surely point to the understanding that the loved-one is her husband, as reflected in the poem's title *The Wife's Lament*, devised by nineteenth-century scholars. For whatever reason, the husband has departed from his wife and his homeland, leaving the wife in a hostile environment, apart from society; in this dismal setting, in a place of lonely enclosure, nature and atmosphere are depicted poetically as reflecting the speaker's unhappy state of mind.

In developing her *giedd*, 'song' (line 1), the wife draws upon the male language of exile and of the heroic *comitatus* of the Germanic lord and his retainers, portraying herself as her husband's loving follower, cruelly parted from him. By the end of the poem, it is clear that she is bitterly alienated from this male world. What critics disagree about is whether her feelings of bitterness also extend to her absent husband. She is still overwhelmed by her feelings for him but some argue that she also blames him for her present sorry situation, feeling anger and hatred towards him, or at least having an ambivalent attitude. Rather than coherently outlining the woman's story, however, or even clarifying her emotions about the husband, the poem is dominated by the intensity of the speaker's distress and agitation, its apparent lack of controlled structure reflecting this distress and agitation.

Religious elegy: The Seafarer

The Wife's Lament and *Wulf and Eadwacer* were evidently thought by the compilers of the Exeter Book to be worthy of inclusion in an edifying anthology with a predominantly religious subject matter, and the poems would have been read in it by monastic readers in the tenth and eleventh centuries. These lyric pieces must have been considered valuable for the Exeter Book compilers and readers, perhaps because they alluded to stories (now lost) from the still-cherished Germanic past, perhaps simply because they were prized for their poetic qualities and expression of emotion. Some readers might have allegorized or moralized them, finding religious meaning in their non-religious content, though the poems also seem to resist this in their insistence on a this-worldly perspective. Someone like Ælfric would surely not have thought these secular elegies to be suitable reading material for his monks but a more inclusive attitude is reflected in the Exeter Book, even though some of its poems, for example the *Advent Lyrics* (also referred to as *Christ I*), reflect the influence of Benedictine reform ideals that Ælfric would very much have approved of, while others, including some of the elegies themselves, express strongly renunciatory messages.

Among the latter group is *The Seafarer* (trans. Bradley 1982, pp. 329–35; for original text, see Marsden 2004, pp. 221–30), the most admired, and the most complex, of the elegies, to which it is appropriate briefly to turn in concluding the present section. As noted in a previous chapter (see above, pp. 68–9), *The Seafarer* exploits imagery and themes from Germanic heroic tradition in developing its Christian message, which is a homiletic one, urging its audience to reject the seductive attractions of the world and to strive for the reward of life in heaven, where it insists that we have our true home. *The Seafarer* adopts the language of heroic tradition to invert or transform heroic desires – which represent worldly desires – showing them to be inadequate in their own terms but simultaneously turning them into a metaphor for the life of spiritual striving that the poem presents as the only life that can bring fulfilment of human yearning.

The conclusion of *The Seafarer* is both stark and triumphant:

> Let us think where we may have our home,
> and then let us reflect how we may come there;
> and let us then also work that we may enter
> into that eternal blessedness,
> where is the source of life in the love of the Lord,
> joy in heaven. For this, thanks be to the Holy One
> that he has honoured us, the Prince of glory,
> the eternal Lord, for all time. Amen.   (lines 117–24)

To get to this point of perception and heavenly vision, the 'voice' of the poem has had to move from preoccupation with personal individual hardship and misfortune – the first line is 'I can tell a true tale (*soðgied*) about myself' – to a recognition that hardship and misfortune are the reality of life on earth, despite life's fleeting pleasures, and to the understanding that the community and 'home' that we vainly seek in the world are to be found in heaven and are to be gained precisely through embracing a life of exile on earth, which becomes a meaningful heroic life, bringing praise (*lof,* lines 73, 78) not in this world but the next.

The language of exile features centrally in the poem. At the beginning the speaker unhappily treads the paths of exile (*wræccan lastum,* line 15) in a winter seascape, contrasting his miserable experience with the joys of society: he has only the sea-birds for his 'entertainment' (*to gomene,* line 20):

> the noise of the swan instead of the laughter of men,
> the mew singing instead of the drinking of mead.   (lines 21–2)

As in the secular tradition, as represented in heroic poetry and in elegies such as *The Wife's Lament,* the idea of exile at the beginning of *The Seafarer* is presented as a deeply distressing one. In the tradition that *The Seafarer* is drawing upon here, exile and alienation from community provide the archetypal expression of unhappiness. In this tradition life has no meaning away from community, and solitude has no attractions. Community is the basis of cultural life, and life away from community is engaged in only by outcasts, fugitives and tragic figures, who strive to gain re-admittance into community (like the man in *Beowulf* who steals a rich object from the dragon's hoard in order to use it as a gift to win back the favour of his lord) or who work to reestablish community in their place of exile (as the 'husband' appears to have done in *The Husband's Message* when he asks his partner to rejoin him in a new life). Some figures of exile, like Grendel, descended from the cursed race of Cain, wage war from the wilderness against the bright human world from which they are excluded.

Uniquely in *The Seafarer*, however, the speaker goes on willingly to impose a kind of exile on himself. After the description of the harsh life endured at sea with which the poem opens (lines 1–33a), and in the light of this description, the speaker immediately proceeds to express his passionate wish to set sail on the high seas, turning his back on land and home and seeking the place of foreigners:

> And so thoughts now
> beat against my heart, that I should venture for myself
> onto the towering seas, the tumult of the salt-waves –
> on every occasion the desire of my mind urges
> my spirit to travel, so that far from here
> I may seek the homeland of alien people.   (lines 33b–8)

This is paradoxical in the context, and from the perspective of the secular tradition, it is an incomprehensible choice. In *The Seafarer* the revolutionary nature of this choice is highlighted by the poem's awareness of the hardships that the exile will endure in venturing on a sea-voyage and by its appreciation of how appealing are the joys of life 'on land'.

The choice of *The Seafarer* makes no sense from the secular perspective, but it makes very great sense from the perspective of renunciatory Christian spirituality, which forms a key context for the interpretation of the poem. In rejecting earthly comfort and community and embracing hardship the speaker of *The Seafarer* is doing what ascetic Christians had done at least from the third century when the monks of the Egyptian desert were seeking salvation through renunciation. The fathers of monasticism of this time, most famously the hermits Antony and Paul, lived lives of heroic striving in the solitude of the desert. According to his biographer Athanasius of Alexandria, Antony experienced the ascetic impulse from an early age: 'He was not content to stay at home but ..., released from all worldly ties, eagerly entered upon a harsh and arduous way of life' (trans. White, p. 10). Jerome relates that Paul retreated further and further into the desert, eventually finding the remote spot where he 'spent the rest of his life in prayer and solitude' (trans. White 1998, p. 77).

This impulse was strongly reflected in Britain and Ireland in the early Middle Ages. In Anglo-Saxon England it is seen in the lives of the popular saints Cuthbert and Guthlac, for example, both of whom actively chose the ascetic life of solitude. And the tradition of voluntary *peregrinatio pro amore Dei*, 'exile for the love of God', according to which individuals would entrust themselves to the sea in boats and travel to wherever the Lord brought them, is a particularly striking Irish and Anglo-Saxon instance of the renunciatory impulse. Indeed, in a celebrated article, Dorothy Whitelock argued that this very custom is what is literally being described in *The Seafarer* (Whitelock 1950). While it is now accepted that *The Seafarer* should be interpreted symbolically and not as a call for actual *peregrinatio*, the custom does throw light on the outlook of the poem.

In another way too (i.e., as well as supplying an image of earthly hardship and unhappiness), the secular theme of exile provides a powerful literary tool for the poet of *The Seafarer*. This theme is used in the poem to give imaginative expression to the profound *Christian* concept of exile, as inherited from the Bible and the writings of the fathers of the church. According to this meta-phorical concept, which is widely represented in Anglo-Saxon homiletic writings, the human race was put into exile by the fall of Adam and Eve and yearns to return to its true home, which is with God. The possibility of such a return, a journey home from exile, was opened up for members of the human race by the atonement of Christ. The great narratives of exile and journey in the Old Testament were seen in Christian tradition as figures of this universal human condition, to which Christianity itself offered the only remedy. According to this tradition, we are all in exile, and death is the solitary journey which may lead to salvation. *The Seafarer* dramatizes this solitary journey, giving a vivid representation, indeed, of the onset of death itself and present-ing an urgent message of salvation in the light of the recognition of life on earth as a life of exile. Thus Christian and Germanic concepts of exile, along with the related idea of a sea journey, interact in a dynamic and shifting way in building towards the poem's Christian message.

Life on earth as exile, in some Old English homilies

Because of the sins of the first man, Adam, we were cast out of the homeland of Paradise and sent into this world of exile, and we are thus in this world as if we have here no homeland. Concerning this, the apostle Paul said, *'Dum sumus in corpore peregrinamur a domino'*. He, St Paul, said, 'While we are in the body, we are in exile from God'. From here we may earn for ourselves the eternal homeland and true joy. (*Vercelli Homilies*, XI [ed. Scragg 1992, p. 223])

We are in the foreign land of this world – we are exiles in this world, and so have been ever since the progenitor of the human race broke God's behests, and for that sin we have been sent into this banishment, and now we must seek hereafter another kingdom, either in misery or in glory, as we may now choose to merit. (*Blickling Homilies*, II, trans. Morris 1874–80, p. 22 [modified])

For our country is Paradise, to which we cannot return by the way we came. The first-created man and all his offspring were driven from the joy of Paradise, through disobedience, and for eating the forbidden fruit, and through pride, when he would be better than the Almighty Creator had created him. But it is greatly needful to us that we should, by another way, avoid the treacherous devil, that we may happily come to our country, for which we were created. (Ælfric, *Catholic Homilies* I, VII [trans. Thorpe 1844–6, I, 119])

Such a homiletic message is highly relevant in the monastic context in which the Exeter Book would have been read. We might puzzle about the place of *The Wife's Lament* and *Wulf and Eadwacer* in the manuscript but *The Seafarer* 'speaks the language' of those who have withdrawn from the world, seeking salvation through renunciation. It should also be said, however, that the message of the poem is not only for monks and nuns. In *The Seafarer* it is stated that *everyone* has anxiety about their 'sea-voyage' (*sæfore*, line 42). In this statement the poem universalizes the theme of seafaring in a way that demands non-literal interpretation, but *The Seafarer* does not specify what form such renunciation should take for people reading or hearing the poem, as they strive to attain the bliss of their heavenly home.

Postscript: genre and manuscripts

Dividing them into genres or types has long been recognized as presenting a valuable perspective on the writings of Anglo-Saxon England (and elsewhere, of course), allowing critics to group works together and thereby enabling the modelling of literary traditions and affiliations. The present chapter and the previous one have aimed to offer an understanding of Anglo-Saxon literature by adopting such an approach. The generic approach gives a valuable intertextual perspective, but it must be acknowledged that, like the editing of individual texts, in doing so it runs the danger of abstracting works too much from their manuscript context. Considering the make-up of manuscripts and viewing individual items and groups of items in relation to their codicological environment are also vital in throwing light on Anglo-Saxon literature and its uses, and these circumstances must be taken account of along with any discussion of kinds of literature; and indeed they must feed into such discussion, as I hope they have in these chapters.

Thus, as well thinking about the Vercelli Book homilies, say, in relation to other homilies, it is highly relevant to read them in the context of the manuscript as a whole in which they occur and in relation to the poems that it also contains. Such perspectives are increasingly throwing interesting light on individual works and on groups of works that appear together, providing compelling evidence about their purpose and reception (see, for instance, with reference to the Vercelli Book, Zacher and Orchard 2009) and about perceptions of literature in the period. To highlight just a few examples, researchers have recently used manuscript evidence to ask questions about the use and afterlife of works by Ælfric (e.g. Kleist 2009) and Wulfstan (e.g. Wilcox 1992); the religious themes that particular manuscript compilers are drawn to (for views about the Exeter Book, for example, see Conner 1993, Muir 2000); the way *Beowulf* might have been read (see above, p. 93); and, more generally, structural patterning in Old English poetry (Pasternack 1995).

Scholars debate principles of organization and structure within manuscripts, particularly those that contain a wide range of kinds of literature. One example among many is the mostly Old English manuscript Cambridge, Corpus Christi College 201, put together in the mid eleventh century with contents that include a translated fragment of the *Monastic Agreement*, homilies and laws by Wulfstan, other legal texts, the romance *Apollonius of Tyre*, items on English saints, an excerpt from the translation of Genesis, some religious poetry, and material in Latin. The manuscript has been characterized as a 'hodge-podge' (Clemoes 1960) but one recent commentator persuasively argues that a penitential theme in a Lenten setting underlies the collection and that forgiveness is a recurring theme across its apparently disparate items (Anlezark 2006).

Some manuscripts were evidently carefully organized, for example according to the church calendar, others have close thematic unity, such as collections of selected homilies, while others can be shown to have been composed incrementally, with material added on to an existing core (Scragg 2009, pp. 61–2). Manuscripts represent the material remains of literary history and analysis of them provides a key means of locating and historicizing the literature. The manuscript context of Anglo-Saxon writings has traditionally been somewhat neglected by literary critics but is now receiving concentrated attention, especially as the resources and tools of the digital age increasingly make new possibilities available for studying manuscripts, and indeed for giving wide access to images of them (Treharne 2009, p. 111; see further Lee and O'Donnell 2009).

Aspects of the visual appearance and layout of manuscripts were touched on earlier. In concluding the present postscript it is worth emphasizing the point that Old English texts, particularly poetry, look very different in their manuscripts from the way they do in modern editions and translations. Not only do the original manuscripts lack the titles, paragraphing, punctuation and capitalization that we find in printed editions and translations but, as was pointed out with reference to Figure 2.5 above (p. 71), in the case of poetry they are not even set out in verse lines but are written continuously, like prose. A modern printed edition or translation recreates the text according to the principles and conventions of print technology, effacing the manuscript context and the particularities of manuscript presentation in the process. We need the printed edition, as we need the translation, but should be aware that even an edition is a kind of translation. It mediates a text that would otherwise have been inaccessible but in doing so it incorporates a particular interpretation of that text. Interpretative possibilities were more open for the Anglo-Saxon readers of the original manuscripts. It has been suggested that hypertext digital editions offer a more enabling way of presenting manuscript texts than does print (see especially Foys 2007); this may well be the case and such editions have begun to appear (e.g. O'Donnell, ed., 2005, Muir, ed., 2006; see further Lee and O'Donnell 2009), though it is still very early days in the digital age for us to know how editing techniques will develop. It should be added, however, that digital technology mediates too, if in a different way from print technology.

Chapter 5

Anglo-Saxon afterlives, medieval to modern: later uses and appropriations of Anglo-Saxon writings

This chapter offers a brief overview of the perception and reception of Anglo-Saxon England and its literature after the Anglo-Saxon age itself. Anglo-Saxon literature has been read and used in one way or another throughout later history, and images of Anglo-Saxon England have been wielded politically in a succession of cultural contexts, with the idea of pre-Conquest England often being invested with symbolic significance. Today Anglo-Saxon artefacts are among the most popular exhibits in museums in Britain, and when the Staffordshire Hoard was first put on display in 2009 people queued around the block to see its treasures. In recent generations Anglo-Saxon writings have fired the imagination of creative writers, most famously perhaps Tolkien and Heaney, and we have got used to appropriations, particularly of *Beowulf*, in popular culture. Such appropriations have included novels, comic books and graphic novels, retellings for children, animated films, illustrated translations and adaptations, computer games, musical versions, and Hollywood movies (see Staver 2005, George 2010, Clark and Perkins 2010).

To mention only the latter, there have been five *Beowulf* films in the past decade or so. Of these the most high-profile has been Robert Zemeckis's 2007 version, a big-budget production in a 'performance-capture' animation format, but other cinematic adaptations have proved popular as well. Particularly notable, and interesting I think, are *The 13th Warrior* (1999), with

Antonio Banderas, directed by John McTiernan, and *Outlander* (2008), with Jim Caviezel, directed by Howard McCain. The latter uses a science-fiction plot framework to render the monster theme plausible for a twenty-first-century audience and incorporates ecological and postcolonial themes, as well as plenty of violence. The former is based not directly on *Beowulf* itself but on the 1976 thriller *Eaters of the Dead* by the best-selling novelist Michael Crichton, who blends story elements from *Beowulf* with documentary information from a tenth-century source written by an Arabic traveller. The novel is intriguingly postmodern in its blurring of fact and fiction, which disconcerted Crichton in retrospect, and the novel and the film take on new resonances in the post-9/11 cultural context: Banderas plays a sophisticated Muslim observer of a Germanic culture presented as alien and undeveloped. There has also been a Canadian–Icelandic co-production, *Beowulf and Grendel*, directed by Sturla Gunnarsson (2005), a muscular if somewhat ponderous retelling, with Gerald Butler, and one other Hollywood version, Graham Baker's *Beowulf* (1999), with Christopher Lambert (the less said about the latter, the better, I think).

Recent appropriations bring out the otherness of the Anglo-Saxon and Germanic past (at the beginning of this book I quoted Heaney referring to the 'remoteness' of *Beowulf*) as well as its perceived nobility. Such themes are not new. Anglo-Saxon writings and the world associated with them were also being appropriated in comparable, though also in contrary, ways in earlier periods, influencing important literary figures and playing significant roles in intellectual life and popular culture.

Medieval continuities

As pointed out in Chapter 1, Old English literary traditions persisted after the Norman Conquest for up to two centuries in some places. There was continuity in the copying, revision and composition of Old English texts, particularly, but not only, of homiletic and hagiographical material. And long after the Conquest we also find careful scholarly glossing and annotation of Old English manuscripts from earlier centuries, most notably by the figure identified from his trembling script as the 'Tremulous Hand' of Worcester, a learned monk with mastery of the older language, working in the late twelfth and early thirteenth century to facilitate the continuing use of Anglo-Saxon writings among contemporary readers (Franzen 1991). Eventually knowledge of Standard Old English fades and the language of vernacular texts becomes identifiable as Early Middle English, a process that we can see taking place in the *Peterborough Chronicle*, for example. A poem like *The Grave* (mid-twelfth century) exhibits a transitional form of early English while still preserving Old English forms. Developing the metaphor of the grave as a house, the poem (ed. Short 1976, pp. 292–3) begins,

> Ðe wes bold ȝebyld   er þu iboren were,
> ðe wes molde imynt   er ðu of moder come.

[For you a house was built before you were born; the ground was intended for you before you came from your mother.]

Old English spelling appears here in a modified form (with *e* for *æ*, for example), but the grammar is essentially that of Old English, and the Anglo-Saxon poetic metre is still recognizable.

The interest in the English past in the eleventh and twelfth centuries is not confined to non-Norman outposts but is also very much in evidence in Anglo-Norman circles. This is a period highly productive in Latin writings about Anglo-Saxon saints, for example, most of them written by Normans. Indeed it has been remarked that '[t]he vast output of this period makes the pre-Conquest Latin hagiography of England seem meagre by comparison' (Love 1999, p. 227). And there is a wave of large-scale Latin histories of England, which make informed use of Anglo-Saxon sources, some of which sources are no longer extant. The leading figure among this group of writers is William of Malmesbury (*c.* 1085/90–*c.* 1143), a monk of mixed Norman–English parentage, whose *History of the Kings of England* (*Gesta regum Anglorum*) and *History of the Bishops of England* (*Gesta pontificum Anglorum*) are key works of medieval historiography. William draws upon Bede, the *Anglo-Saxon Chronicle*, Asser and other sources, some unidentified, to tell the story of English history down to the early twelfth century, later bringing it up to date with his *Contemporary History* (*Historia novella*). He views England as having a proud history but for William the country went into decline in the later Anglo-Saxon centuries and the Normans brought welcome new life. He castigates the behaviour of clergy, monks, nobles and common people in the period before the coming of the Normans (see especially *Gesta regum*, III. 245; ed. and trans. Mynors 1998, pp. 458–61). William has some criticisms of the Normans too but they are mild by comparison. He writes of the Normans indeed that 'they are of all nations the most hospitable, they treat strangers with the same respect as each other'. He adds, 'The standard of religion, dead everywhere in England, has been raised by their arrival: you may see everywhere churches in villages, in towns and cities monasteries rising in a new style of architecture; and with new devotion our country flourishes, so that every rich man thinks a day wasted if he does not make it remarkable with some great stroke of generosity' (III. 246; ed. and trans. Mynors 1998, pp. 460–1).

William is profuse in his praise of Bede, in whose steps he sees himself as following, and other historians of the period were equally in Bede's debt, and equally admiring of him. The *Ecclesiastical History* was a major object of study in Anglo-Norman England, to the extent that by the mid-twelfth century, as N. J. Higham writes, Bede 'was well established in the role of the founding father of English History, mined comparatively indiscriminately for stories and "facts" and widely subjected to the plagiarism by which intellectuals of the period showed their appreciation' (Higham 2006, p. 28).

The use of Anglo-Saxon literature and history in the later Middle Ages is a topic that was opened up by some of the contributions in a volume published in 2000 (ed. Scragg and Weinberg 2000) and that is being pursued in current research. Chaucer and Gower may not seem to offer promising avenues for such research but Chaucer's *Man of Law's Tale* and its analogue, Gower's *Tale of Constance*, feature Anglo-Saxon Northumbria, a remote land where heathens, having previously expelled the British Christians, are themselves beginning to convert to Christianity. Both these versions have been seen as using images of Anglo-Saxon England to highlight concerns about sovereignty and identity in the late fourteenth century (Lavezzo 2006; Lees forthcoming), though the emphasis on Anglo-Saxon England and its history is more pronounced in the source of the Chaucer and Gower tales, the early fourteenth-century Anglo-Norman *Chroniques* of Nicholas Trevet, than in the Middle English versions themselves (Frankis 2000).

By the time of Chaucer and Gower, Old English texts had become a closed book, so to speak, though vernacular literary traditions of alliterative poetry showing continuity with Old English verse were still flourishing in late medieval Britain, and Bede's *Ecclesiastical History* remained popular (Gransden 1992, pp. 1–29). Anglo-Saxon England also features in Middle English romance (Rouse 2005). It is only with the efforts of Tudor antiquarians in the sixteenth century that knowledge of the Old English *language* begins to be recovered, however, and that Anglo-Saxon England begins to be perceived as constituting a subject of special interest and relevance to the concerns of the present.

Early modern: recovering Anglo-Saxon England

The early modern recovery of Old English can be traced back to the studies in the 1540s of a group of antiquarians interested in the early history of regions and places in England, of whom the churchman Robert Talbot was the most advanced in his knowledge of the language, having taught himself Old English inductively from the texts themselves (there were no other resources for him to draw upon). These scholars were followed in the 1560s by a 'second generation', referred to as the Parker circle. Under the auspices of Matthew Parker, archbishop of Canterbury 1559–75, this group established the study of the Old English language on a firm footing and brought Old English writings into the public domain. The major themes of this second phase of activity have been identified as 'the focused study of legal texts and the *Anglo-Saxon Chronicle*, the examination and exploitation of manuscripts for the evidence that they could contribute to contemporary religious debates, and the appearance of the first printed editions of Old English texts' (Graham 2001, p. 418). Parker himself was a tireless collector of manuscripts in the period after the monasteries had been dissolved and much of their contents destroyed or lost; it is thanks to him that we have one of the great collections of medieval English manuscripts, now in the Parker Library at Cambridge. A second great collection would be assembled in the early seventeenth century by Sir Robert Cotton (1571–1631), now in the British Library, though part of it would be lost in a fire of 1731.

The study of writings from Anglo-Saxon England participated in the politics of the time, both secular and religious. The era of Parker was one of fierce religious controversy, of course, with the Protestant Reformation in England at its height. Parker had succeeded the Catholic Robert Pole as archbishop and was zealous in championing Protestant teaching. It was under his direction that the Thirty-nine Articles that defined English Protestantism were established. The first Old English texts to be edited and printed (by Parker and his associate John Joscelyn, in 1566 or 1567) were works by Ælfric, of which the most prominent was his homily for Easter from the Second Series of *Catholic Homilies*, a homily on the Eucharist. This homily was presented to the public, though not without some judicious tweaking in the editing (see Leinbaugh 1982), as evidence that the ancient English church did not subscribe to the popish doctrine of transubstantiation but understood the sacrament to represent the body and blood of Christ symbolically. The homily was popular with religious polemicists throughout the next century and beyond, serving to draw an emphatic line between England and Rome. Not for these early modern ideologues the idea of Rome as 'capital of Anglo-Saxon England' (see above, p. 101): it was a case of 'not Angles, but Anglicans', as it were.

For Elizabethans like Parker the distinctive Englishness of the English church was already apparent in the Anglo-Saxon centuries. The fact that that Englishness was expressed in the vernacular 'Saxon' language would also have been seen as highly relevant in this period, when English was coming out of the shadow of Latin both academically – suitably 'enriched' – and ecclesiastically. The Tudor period was the great period of sustained Bible translation in England, of the Book of Common Prayer and of English as now the language of the liturgy. Parker himself sponsored the 'Bishops' Bible' of 1568, which was to be kept in all churches. In 1571 John Foxe, chronicler of Protestant martyrdoms, brought out an edition of the Old English Gospels, with the text of the Bishops' Bible given as a gloss in the margins. Both the English church and the English language served to define Englishness, and both could be traced back to the Anglo-Saxons. So too could English law, in contrast to the codified Roman law in operation on the Continent. Thus it is not surprising that Anglo-Saxon laws were among the first Old English texts to be edited (with a Latin translation), by a leading member of the Parker circle, William Lambarde, in 1568; Lambarde was building on the pioneering work of his learned associate Laurence Nowell.

The key Anglo-Saxon historical sources were carefully studied by these reformist scholars: the *Anglo-Saxon Chronicle* (though no edition was published at this stage; see Lutz 2000), Asser (Parker's edition of Asser and of Alfred's *Preface to the Pastoral Care* appeared in 1574), and Bede. Bede was a problematic figure for Parker and his circle, however, even though he had been praised by that earlier scourge of the medieval church, John Bale, as a writer who, like Lot among the Sodomites, did good work in evil times (Happé 1996, p. 67). Parker and company objected to him because of his monasticism and his attachment to Rome. Bede was enlisted on the Catholic side in the religious controversy, with the first translation of the *Ecclesiastical History* into Modern English being produced, in 1556, by Thomas Stapleton, a Catholic churchman in exile in the Low Countries and France; the Latin text had been printed on the Continent as early as 1480 or so, and again in 1550. Later, however, Bede was appropriated to the Protestant cause as a prophet-figure (Higham 2006, p. 33), and he came to be associated with ideals of English identity. The *Ecclesiastical History* was published by Abraham Wheelock in 1643 in an edition that gave both the Latin and Old English versions of it and that also included the *Anglo-Saxon Chronicle*. In the prefatory epistle to the publication Wheelock declares that this supplementary material 'will show you the antiquity [of current Anglican doctrine] which will remove the accusation of novelty; will show truth (if the accusers wish to be self-consistent) as the expeller of heresy; will show harmony, by amply demonstrating our communion with the ancient mother Church (*cum grand-æva matre Ecclesia communionem*)' (quoted in Plumer 2000, p. 255).

What we do not get in Anglo-Saxon studies in the sixteenth century, and for the most part in the following two centuries either, is much interest in the Anglo-Saxon documents as literature: the interest is historical, theological and linguistic. Even when the Anglo-Saxon world began to attract the attention of creative writers and artists, as it did from the mid eighteenth century on, it was historical figures that they were attracted to, above all King Alfred, who stimulated a veritable industry of drama, poems, fiction and art, increasing in the nineteenth and twentieth centuries and thereby cementing Alfred's reputation as Alfred the Great, England's greatest king and the greatest Englishman ever (Keynes 1999). In the political context of the later eighteenth and early nineteenth century Alfred became by extension a symbol of British identity and achievement (Pratt 2000; on the construction of Britishness in this period, see Colley 2005).

Old English literature, however, did not seize the imagination; it was valued for its documentary content, and for the fact that it was written in the vernacular, rather than for its form. Indeed, Old English poetry was not recognized as such until the work of Francis Junius, who brought out an edition of the poems of the 'Cædmon' manuscript in 1655, in which the half-line units are indicated by pointing. Old English poetry is not lineated in the original manuscripts, of course, and previous editors had taken it to be prose. Wheelock, for example, prints the *Chronicle* poems and Cædmon's *Hymn* without recognizing them to be verse, though he comments on the 'ancient and rough' (*perantiquum, & horridum*) quality of the style of *The Battle of Brunanburh* and other *Chronicle* texts later found to be poems (Plumer 2000, p. 254). The first discerning account of the workings of Old English poetry came from George Hickes, the great figure in Anglo-Saxon studies at the end of the seventeenth century and the start of the eighteenth, whose monumen-tal *Thesaurus* 'of ancient northern languages' (Hickes and Wanley 1703–5, vol. I) contains a chapter on the poetry, in which Hickes discusses diction, metre and rhythm, noting, crucially, that Old English metre is stress-based rather than syllabic. This was just the beginning of the scholarly understand-ing of Old English poetry, but it was a beginning – though more than a hundred years later the influential historian Sharon Turner could write that the poetry of the Anglo-Saxons had 'no rules at all' (Turner 1820, III, 301); an understanding of the complexity of Old English metre would come only in the later 1800s. Hickes and his associate Christopher Rawlinson also insti-tuted the practice of setting out Old English poetry as verse in half-lines, a practice that would be followed until the later nineteenth century, when the modern convention of taking each pair of half-lines together as a single line gained acceptance.

In the early seventeenth century interest in Anglo-Saxon England had continued but at a more subdued level than previously. In James I England had a non-English king, who had a political interest in espousing the idea of Britain rather than England. It is notable that in the context of the growing friction between parliament and the king Anglo-Saxon studies, and perceived

Anglo-Saxon values and free institutions, were embraced by scholars associated with parliamentary opposition to the crown (Horsman 1981, pp. 12–14). A concern with the ancient *British* past is reflected in literature of James's reign, notably in Shakespeare's plays *King Lear* and *Cymbeline*, the latter of which in particular has been seen as supportive of British union; earlier in his career Shakespeare had written much on *English* medieval history, and appears to have been sceptical about union with Scotland (Hadfield 2004, pp. 151–68). Anglo-Saxon England, however, provides the setting for only one scene in a play by the Bard, *Macbeth*, a work of the Jacobean period. In *Macbeth* England is a haven of tranquillity compared to Macbeth's Scotland. The relevant scene (IV, iii) mentions the power of King Edward the Confessor to cure illness (the 'king's evil'); and the reference to Edward as 'gracious England' in this scene may be viewed as, by association, presenting the country itself in a good light (England appears off-stage in *Hamlet* but the historical period is unspecific).

In later literary history there would be a continuing flow of plays and poems – and, later, novels – on Anglo-Saxon topics (Scragg 2000) but the Anglo-Saxon period does not attract Elizabethan or Jacobean playwrights. Even Thomas Middleton's chronicle play *Hengist, King of Kent* (the main plot of which is based on an episode in Holinshed that goes back ultimately to Geoffrey of Monmouth) is predominantly British rather than Anglo-Saxon in its focus. This play is set at the time of the Anglo-Saxon invasions of Britain but the main interest in it is in the Britons, among whom the dominant figure is the treacherous and lustful Vortiger, who comes to the throne after having the saintly King Constantius murdered and who with other scheming characters meets a suitably unpleasant end (in a fire). *Hengist* shows little sign of identification with the Anglo-Saxons, who are portrayed negatively. As noted by Julia Briggs (Briggs 2000), the play contains some Old English words – a first in modern literature – inherited from its sources: as a signal for the Saxons to mount a surprise attack on British lords, Hengist calls out to his men, 'Nemp your sexes!' (IV, iii, 35, 52: 'Seize your seaxes', a *seax* being a type of short sword used by the invaders); but the effect of these strange words is to distance their (heathen) speakers from the audience.

The long eighteenth century: history and politics

Scholarly interest in Anglo-Saxon England continued steadily in the seventeenth century, however, increasing in intensity as it went on and especially at the end of it and into the 1700s, with foundational publications on grammar, lexicography and manuscript studies being produced, while an increasing number of Anglo-Saxon texts were edited. The period of the brilliant Hickes and his group of scholarly associates was one of the key ones in the history of Anglo-Saxon studies. As Mechthild Gretsch has written, at the beginning of the eighteenth century Anglo-Saxon studies 'were the domain of some of the intellectually most active scholars of the age' (Gretsch 1999, p. 201). One of the most interesting of these scholars is Elizabeth Elstob, who was motivated by a love of the subject and a desire to popularize it. Like other Anglo-Saxonists of the period, she also had theological and nationalistic motivations for studying and promoting Old English. She writes in the preface to her edition and Modern English translation of Ælfric's *Life of St Gregory*, 'This is some, no small Satisfaction that we reap, from Saxon Learning: that we see the Agreement of the reformed and the ancient Saxon Church. That it is no new Church, but the same it was before the Roman Church was corrupted' (Elstob 1709, p. xiv; quoted Gretsch 1999, p. 503). The Gregorian mission brought an uncorrupted form of Christianity, thus linking the Anglo-Saxon church backwards to what Elstob calls 'the Primitive Church of Christ' as well as forward to reformed Anglicanism.

Elstob also wrote *The Rudiments of Grammar for the English-Saxon Tongue* (1715), the first Old English grammar in Modern English as opposed to Latin, and she prepared an edition of Ælfric's *Catholic Homilies*. The flowering of Anglo-Saxon studies in the period rapidly came to an end, however, after the death of Hickes in 1715. Elstob herself gave up scholarship and her edition of the *Catholic Homilies* never came out. Despite her efforts Anglo-Saxon studies did not succeed in appealing to a wider audience. In some quarters the subject may even have been regarded as politically suspect by association, since leading proponents of it, notably Hickes himself and Thomas Hearne, were 'nonjurors', having refused to swear the royal oath of allegiance; Hickes spent a number of years in concealment. The study of 'Saxon' was also denigrated by the emerging prescriptive grammarians of the period and by those, led by Jonathan Swift, who sought to improve – 'ascertain' – the English language. As pointed out by Danielle Plumer, 'Swift referred to antiquarians as "Laborious Men of low Genius" and took a contemptuous stance toward the studies of "the vulgar Tongue"' (Plumer 2000, p. 271). Elstob was responding to the wider public perception of Anglo-Saxon studies when she asked rhetorically in the preface to her edition of the St Gregory homily, 'What is this Saxon? what has she to do with this barbarous antiquated Stuff? So useless, so altogether out of the way?' (Elstob 1709, p. vi).

The idea of Saxon 'Stuff' as barbarous was, more generally, a reflection of the neoclassical aesthetic that reigned in the Enlightenment era. Saxon writings might have served theological and historical purposes but they did not conform to classical principles. And even when a vogue for writings from the later Middle Ages developed in the pre-Romantic period, most commentators gave Anglo-Saxon literature, and Anglo-Saxon England, a wide berth. For the antiquary Joseph Ritson, writing in 1803, the Anglo-Saxons were 'for the most part, an ignorant and illiterate people', and Ritson was caustic about the quality of their literature: 'it will be vain to hope for proofs, among them, of genius, or original composition, at least in their native tongue' (quoted by Shippey and Haarder, eds., 1998, p. 3). The *Ecclesiastical History* of Bede, which had been available in a new edition by John Smith from 1722, might be acceptable, but writings in the 'native tongue' were not to the taste of cultivated readers, especially poetry. Even Sharon Turner, the first major historian of Anglo-Saxon England and an admirer of his ancestors, could refer to the rude state of poetical genius and taste in the Anglo-Saxon period (Turner 1820, III, 299); with particular reference to *The Battle of Brunanburh* and other *Chronicle* poems, he writes, 'we see poetry in its rudest form, before the art of narration was understood' (Turner 1820, III, 322). The Anglo-Saxon past was to be cherished as formative; it should not be expected to have progressed to an advanced stage of civilization: 'Why should [the reader] then despise the first state, and the improving progress of his Saxon ancestors?' Turner asks. 'This nation exhibits the conversion of ferocious pirates, into a highly civilized, informed, and generous people – in a word, into ourselves. Can it be frivolous to depict the successive steps of this admirable change?' (Turner 1799–1805, II, xii).

J. J. Conybeare, who produced in his *Illustrations of Anglo-Saxon Poetry* (1826) the earliest translations from *Beowulf* and other Old English poems into Modern English verse, makes the best case he can for Old English poetry but still acknowledges its rudeness: 'he who makes due allowance for the barbarisms and obscurity of the language . . . and for the shackles of a metrical scheme of extreme difficulty, and, to our ears at least, totally destitute of harmony and expression, will find that *Beowulf* presents many of those which have in all ages been admitted as the genuine elements of poetic composition' (Conybeare 1826, pp. 80–1). Conybeare's *Illustrations* prints passages from *Beowulf* in the original accompanied by a literal translation into Latin and with selected extracts translated into Modern English in iambic pentameter:

> Thus fared the chieftains in their days of bliss
> Right gallantly, till that foul and hateful fiend
> Wreak'd on them his sad vengeance; that fierce spirit
> Roaming the marches in his lonely might –
> The Grendel – he that by the Fifel tribe
> Fastness and fen-land held and dark morass,
> Unholy wanderer.   (pp. 36–7; = lines 99–105a)

Conybeare also provides selections from a range of other poems, again printing the Anglo-Saxon original along with a literal Latin translation and a version in Modern English iambic pentameter, including Cædmon's *Hymn*, 'The Song of the Traveller' (*Widsith*), 'The Battle of Finsborough', passages from the Junius and Exeter manuscripts, the metrical *Boethius* and the 'Norman-Saxon' fragment, *The Grave*.

Elizabeth Elstob had tried to counter criticisms of the Anglo-Saxon age a century earlier. In response to the characterizing of Anglo-Saxon England as barbarous, she wrote spiritedly in the preface to the St Gregory homily, 'I fear, if things were rightly consider'd, that the Charge of Barbarity would rather fall upon those who, while they fancy themselves adorn'd with the Embellishments of foreign Learning, are ignorant, even to Barbarity, of the Faith, Religion, the Laws and Customs, and Language of their Ancestors' (Elstob 1709, p. vi). Even Elstob did not attempt to defend Anglo-Saxon literature on aesthetic grounds, however.

Nineteenth- and twentieth-century perspectives

In the 1800s Old English poetry moved centre-stage in Anglo-Saxon studies. As the new science of philology developed and flourished (see above, pp. 11–13), editions and discussions of most of the surviving poems were produced and a basic understanding of the structural principles of the verse worked out. The poetry was still believed to be primitive and unsophisticated, as remained the view of many scholars and literary people until well into the twentieth century. Old English poetry was primitive but it was considered to be a precious heritage reflecting the beliefs and ideas of archaic pre-Christian times, which were now – in contrast to previously – of great interest to researchers. Philology developed in an intellectual climate powerfully affected by the ideas of the Romantic movement, and in this context literature that could be identified as the product of Germanic paganism was a particular fascination. This literature was noble and inspiring. Some of it had been contaminated by monkish editors but it still provided a window on the pagan past; Christian religious writings were no longer seen as the glory of the Anglo-Saxon age. In his classic study *The Search for Anglo-Saxon Paganism*, Eric Stanley refers to a review by the magisterial Ludwig Ettmüller of an anthology of Old English literature published in 1838, in which Ettmüller takes the editor to task for including religious as well as secular texts in his selection: he exclaims with distaste, 'Surely such things could today only find acceptance and praise from brain-sick conventiclers' (Stanley 1975, p. 14). As Stanley goes on to point out (p. 15), Ettmüller's was the dominant view at the time.

In this context of interest in the archaic past, Old English poetry and Anglo-Saxon culture were appropriated by emerging ideologies of nationalism and racialism. German scholars came to regard the poetry and the culture, along with those of Scandinavia and other areas of early Germanic population, as monuments of an inclusive German antiquity. As the great philologist Jacob Grimm wrote in 1840, 'Anglo-Saxon poems need no recommendation for anyone whose interest lies in the history and language of our antiquity; they belong to all Germany as much as to England; indeed, they belong to us more than Old Norse poems in so far as their language is closer to ours' (quoted Stanley 1975, p. 16). Karl Simrock, translator of *Beowulf* and of works in medieval High German, entitled his translation of *Beowulf* (1859), *Beowulf. Das älteste deutsche Epos* (*Beowulf: The Oldest German Epic*), following the practice of other scholars in doing so. The language of the early Germanic people and their literature provided a key foundation for ideas of distinctive German – or, later, 'Aryan' – identity, which were expressed with increasing zeal as the 1800s went on and were to be eagerly appropriated, with sad consequences, in the 1900s (Benes 2008, especially pp. 197–239).

In nineteenth-century Britain the Anglo-Saxon past was embraced as formative in the establishment of English and British identity, with considerable slippage in the use of the terms England/English and Britain/British in the period (as later). Enthusiastic 'Saxonism' is apparent in the writings of the influential philologist John Mitchell Kemble (who produced the first properly scholarly edition of *Beowulf*), especially in his popular *The Saxons in England* (1849). This historical work, written at a time of shattering revolution across Europe, 'attributes the political stability of England to the permanence and power of endurance of its Saxon institutions, in particular its system of land laws, as well as its language, and its municipal, religious and social institutions' (Young 2008, p. 33). Kemble was among those who used the popular metaphor of early England as the 'childhood' of the nation (MacDougall 1982, p. 96; Young 2008, p. 33), thereby expressing the kind of progressivist view of history that is also strongly evident in Turner, who compares the style of Old English poetry to that of a child learning to talk (1820, III, 308–9).

Contemporaries of Kemble went further, converting admiration for Anglo-Saxon institutions, which they saw as continuing in their own time, to a perception of inherent superior racial characteristics of the English traceable back to the Anglo-Saxons. Fiction writers, led by Sir Walter Scott, writing for an even wider audience than that of Kemble's *The Saxons in England*, popularized this view, which was developed in the Victorian period to glorify 'Anglo-Saxon' character and achievement throughout history. Scott and other novelists eulogized the manliness and love of freedom of the original

Anglo-Saxons and strove to integrate the reality of their defeat by the Normans with an understanding of English history as 'a great unbroken sweep' from the virtuous Anglo-Saxon age to the present (Sanders 2000, p. 172).

Some of the key ideas of nineteenth-century Anglo-Saxon racial superiority are there in embryonic form in Turner. To quote Hugh MacDougall, 'In Turner's *History* one can find all the ingredients necessary for an explicitly racist interpretation of English history: the common Germanic origin of the English people; the exceptional courage and manliness of the Saxons, their predilection for freedom and the inherent excellence of their language and social institutions; the special affinity of the transmitted Saxon genius for science and reason; the inevitability of the ultimate triumph of a people so superbly endowed and directed by a kindly providence' (MacDougall 1982, p. 94). In the nineteenth century such ideas found support in evidence from philology (selectively deployed) and anatomy (which presented the Caucasian race as superior to all others). They were confidently placed on a scientific basis, according to which people of Anglo-Saxon stock, in Britain and around the globe, could see themselves, as Reginald Horsman puts it, as 'the elite of an elite' (Horsman 1981, p. 38).

As Horsman has explained, it was not least in the United States of America that the far-reaching effects of an increasingly scientific – and indeed theological – 'Anglo-Saxonism' were to be found. Anglo-Saxon England had been admired by Thomas Jefferson, a 'founding father' of America, who idealized the pre-Conquest age as a time of freedom and law based on the natural rights of man and who believed that 'the Anglo-Saxon government and way of life should become a model for the new America' (Horsman 1981, p. 21). Jefferson wrote a grammar of the Old English language (making use of Elizabeth Elstob's *Rudiments*) and included study of the language on the curriculum of the University of Virginia, which he set up. He even had the idea of having Hengist and Horsa, legendary founders of Anglo-Saxon England, on the Great Seal of the United States (on Jefferson and Old English, see further Hauer 1983).

The academic study of Old English did not make much impression in the early Republic immediately after Jefferson but it began to establish itself in universities as the century went on, influenced by philological developments in Germany, where many American scholars studied (Frantzen 1990, pp. 74–7; Hall 2001, pp. 447–9). By 1899 Old English was taught at some three dozen American universities and was more widely available than anywhere else in the world (Hall 1997, p. 133). Anglo-Saxon studies appear to have had a particular resonance in the Southern States, where, after the Civil War, intellectuals identified the South with the Anglo-Saxons, who were defeated by the tyrannical Normans but eventually proved victorious in terms of language and culture (VanHoosier-Carey 1997). It wasn't just the South that looked to Anglo-Saxon England, however. The culturally dominant population of the country as a whole saw itself as being of Anglo-Saxon descent and as racially superior to other people. To quote Horsman, 'By 1850 the emphasis was on the American Anglo-Saxons as a separate, innately superior people who were destined to bring good government, commercial prosperity, and Christianity to the American continent and to the world' (Horseman 1981, pp. 1–2). This perception of racial superiority became increasingly accepted as self-evident.

The picture of Anglo-Saxon history, language and literature that nineteenth-century intellectuals and their gratified audiences derived from the sources and appropriated for their own political purposes is of course very unlike that described in earlier pages of this book. Today we have a different appreciation of the writings of the Anglo-Saxons, and the idea of a pure Anglo-Saxon race obviously does not stand up with reference to the early Middle Ages, never mind with reference to the ethnic intermingling of later centuries. Anglo-Saxonism was comprehensively discredited in intellectual circles in the twentieth century, with Anglo-Saxon studies itself serving to demonstrate the spuriousness of earlier ethnic claims. Forms of Anglo-Saxonism and the like live on, however, as a browse of the world wide web will quickly confirm.

Critics at the time also raised objections to the racial myth (see, for example, Hall 1997, pp. 134–7), though the belief in the innate superiority of Anglo-Saxon peoples was judged 'universal' in America in the mid nineteenth century and later (Hall 1997, p. 136), conveniently authorizing the world view of those who subscribed to it. In Britain, as Andrew Sanders points out in the light of the project of forging British as opposed to English identity, 'To proclaim an exclusive cultural inheritance as a birthright of the unadulteratedly Teutonic English race appeared to many Victorians to be a dull, perverse and unnecessary exercise' (Sanders 2000, p. 163), but nonetheless the Saxon genius was seen as providing the basis for deserved British success in the modern period.

In the first chapter of this book I discussed the literary turn in Old English scholarship that took place in the twentieth century and I outlined some subsequent developments in the field, particularly since the Second World War; there is no need to go over that ground again here. Crucially, however, Old English literature became interesting as literature, and in this context the study of it found its institutional location, as part of the new subject of English studies (Palmer 1965), predominantly in university English departments, where it still tends to remain. The prodigious achievements of nineteenth-century philologists had provided an essential foundation for later scholars but these scholars now took their subject through progressive processes of reinvention. Meanwhile in the wider culture, in reaction to the earlier glorification of Anglo-Saxon England, the period and its literature became increasingly marginalized in the course of the twentieth century, finding little if any place on school curriculums in the later decades and providing few sources for popular education and entertainment, though, as evidenced at the beginning of this chapter, the new century has witnessed something of an upturn in interest.

Creative writers and Anglo-Saxon literature: from Wordsworth and Longfellow to Heaney and the present

Among the students encountering Old English literature in English departments have been many creative writers, who have been influenced and stimulated by it. My own department at Queen's University Belfast is known for the major poets who studied and worked there in the past couple of generations. Three of the most distinguished of these, Seamus Heaney, Paul Muldoon and Ciaran Carson, have engaged creatively with Old English poetry to a greater or lesser extent, and other modern poets were influenced by their study of Old English at other universities. The beginning of the story of creative engagement with the Anglo-Saxons and their literature pre-dates the rise of modern Old English studies, however, and such engagement has continued alongside the academic subject as well as in relation to it. A wealth of Anglo-Saxon-related creative material has been produced in the past two centuries and it is relevant in concluding this overview of perceptions and receptions to refer, albeit necessarily briefly, to some appropriations which may be considered particularly significant and interesting. It is notable that writers who have made use of Anglo-Saxon material include many of the major figures in modern literature, who have pondered the links between the Anglo-Saxon world and the present and have been attracted to the sound and language of Old English poetry.

The first nineteenth-century poets to be attracted to Anglo-Saxon England were interested in the originary historical significance of the period rather than in its literature as such. At the very beginning of the century we get patriotic epic poems on King Alfred from Joseph Cottle (1800) and Henry James Pye (1801), both of which received favourable reviews at the time (Pratt 2000), though they subsequently sank without much trace. Then in 1822 William Wordsworth published his *Ecclesiastical Sketches*, later re-titled *Ecclesiastical Sonnets* (ed. Hayden, II, 447–503), a long sequence of sonnets tracing the glorious course of the history of the church in England from the beginnings down to modern times and celebrating its places and practices.

In the *Ecclesiastical Sonnets* we see Wordsworth the conservative, embracing the Anglican tradition and its role in English life. As Bernard Groom writes, 'The origin of the *Sonnets* lies in Wordsworth's lifelong sense of what the "spires", the "steeple-towers", and the "chapels lurking among trees", meant to the rural life of England, and thence to the whole body politic' (Groom 1966, p. 160). Wordsworth views Saxon England as foundational in England's ecclesiastical history and, guided by Turner and by his own reading of Bede, he identifies key moments and individuals of the era. By the late-Saxon period, insists Words-worth (adopting a familiar reading of history), decline has set in, so that

> The woman-hearted Confessor prepares
> The evanescence of the Saxon line.   (XXXI, lines 1–2)

In the *Ecclesiastical Sonnets* Wordsworth extols the 'primitive Saxon clergy', praises the scholarly life of Bede and particularly lionizes King Alfred. He pauses at famous episodes in Bede's *History*, notably the story of Gregory and the slave-boys –

> A bright-haired company of youthful slaves,
> Beautiful strangers, stand within the pale
> Of a sad market, ranged for public sale,
> Where Tiber's stream the immortal city laves   (XIII, lines 1–4)

– and the simile of man's life as the flight of a sparrow through a hall (though in Wordsworth it is, clumsily, the sparrow that man's life is like: 'Man's life is like a sparrow, mighty King!', XVI, line 1). A little later Longfellow translated the same passage from Bede into prose, commenting approvingly on the counsellor's speech: 'This brave man spake well; and how like an American Indian' (Longfellow 1838, p. 98).

Wordsworth is hardly at his best in the *Ecclesiastical Sonnets* but, following Turner, he was bringing knowledge of Anglo-Saxon England and its church to a wider audience at what was an important time for the development of modern understandings of history and identity. As Groom points out, 'In bringing church history into the sphere of general literature he was a pioneer, especially in respect of the earlier stages of the subject' (Groom 1966, p. 160).

Not long afterwards, the sound and language of Old English verse, though appreciated at a fairly rudimentary level, began to capture the attention of nineteenth-century poets as Old English poetry started to appear in print and to be treated in scholarly discussion. The poetry was thought to be crude but it fired the romantic imagination. The American literary giant Henry Wads-worth Longfellow could write as early as 1838 of the 'great energy and vivacity' of Anglo-Saxon poetry (Longfellow 1838, p. 100). The lines of verse,

which are 'short, emphatic', 'ring like blows of hammers on an anvil', exclaims
Longfellow (p. 100). In his 1838 overview of the language, customs and
literature of 'our Saxon forefathers in England' (p. 93), Longfellow includes
for his American readers a translation of lines 189–257 of *Beowulf* (fitt 3,
describing Beowulf's voyage to and arrival in Denmark) (Longfellow 1838,
pp. 104–6; 1910, pp. 739–40), enthusing, 'We can almost smell the brine, and
hear the sea-breeze blow, and see the mainland stretch out its jutting prom-
ontories, those sea-noses (*sæ-næssas*), as the poet calls them, into the blue
waters of the solemn main' (p. 104). Longfellow declares at the end of his
translation, 'We fear, that many of our readers will see very little poetry in all
this', but he appeals to the verdict of J. M. Kemble, whose 'very beautiful'
edition of *Beowulf* had recently come out: Longfellow quotes Kemble
exhorting the reader of *Beowulf* 'to judge this poem, not by the measure of
our times and creeds, but those of the times which it describes; as a rude, but
very faithful picture of an age, wanting indeed in scientific knowledge, in
mechanical expertness, even in refinement; but brave, generous, and right-
principled' (Longfellow 1838, p. 106, quoting Kemble 1833, pp. xxxi–xxxii).

Longfellow strove to popularize Anglo-Saxon England, home of 'our forefathers', in America. He romanticized the Anglo-Saxons – 'brave, rejoicing in
sea-storms, and beautiful in person, with blue eyes and long, flowing hair'
(1838, p. 95) – and their era, a time when mankind went 'reeling through the
Dark Ages; quarrelling, drinking, hunting, hawking, singing psalms, rocked in
cradles, buried in coffins, – weak, suffering, sublime' (1838, pp. 98–9). And he
worked hard to bring Anglo-Saxon poetry to new readers, producing verse
translations not only of the passage from *Beowulf* mentioned above but also
of *The Battle of Brunanburh*, *Maxims II*, *Cædmon's Hymn*, part of *Exodus* and
snippets from other poems (as well as prose). He was particularly attracted to
The Battle of Brunanburh – 'the whole ode is striking, bold, graphic' (1838,
p. 116). His clunky and abrupt version of *Brunanburh* (the lines might be said
to 'ring like blows of hammers on an anvil'), which follows as closely as
possible the half-lines of the original, begins,

> Æthelstan the king,
> lord of earls,
> bracelet-giver of barons,
> and his brother eke,
> Eadmund the prince,
> very illustrious chieftain,
> combated in battle,
> with edges of swords,
> near Brunanburh.   (Longfellow 1838, p. 116)

This is hardly impressive verse but conveys something of the alterity of Old English poetry, as well as mostly getting the sense right: here only 'very illustrious chieftain' for *ealdorlangne tir*, 'life-long glory', is wide of the mark in its meaning.

Longfellow also published a translation of the very late Old English (or early Middle English) poem which I referred to at the beginning of this chapter, *The Grave*, in a version which is not without bathos but which strives to capture the salutary tone of the original. The opening lines read,

> For thee was a house built
> Ere thou wert born,
> For thee was a mould meant,
> Ere thou of mother camest.   (Longfellow 1838, p. 124; 1910, p. 40)

The most celebrated British poet of his period, Alfred Lord Tennyson, also produced a translation of *The Battle of Brunanburh* (ed. Ricks 1987, III, 18–23; also printed in Irving 2000, pp. 189–93). As Edward Irving comments, with the publication of this translation by the famous poet laureate in 1880, 'familiarity on the part of general readers with Old English poetry must have expanded suddenly by a quantum leap' (Irving 2000, p. 174). The translation brought Old English poetry to a wider audience than it had ever had before; we might compare its impact with that of Nobel laureate Seamus Heaney's *Beowulf* in 1999 and 2000 when it topped best-seller lists on both sides of the Atlantic Ocean. And Tennyson's translation was in verse of a kind that Victorians would not have encountered before:

> Athelstan King,
> Lord among Earls,
> Bracelet-bestower and
> Baron of Barons,
> He with his brother,
> Edmund Atheling,
> Gaining a lifelong
> Glory in battle.   (lines 1–8)

Tennyson had sketched a translation of ten half-lines from *Beowulf* as early as 1830–1 (they survive in one of his notebooks now at Harvard University: see Ricks 1987, III, 18; Magennis 2011, pp. 62–3); he would have read selections from *Beowulf* and other poems in Conybeare's *Illustrations of Anglo-Saxon Poetry*. The 'Battle of Brunanburh' dates from late in his career, from the time he was also working on his play *Harold*, on the Norman Conquest of Anglo-Saxon England. Written, as suggested by Michael Alexander, as 'a patriotic celebration of Brunanburh as a crucial English triumph' and because he was attracted to *The Battle of Brunanburh* as a 'war-song' (Alexander 1985, p. 151), Tennyson's 'Battle of Brunanburh' is based on a prose translation of the Old English poem published a few years earlier by his son Hallam but also on his study of *Brunanburh* itself. The translation was well received at the time and has been much praised since: it is 'probably the best verse-translation of any Anglo-Saxon poetry', in the view of Christopher Ricks (1972, p. 292). Criticism has been made of its quaint archaic vocabulary and of the 'monotonous hammering effect' of its rhythm (Irving 2000, p. 186) – 'blows of hammers on an anvil' again – but the translation engages creatively with the original. It changes that original, which is a carefully wrought celebration of victory rather than a 'war-song', but the result is arresting and compelling:

> Bowed the spoiler,
> Bent the Scotsman,
> Fell the shipcrews
> Doomed to the death.
> All the field with blood of the fighters
> Flowed, from when the first great
> Sun-star of morningtide,
> Lamp of the Lord God
> Lord everlasting,
> Glode over earth till the glorious creature
> Sank to his setting.   (lines 20–30)

Also arresting and compelling is William Morris's 1895 translation of *Beowulf*, only more so. Having collaborated with the scholar A. J. Wyatt, Morris produced an experimental, deliberately alienating kind of verse in order to suggest the medieval alterity of the Old English poem. The result is a work that many have found unreadable, especially since it is so large in scale, but it certainly gets away from the insipidness that had characterized previous verse translations of *Beowulf*. It is syntactically cumbersome, rhythmically abrupt and extremely mannered and archaic in expression, as illustrated in its opening lines:

> WHAT! We of the Spear-Danes of yore days, so was it
> That we learn'd of the fair fame of kings of the folks
> And the Athelings a-faring in framing of valour.

But Morris was attempting to reflect perceived qualities of the original poem. As Roy Liuzza puts it, Morris was seeking 'to respect and recreate the strangeness of the reading encounter with an ancient poem' (Liuzza 2002, p. 293; see further, Magennis 2011, pp. 57–62).

With Tennyson and Morris, Old English poetry is taken seriously as poetry worth recreating in a new idiom, and as capable of inspiring new kinds of stress-based (as opposed to syllabic) modern poetry. Gerard Manley Hopkins was also affected by Old English poetry, declaring that something like his 'sprung rhythm' 'existed in full force in Anglo-Saxon verse and in great beauty' (quoted in Gardner 1958, II, 158). And, of course, Ezra Pound was significantly influenced by Old English poetry, most obviously in his translation of *The Seafarer* and his epic poem *The Cantos* but, as Chris Jones points out, 'his whole career is a feeling back along ancient lines of advance', necessitating 'the reanimation of the earliest form of English' (Jones 2006, p. 67); Pound's 'The Seafarer' (Pound 1948 [originally published 1909], pp. 18–21), though it has received harsh criticism from some Anglo-Saxonists, is a powerful piece of writing, disorientating and exciting and – unlike *The Seafarer* itself – resolutely pagan:

> May I, for my own self, song's truth reckon,
> Journey's jargon, how I in harsh days
> Hardship endured oft.
> Bitter breast-cares have I abided,
> Known on my keel many a care's hold,
> And dire sea-surge, and there I oft spent
> Narrow night-watch nigh the ship's head
> While she tossed close to cliffs.

A slightly younger contemporary of Pound's who merits special consideration in this survey of creative writers in view of the depth of his knowledge of and attachment to the Anglo-Saxon world and its literature is J. R. R. Tolkien. Tolkien's fiction is not to everyone's taste and he has been treated with considerable disdain by influential voices in the literary establishment. He is a writer who deals with such serious and profound themes, however, and whose works in the major genre of fantasy fiction – which burgeoned spectacularly under his influence – are of such abiding popularity that Tom Shippey can present him not only as *a* writer of the twentieth century but, provocatively, as *the* writer of the twentieth century (Shippey 2000). Steeped in the literature of early England and Scandinavia and exploiting his formidable mastery of philology for creative purposes (Shippey 1979, 2005), Tolkien produced in *The Lord of the Rings* a classic of imaginative writing. Shippey demonstrates in particular the influence of *Beowulf* on it and shows how the poem is drawn upon in the presentation of the 'Riders of the Mark', for example, who are themselves an 'image of Englishness' (2000, p. 91). Englishness presents for Tolkien a precious heritage in the aftermath of destructive world wars. As Charles Moseley writes, in his major fictions Tolkien fashioned a myth to which his experience committed him at a deeply emotional level, 'a myth which expressed some of his fears about the world he experienced and the England he loved, and one which many accepted as a map of their own fears' (Moseley 1997, p. xv).

The Lord of the Rings incorporates much use of the Old English language and it contains passages written in a form of the traditional Old English poetic metre, deployed with considerable skill. Less well known but worthy of note is Tolkien's separate poem inspired by *The Battle of Maldon*, 'The Homecoming of Beorhtnoth Beorhthelm's Son' (Tolkien 1953). This poem was written as a radio play around 1945 and takes the form of a drama with two main speakers, servants of the slain Beorhtnoth (Byrhtnoth) who, after the battle of Maldon, go to the battlefield in the darkness to recover their lord's body. One of them is Torhthelm, a youth, 'his head full of old lays concerning the heroes of northern antiquity', as Tolkien puts it in his introduction (p. 2); the other, Tidwald, is 'an old *ceorl* ['churl', i.e. peasant freeman], a farmer who had seen much fighting in the English defence-levies' (p. 2). As Tolkien notes (p. 3), the poem is composed in a metre 'little if at all freer (though used for dialogue) than the verse of *The Battle of Maldon*'. Tolkien uses the metre to express a range of moods from aggressive to tender, achieving considerable eloquence in what might appear to be too unwieldy a medium. The young Torhthelm makes a moving speech when the body of Beorhtnoth is finally found:

> His head was higher than the helm of kings
> with heathen crowns, his heart keener
> and his soul clearer than swords of heroes
> polished and proven; than plated gold
> his worth was greater. From the world he passed
> a prince peerless in peace and war,
> just in judgement, generous-handed
> as the golden lords of long ago.
> He has gone to God glory seeking,
> Beorhtnoth beloved.   (p. 6)

The passage has a calm dignity and is richly resonant for readers of *Beowulf*, *The Battle of Maldon* and other Old English poems.

At the very end of the piece a third voice is heard singing out in the dark, using not alliteration but rhyme (p. 13):

> Sadly they sing, the monks of Ely isle!
> Row men, row! Let us listen here a while.

The words (echoing a fragment of Middle English verse from Ely) introduce a different register. Tolkien describes them as 'presaging the fading end of the old heroic alliterative measure' (p. 3). 'The Homecoming' is itself an elegy to the heroic world, as perhaps Tolkien's work more generally may be seen to be.

The Anglo-Saxon world and its literature have continued to influence literary figures of major significance. Adopting a phrase from the *Mercian Hymns* of English poet Geoffrey Hill (G. Hill 1985, p. 133), Chris Jones discusses the 'strange likeness' between important strands of modern poetry in English and the verse of the Anglo-Saxons, tracing the continuing and developing use of Old English by distinguished poets of the twentieth century, specifically Pound, W. H. Auden, Edwin Morgan and Seamus Heaney (on Heaney, see also McCarthy 2008, Magennis 2011, pp. 161–84).

Other twentieth-century poets were also drawn in various ways to Anglo-Saxon England and its literature, including Basil Bunting, Louis MacNeice, Richard Wilbur, Denise Levertov and Geoffrey Hill (see Clark and Perkins, eds., 2010). Bunting and Hill link the Anglo-Saxon past and the present, while in his poem *Beowulf* Wilbur looks at Beowulf from a twentieth-century perspective (Wilbur 1988, p. 484). Levertov revisits the miracle of Cædmon and his apparition (as does Heaney in his poem 'Whitby-sur-Moyola', as mentioned below). In *Dark Age Glosses*, as Edna Longley notes, MacNeice 'conjures up the so-called "dark ages" of England, Iceland and Ireland in order to expose what is in fact dark to modern man' (Longley 1988, p. 124). MacNeice considers Bede's sparrow flying through the hall again, finding a new comfortless meaning in its flight:

> This indoors flying makes it seem absurd,
> Although it itches and nags and yearns,
> To postulate any other life than now.   (ed. Dodds 1966, p. 484)

An important figure whose evidently profound relationship to Anglo-Saxon literature would merit detailed exploration is Jorge Luis Borges. In his poem 'To a Saxon Poet', for example (as translated by Alastair Reid), Borges pictures an Old English poet, 'my ghostly companion', and imagines him at work. Elaborating the Anglo-Saxon theme of mutability, Borges contemplates the great chasm 'between your time and mine':

> Where can your features and your name be found?
> These things are buried in oblivion.
> Now I shall never know how it must have been
> for you, as a living man who walked his ground.
>
> (ed. di Giovanni 1972, pp. 238–9)

In the work of Borges and of other modern writers there is a detachment from, as well as fascination with, the Anglo-Saxon world absent in earlier appropriations, which were keen to identify with that world in some way. Earlier paradigms are superseded, above all perhaps in the poetry of Heaney, an Irish poet who has interacted with Anglo-Saxon England and its poetry throughout his career. In his poem 'Whitby-sur-Moyola' Heaney even relocates Bede's Cædmon to Ireland, an imaginative move towards which he is likely to have been encouraged by the fact that Cædmon – Bede's originary English poet – has a Celtic, not an Anglo-Saxon name (see Jones 2006, pp. 182–6). Much interesting work is being done today by Jones and others on the place of Anglo-Saxon England and its literature in modern writing. Here I have been able only to scratch the surface of what is a topic of lively current interest among critics. Meanwhile modern poets today continue to seek new ways to translate and rework the poetry of the Anglo-Saxon past, as the forthcoming anthology edited by Delanty and Matto, and indeed our postscript, below, eloquently illustrate.

Anglo-Saxon literature continues to fascinate modern creative writers, and modern readers more generally. Anglo-Saxon studies do not have the privileged place in academia today that they had a hundred years ago, and indeed their survival is under threat in some places in a context of rethinking and revision going on in English studies, though they continue to flourish widely in great seats of learning and also in new institutional contexts. In a sense they have made the interesting shift from mainstream to alternative, and taken on new life in the process. Today popular and scholarly interest in Anglo-Saxon literature is greater than ever and understanding of it is on a sounder basis than formerly, though we are still learning. The area of literary Anglo-Saxon studies is a vigorous and intellectually exciting one, as I hope this book has suggested, and one that has become both more interdisciplinary in terms of attention to the Latin dimension of Anglo-Saxon culture and to political and social history and also more keyed in to wider issues in current literary and cultural theory than was the case in the past. The subject continues to attract bright and imaginative students at all levels, who contribute to its reinvention. The writings of our 'ghostly companions' of the past can speak powerfully to today's readers and can be given new form in exciting translation.

Postscript: *Riddle 60* and *The Husband's Message* translated by Ciaran Carson

[This sequence from the Exeter Book is usually taken as two poems, a riddle (the first seventeen lines) and an 'elegy', and the solution to the riddle is generally given as 'reed/reed-pipe/reed-pen'. As with all surviving Old English verse, the titles are supplied by modern editors. Some critics would argue that the sequence may be read appropriately as a single poem. The sequences of dots in the translation reflect the fact that the original manuscript has suffered damage to the relevant pages and the text is not recoverable in places. (H. M.)]

I was by the sand, near the sea-wall
at the waters' edge; steadfast I dwelt
where I first stood. Precious few
in this wide world came to that place
to behold my lonely station. Only the dark waves
threw their arms around me, morning twilight
after twilight. Little did I think
that mouthless I would ever speak
across the mead-bench, giving word for word.
A wondrous thing to baffle those who do not know,
how blade-point and right hand
brought a lord's deep thought to this point,
and cut me to this purpose: that I
should share with none but us two
this bold message, that the many might not
broadcast to the wider world
the words that were between us two alone.

Now will I impart to you apart
..... from tree-stock was I reared.
In me ..... of men ..... must in the land of elsewhere
set ....
salt streams..................
In the hold of boat after boat ... sought
where my liege-lord ....
over the high seas. I have come here now
in a keeled craft; now you must weigh
what you feel for my lord, what words you have for him
who minds his love for you. I undertake that you
will understand from this how true he is to you.
     Listen then: he that engraved this stave
bade me tell you, O bejewelled one, to look into
the casket of your mind and be reminded of
the bond of words you made between you both
before, when in the merry strongholds as a twosome
you bespoke your home in one land, there to live
your love as one. But feud drove him

from that proud people. Gladly he commanded me
to urge your keel to cleave the sea
when on the sheer cliff edge you hear
the lonesome cuckoo sounding through the wood.
Let no man sway your course or stay your sail.
    Look to the waves, the abode of the seagull.
Go on board a ship, so that south from here
a sea-lane will steer you to the man,
that overlord who has been thinking long of you.
Nor could he wish for anything in this wide world,
in his own mind – these are his words –
than that Almighty God grant you both a future
where you hand out wealth and studded armlets
to the company at large. He has this much
burnished gold . . . .
. . . . he rules the homeland of a foreign tribe,
a fair land . . . .
. . . . . . loyal warriors, although here my lord
. . . .
driven by his need, pushed out his boat
upon the wide expanse of waterway to undertake
the eager journey all alone. No worries now
for that man; he wants for nothing,
neither horses nor store nor the joy of strong drink,
all the lordly treasure in the world,
O daughter of a prince, so long as he had you.
    As for that long-sworn vow between you two,
I hear the runes of S for sun conjoined with R for road,
and E for earth and B for bliss and M for man
declare this solemn oath together,
that while life is in his body he will hold dear
those bonds of true fidelity the two of you
in former days delighted to repeat.

Appendix: resources for studying Anglo-Saxon literature

The most important resources for studying Anglo-Saxon literature are the texts themselves, which are widely available in print both in good editions in the original languages and in translations stretching from the serviceable to the inspiring. Beginning students wishing to experience selections of key Old English texts in the original have a number of 'readers' at their disposal, of which the one I have referred to particularly in this book has been that of Marsden (2004). Other useful Old English readers include those by Mitchell and Robinson (2006) and Baker (2007), both of which also provide authoritative introductions to the Old English language; Baker's volume is also linked to the author's Old English website, which features additional readings and exercises, http://faculty.virginia.edu/OldEnglish/.

Today editions and translations are increasingly becoming available in electronic form – online and on disk. The online ones are of variable quality and include, as well as new editions, scans of out-of-copyright publications (available, for example, as Google books). They also include the superb *Dictionary of Old English Corpus*, an electronic resource, developed as part of the work of the ongoing *Dictionary of Old English* project, that gives searchable access to the complete range of surviving Old English writings. The *Corpus*, invaluable to scholars, is available in web and CD-ROM versions (ed. Healey 2000, 2004).

Among electronic editions are 'hypertext' productions, which offer exciting new ways of presenting and studying manuscript works (see Foys 2007, Lee and O'Donnell 2009). The first hypertext CD-ROM edition of an Old English text was Kevin Kiernan's *Electronic Beowulf* (1999, 2011), a groundbreaking production that includes high-resolution digital images of the manuscript, a translation, and a range of other supplementary material. Kiernan's *Beowulf* has been followed by two other large-scale digital editions on disk by Bernard Muir, *MS. Junius 11* and *The Exeter DVD*, and a number of current projects involve this kind of electronic publication; major libraries are also in the process of digitizing their manuscript holdings.

The standard collected edition of the vast majority of surviving Old English poems is the six-volume *Anglo-Saxon Poetic Records* (ASPR) (ed. Krapp and Dobbie 1931–53), which is now quite long in the tooth, however, and, like most editions of Old English poems, does not supply a Modern English translation. There are reliable separate editions of the poems individually or in small groups, of which particularly notable are the recent revised edition of Klaeber's *Beowulf* (Klaeber 2008), replacing the 1936/1950 version by Klaeber that had served generations of students of the poem; the series Exeter Medieval Texts (which also includes prose), whose editions include updated versions of previous publications (for example, Woolf 1977, Gordon 1996), as well as brand-new ones (such as Griffith 1997, Upchurch 2007); and accessible scholarly editions of groups of poems, such as Tom Shippey's edition (with translation) of *Poems of Wisdom and Learning* (1976) and Anne Klinck's of the Exeter Book elegies (1992). All the ASPR poems are available in an e-edition accessible in the Old English section of the Georgetown University website *The Labyrinth*, http://labyrinth.georgetown. edu/. *The Labyrinth*, the richest online resource for studying the medieval world, also contains editions and some translations of a range of other Old English texts. Readers will be aware that not all online material is academically respectable. *The Labyrinth* can be recommended, as can other websites associated with leading universities. A number of links to reliable sites can be found conveniently on the web pages of TOEBI (Teachers of Old English in Britain and Ireland), http://www.toebi.org.uk; see too Carl Berkhout's site at http://www.u.arizona.edu/~ctb/.

As with Old English poetry, most works in Old English prose and in Latin are easily available in editions in the original languages, though many such editions are quite old by now. And, again as with Old English poetry, many editions do not contain translations. In the case of Latin, in the nineteenth century and the early twentieth it was assumed that educated readers did not need translations from Latin, while early editions of Old English texts did tend to supply parallel translation. Nowadays the situation is largely reversed, with editions of Anglo-Latin texts very often coming with a translation but many editions of Old English prose, such as the important ones in the EETS series, not supplying translations. Thus in his 1844–6 edition of Ælfric's *Catholic Homilies* Benjamin Thorpe translates all the Old English material but leaves the Latin untranslated; in Jonathan Wilcox's 1994 edition of Ælfric's *Prefaces*, on the other hand, the Latin prefaces are translated but not the Old English ones. Collections of translations, such as those by Crossley-Holland (1984), Keynes and Lapidge (1983) and Swanton (1993), are invaluable here, as are old editions. For example, in the present book

I have quoted from Thorpe's translation of Ælfric's *Catholic Homilies*, now otherwise superseded by the EETS edition of Clemoes (1997) and Godden (1979, 2000). There are still important Old English prose and Anglo-Latin texts for which satisfactory translations are not available – one thinks of works of Alcuin, for example, a number of Alfredian translations, and homilies by Ælfric and Wulfstan as conspicuous cases in point – but much work has been done on translation particularly in recent decades, so that most of the texts discussed in this book can be accessed in Modern English versions, including key works of Bede (see, for example, Farmer 1983, Wallis 1999; Lifshitz 2001), the prose and verse writings of Aldhelm (Lapidge and Herren 1979; Lapidge and Rosier 1985), and a range of Latin saints' lives (for example, Talbot 1954; Colgrave 1956; Lapidge and Winterbottom 1991 [the latter two also having the Latin originals]). One of the most useful collections of translated material based on Anglo-Saxon originals is Dorothy Whitelock's substantial *Anglo-Saxon Documents* (1979), an essential source for historians but also a treasury of material of literary relevance.

The most used collected translation of Old English poetry is probably S. A. J. Bradley's thoughtfully rendered *Anglo-Saxon Poetry* (1982), which is comprehensive in its coverage and accurate in translation but, being in prose, does little to bring the verse to life. Some Old English poetry has been turned enablingly into modern verse by gifted poets, though the vast majority of translations of the poetry are in prose. *Beowulf* has inspired a stream of verse translations but other poems have not fared so well. Many of the *Beowulf* translations are excellent, as for example the contrasting versions by Michael Alexander (1973, 2001), Kevin Crossley-Holland (in Crossley-Holland, trans., 1984) and Seamus Heaney (1999), to name just three. Some verse translations of *Beowulf* come with a range of useful supplementary material, as is the case with Roy Liuzza's version (2000), which also reads very well as a translation. For poems other than *Beowulf* the best represented in verse translation are the elegies, the riddles and *The Dream of the Rood*. The most wide-ranging collections of translations into verse in use today are probably still those by Richard Hamer (1971) and Kevin Crossley-Holland, the latter of which includes prose as well. A welcome forthcoming publication is the anthology of translations by an impressive group of contemporary poets, edited by Matto and Delanty.

In the course of this book I have referred to many important secondary sources – works of criticism and scholarship – all of which are listed in the bibliography. These are writings that have informed my own discussion of Anglo-Saxon literature and they can usefully be explored further by interested readers. There is a host of definitive criticism and scholarship that

I have not had occasion to cite, of course. I can't cover every indispensable publication in these few closing paragraphs either, but it may be relevant to point the beginning reader towards a few accessible high-quality accounts of Anglo-Saxon literature and its background (in book form as opposed to individual articles).

An excellent starting point would be two of the 'companion' volumes that are widely in use today, *The Cambridge Companion to Old English Literature*, edited by Godden and Lapidge (1991), and *A Companion to Anglo-Saxon Literature*, edited by Pulsiano and Treharne (2001), both of which provide a wealth of (different) information and insight. Another companion-type volume that can be strongly recommended is *Reading Old English Texts*, edited by O'Brien O'Keeffe (1997), which presents a number of theoretical approaches to the literature. As suggested above, many websites have to be approached with caution; one that provides authoritative articles on Anglo-Saxon writers and works, as well as on literary topics generally, is *The Literary Encyclopedia* (ed. Clark, http:www.litencyc.com).

There are many collections of essays in print containing seminal studies, of which a particularly rich recent example is that edited by Liuzza (2002). Well-written histories of Old English literature have recently been produced by Michael Alexander (2002, revising an existing publication) and by R. D. Fulk and Christopher Cain (2003), superseding that of Greenfield and Calder (1986) – which is still worth consulting, however. Surveys of the literature have gone out of fashion somewhat but one penetrating critical appraisal of the poetry is that of Michael Swanton (2002). Instead of presenting general surveys today's books by Anglo-Saxonists tend (among other things) to focus in detail on particular texts and groups of texts, to study themes and topics of special current interest and to apply specific theoretical approaches. I have drawn upon important strands of such work in this book but have not been able to take account of all the new avenues currently being explored, nor indeed of all the brilliant 'traditional' scholarly work that is being produced. And of course an even better place than secondary literature to start at is with the texts themselves, in a reader such as that by Marsden or an accessible edition, or in translation – Heaney's or Alexander's *Beowulf*, say, or a collection of translations such as those by Keynes and Lapidge (1983) or Crossley-Holland (1984), to name but two. The translation of Bede's *Ecclesiastical History* by Colgrave and Mynors is available not only in their parallel-text edition of 1969 but also in a 'World's Classics' volume edited by McClure and Collins (1994), which also contains the 'Greater Chronicle' from *The Reckoning of Time*; and there is also a convenient Penguin translation of the *Ecclesiastical History* by Sherley-Price (1990).

I hope that my bibliography will prove to be a useful starting point for further study along these and other lines. Readers will also wish to make use of other bibliographical resources, however, and happily such resources are at hand. For writings on Old English literature up to 1972, the Greenfield and Robinson *Bibliography of Publications on Old English Literature* (1980) gives comprehensive coverage. Building on the Greenfield and Robinson *Bibliography*, the journal *Old English Newsletter* has been bringing out annual bibliographies on Old English studies since 1972, and these are available online as a single searchable database at http://www.oenewsletter.org/; *Old English Newsletter* also publishes annually a critical survey of publications, giving reviews of the books, articles, etc. on Old English studies that had been listed in the previous year's bibliography. And the other key bibliography produced every year is that published in the annual journal *Anglo-Saxon England*. The *Anglo-Saxon England* annual bibliography covers not only Old English literature and language but also Anglo-Latin writings, history, archaeology and other strands of Anglo-Saxon studies.

Bibliography

Primary: Editions, Translations, Facsimiles, Modern Appropriations

Alexander, Michael, trans., 1966. *The Earliest English Poems* (Harmondsworth: Penguin); revised and expanded as *The First Poems in English* (London: Penguin, 2008)

trans., 1973. *Beowulf: A Verse Translation* (Harmondsworth: Penguin; revised edn, 2001)

Allen, Michael J. B. and Daniel G. Calder, trans., 1976. *Sources and Analogues of Old English Poetry: The Major Latin Texts in Translation* (Cambridge: D. S. Brewer; Totowa, NJ: Rowman and Littlefield)

Assmann, Bruno, ed., 1889. *Angelsächsische Homilien und Heiligenleben*, Bibliothek der angelsächsischen Prosa 3 (Kassel: H. Wigand); reprinted with supplementary introduction by P. Clemoes (Darmstadt: Wissenschaftliche Buchsellgeschaft, 1964)

Baker, Peter S., 2007. *An Introduction to Old English*, 2nd edn (Oxford: Blackwell)

Barney, Stephen A., W. J. Lewis, J. A. Beach and Oliver Berghof, trans., 2006. *The Etymologies of Isidore of Seville* (Cambridge: Cambridge University Press)

Bately, Janet M., eds., 1980. *The Old English Orosius*. EETS, SS 6 (Oxford: Oxford University Press)

Bettenson, Henry, trans., 1972. *Augustine: Concerning the City of God against the Pagans* (Harmondsworth: Penguin)

Black, Joseph, *et al.*, eds., 2009. *The Broadview Anthology of British Literature*, I, *The Medieval Period*, 2nd edn (Peterborough, Ontario: Broadview Press)

Bradley, S. A. J., trans., 1982. *Anglo-Saxon Poetry* (London: Dent)

Bullough, Donald A., 1993. 'What has Ingeld to do with Lindisfarne?', *Anglo-Saxon England* 22, 93–125 [contains translation of Alcuin's 'Letter to Speratus']

Campbell, A., ed. and trans., 1962. *Chronicon Æthelweardi: The Chronicle of Æthelweard* (London: Nelson)

Clemoes, Peter, ed., 1997. *Ælfric's Catholic Homilies, The First Series: Text*, EETS, SS 17 (Oxford: Oxford University Press)

Colgrave, Bertram, ed. and trans., 1956. *Felix's Life of St Guthlac* (Cambridge: Cambridge University Press)

Colgrave, Bertram and R. A. B. Mynors, eds. and trans., 1969. *Bede's Ecclesiastical History of the English People* (Oxford: Clarendon Press)

Conybeare, John Josias, 1826. *Illustrations of Anglo-Saxon Poetry*, ed. William Daniel Conybeare (London: Harding and Lepard)

Crossley-Holland, Kevin, trans., 1979. *The Exeter Book Riddles* (Harmondsworth: Penguin)

trans., 1984. *The Anglo-Saxon World: An Anthology* (Oxford: Oxford University Press)

Delanty, Greg and Michael Matto, eds., forthcoming. *The Word Exchange: Contemporary Poets Translate Old English Poetry* (New York: W. W. Norton)

di Giovanni, Norman Thomas, ed., 1972. *Jorge Luis Borges: Selected Poems 1923–1967* (London: Allen Lane)

Dodds, E. R., ed., 1966. *Louis MacNeice: Collected Poems* (London: Faber)

Elstob, Elizabeth, ed. and trans., 1709. *An English-Saxon Homily on the Birth-Day of St. Gregory: Anciently Used in the English-Saxon Church. Giving an Account of the Conversion of the English from Paganism to Christianity* (London: W. Bowyer)

Farmer, D. H., trans., 1983. 'Bede: *Lives of the Abbots of Wearmouth and Jarrow*', in *The Age of Bede*, trans. J. F. Webb, revised edn, ed. D. H. Farmer (Harmondsworth: Penguin)

Glosecki, Stephen O., trans., 2009. 'Old English Metrical Charms', in *The Broadview Anthology of British Literature*, I, *The Medieval Period*, ed. Black *et al.*, pp. 41–3

Godden, Malcolm, ed., 1979. *Ælfric's Catholic Homilies, The Second Series: Text*, EETS, SS 5 (Oxford: Oxford University Press)

2000. *Ælfric's Catholic Homilies: Introduction, Commentary and Glossary*, EETS, SS 18 (Oxford: Oxford University Press)

Gordon, Ida, ed., 1996. *The Seafarer*, revised edn, with a Bibliography compiled by Mary Clayton (Exeter: University of Exeter Press; original edn, London: Methuen, 1960)

Griffith, Mark, ed., 1997. *Judith* (Exeter: University of Exeter Press)

Hamer, Richard, ed. and trans., 1970. *A Choice of Anglo-Saxon Verse* (London: Faber)

Hayden, John O., ed., 1977. *William Wordsworth: Poems*, 2 vols. (Harmondsworth: Penguin)

Healey, Antonette di Paolo, ed., 2000. *Dictionary of Old English: Old English Corpus*, website (Ann Arbor, MI: University of Michigan Humanities Text Initiative); *Dictionary of Old English Corpus in Electronic Form*, CD-ROM (Toronto: Pontifical Institute for Medieval Studies, 2004)

Heaney, Seamus, trans., 1999. *Beowulf* (London: Faber and Faber)

Herzfeld, George, ed. and trans., 1900. *An Old English Martyrology*, EETS, OS 116 (London: Kegan Paul, Trench and Trübner)

Hill, Geoffrey, 1985. *Collected Poems* (Harmondsworth: Penguin): *Mercian Hymns* (first published 1971), pp. 103–34

Hurst, D., ed., 1955. *Bedae venerabilis opera rhythmica*, Corpus Christianorum, Series Latina 122 (Turnhout: Brepols)

Kemble, John M., ed., 1833. *The Anglo-Saxon Poems of Beowulf, the Travellers Song, and the Battle of Finnesburh* (London: William Pickering); 2nd edn, vol. 1, 1835; vol. 2, *Beowulf: A Translation and Commentary*, 1837

Keynes, Simon and Michael Lapidge, trans., 1983. *Alfred the Great: Asser's Life of King Alfred and Other Contemporary Sources* (Harmondsworth: Penguin)

Kiernan, Kevin, ed., 2011. *Electronic Beowulf*, CD-ROM, revised edn (London: British Library; original edn, 1999)

Klaeber, Fr., ed., 2008. *Klaeber's Beowulf and The Fight at Finnsburg*, 4th edn, ed. R. D. Fulk, Robert E. Bjork and John D. Niles (Toronto, Buffalo, NY, and London: University of Toronto Press)

Klinck, Anne L., ed., 1992. *The Old English Elegies: A Critical Edition and Genre Study* (Montreal and Kingston: McGill–Queen's University Press)

Krapp, George Philip and Elliott Van Kirk Dobbie, eds., 1931–53. *The Anglo-Saxon Poetic Records*, 5 vols. I, *The Junius Manuscript*, ed. George Philip Krapp (London: Routledge; New York: Columbia University Press, 1931); II, *The Vercelli Book*, ed. George Philip Krapp (London: Routledge; New York: Columbia University Press, 1932); III, *The Exeter Book*, ed. George Philip Krapp and Elliott Van Kirk Dobbie (London: Routledge and Kegan Paul; New York: Columbia University Press, 1936); IV, *Beowulf and Judith*, ed. Elliott Van Kirk Dobbie (London: Routledge and Kegan Paul; New York: Columbia University Press, 1953); V, *The Paris Psalter and the Meters of Boethius*, ed. George Philip Krapp (London: Routledge and Kegan Paul; New York: Columbia University Press, 1932); VI, *The Anglo-Saxon Minor Poems*, ed. Elliott Van Kirk Dobbie (London: Routledge and Kegan Paul; New York: Columbia University Press, 1942)

Lapidge, Michael and Michael Herren, trans., 1979. *Aldhelm: The Prose Works* (Ipswich: D. S. Brewer; Totowa, NJ: Rowman and Littlefield)

Lapidge, Michael and James L. Rosier, trans., 1985. *Aldhelm: The Poetic Works* (Woodbridge and Dover, NH: D. S. Brewer)

Lapidge, Michael and Michael Winterbottom, eds. and trans., 1991. *Wulfstan of Winchester: The Life of St Æthelwold* (Oxford: Clarendon Press)

Lifshitz, Felice, trans., 2001. 'Bede, *Martyrology*', in *Medieval Hagiography: An Anthology*, ed. Thomas Head (New York and London: Routledge), pp. 169–97

Liuzza, R. M., trans., 2000. *Beowulf: A New Verse Translation* (Peterborough, Ontario: Broadview)

Longfellow, Henry Wadsworth, 1910. *The Poetical Works* (London: Oxford University Press)

McClure, Judith and Roger Collins, eds. and trans., 1994. *Bede: The Ecclesiastical History of the English People, The Greater Chronicle, Bede's Letter to Egbert* (Oxford: Oxford University Press); the translation of the *Ecclesiastical History* (pp. 1–298) is that of Colgrave and Mynors, previously published in Colgrave and Mynors, trans., 1969

Magennis, Hugh, ed. and trans., 2002. *The Old English Life of St Mary of Egypt* (Exeter: University of Exeter Press); translation from this also in *The Broadview Anthology of British Literature*, I, *The Medieval Period*, ed. Black *et al.*, pp. 135–48

trans., 2004. 'Ælfric of Eynsham's *Letter to Sigeweard*', in *Metaphrastes, or, Gained in Translation: Essays and Translations in Honour of Robert H. Jordan*, ed. Margaret Mullett (Belfast: Belfast Byzantine Texts and Translations), pp. 210–35

Marsden, Richard, 2004. *The Cambridge Old English Reader* (Cambridge: Cambridge University Press)

Mattingly, H., trans., rev. H. A. Handford, 1970. *Tacitus: The Agricola and The Germania* (Harmondsworth: Penguin)

Mitchell, Bruce and Fred C. Robinson, 2005. *A Guide to Old English*, 6th edn (Oxford: Blackwell)

Morris, Richard, ed. and trans., 1874–80. *The Blickling Homilies*, EETS, OS 58, 63, 73 (London: Oxford University Press; reprinted as one vol. 1967)

Morris, William and Alfred J. Wyatt, trans., 1895. *The Tale of Beowulf, Sometime King of the Weder Geats* (Hammersmith: Kelmscott)

Muinzer, Louis, trans., 1970. '[Ælfric's] *Preface to Genesis*', in *The Literature of Medieval England*, ed. D. W. Robertson (New York: McGraw–Hill), pp. 165–7

Muir, Bernard J., ed., 2000. *The Exeter Anthology of Old English Poetry: An Edition of Exeter Dean and Chapter MS 3501*, 2nd edn, 2 vols. (Exeter: University of Exeter Press)

ed., 2004. *MS. Junius 11*, CD-ROM, Bodleian Digital Texts 1 (Oxford: Bodleian Library)

ed., 2006. *The Exeter DVD: The Exeter Anthology of Old English Poetry* (Exeter: University of Exeter Press)

Mynors, R. A. B., completed by R. M. Thomson and M. Winterbottom, eds. and trans., 1998. *William of Malmesbury: Gesta regum Anglorum: The History of the English Kings*, vol. I (Oxford: Clarendon Press)

O'Donnell, Daniel Paul, ed., 2005. *Cædmon's Hymn: A Multi-media Study, Archive and Edition* (Cambridge: D. S. Brewer, in association with SENET and The Medieval Academy)

O'Neill, Patrick P., ed., 2001. *King Alfred's Old English Prose Translation of the First Fifty Psalms*, Medieval Academy Books 104 (Cambridge, MA: Medieval Academy of America)

Pound, Ezra, 1948. *Selected Poems* (London: Faber and Faber)

Ricks, Christopher, ed., 1987. *The Poems of Tennyson*, 2nd edn, 3 vols. (London: Longman; first edn 1969)

Scragg, D. G., ed., 1992. *The Vercelli Homilies and Related Texts*. EETS, OS 300 (Oxford: Oxford University Press)

Sherley-Price, Leo, trans., 1990. *Bede: Ecclesiastical History of the English People, with Bede's Letter to Egbert and Cuthbert's Letter on the Death of Bede*, revised edn, rev. R. E. Latham, ed. D. H. Farmer (London: Penguin)

Shippey, T. A., ed. and trans., 1976. *Poems of Wisdom and Learning in Old English* (Cambridge: D. S. Brewer; Totowa, NJ: Rowman and Littlefield)

Short, Douglas A., 1976. 'Aesthetics and Unpleasantness: Classical Rhetoric in the Medieval English Lyric *The Grave*', *Studia Neophilologica* 48, 291–9 [contains text of *The Grave*]

Simrock, Karl, trans., 1859. *Beowulf. Das älteste deutsche Epos* (Stuttgart and Augsburg: J. G. Cotta'scher Verlag)

Skeat, Walter W., ed. and trans., 1881–1900. *Ælfric's Lives of Saints*, EETS, OS 76, 82, 94 and 114 (London: Oxford University Press; reprinted as two vols., 1966)

Smyth, Alfred P., trans., 2002. *The Medieval Life of King Alfred the Great: A Translation and Commentary on the Text Attributed to Asser* (Basingstoke: Palgrave)

Swanton, Michael, trans., 1993. *Anglo-Saxon Prose*, revised edn (London: J. M. Dent)

trans., 2000. *The Anglo-Saxon Chronicles* (London: Phoenix Press)

Talbot, C. H., trans., 1954. *The Anglo-Saxon Missionaries in Germany, Being the Lives of SS. Willibrord, Boniface, Sturm, Leoba, and Lebuin, together with the Hodoeporicon of St. Willibald and a Selection from the Correspondence of St. Boniface* (London: Sheed and Ward)

Thorpe, Benjamin, ed. and trans., 1844–6. *The Homilies of the Anglo-Saxon Church: The First Part, Containing the Sermones Catholici or Homilies of Ælfric*, 2 vols. (London: Ælfric Society)

Tolkien, J. R. R., 1953. 'The Homecoming of Beorhtnoth Beorhthelm's Son', *Essays and Studies* 6, 1–18

Upchurch, Robert K., ed. and trans., 2007. *Ælfric's Lives of the Virgin Spouses* (Exeter: University of Exeter Press)

Wallis, Faith, trans., 1999. *Bede: The Reckoning of Time*, Translated Texts for Historians 29 (Liverpool: Liverpool University Press)

White, Carolinne, trans., 1998. *Early Christian Lives* (Harmondsworth: Penguin)

Whitelock, Dorothy, ed., 1979. *English Historical Documents c. 500–1042*, English Historical Documents I, 2nd edn (London: Eyre Methuen; New York: Oxford University Press)

Wilbur, Richard, 1988. *New and Collected Poems* (London and Boston: Faber and Faber)

Wilcox, Jonathan, ed., 1994. *Ælfric's Prefaces*, Durham Medieval Texts 9 (Durham: Durham Medieval Texts) [includes translations of Latin texts]

Williamson, Craig, ed., 1977. *The Old English Riddles of the Exeter Book* (Chapel Hill, NC: University of North Carolina Press)

Woolf, Rosemary, ed., 1977. *Cynewulf's Juliana*, revised edn (Exeter: University of Exeter Press; original edn, London: Methuen, 1955)

Zupitza, J., ed., 1880. *Ælfric's Grammatik und Glossar. Erste Abteilung: Text und Varianten* (Berlin: Weidmann 1880; 4th edn, with introduction by Helmut Gneuss, Hildesheim: Weidmann, 2003)

Secondary

Abels, Richard, 1998. *Alfred the Great: War, Kingship and Culture in Anglo-Saxon England* (Harlow: Longman)

Alexander, Michael, 1985. 'Tennyson's "Battle of Brunanburh"', *Tennyson Research Bulletin* 4.4, 151–61

    2003. *History of Old English Literature*, revised edn (Peterborough, Ontario: Broadview; original edn, London: Macmillan, 1983)

Andersson, Theodore M., 1997. 'Sources and Analogues', in *A Beowulf Handbook*, ed. Robert E. Bjork and John D. Niles (Lincoln, NE: University of Nebraska Press), pp. 125–48

Anlezark, Daniel, 2006. 'Reading "The Story of Joseph" in MS Cambridge, Corpus Christi College 201', in *The Power of Words*, ed. Magennis and Wilcox, pp. 61–94

Bately, Janet M., 1988. 'Old English Prose before and during the Reign of Alfred', *Anglo-Saxon England* 17, 93–138

Belanoff, Patricia A., 1993. 'Judith: Sacred and Secular Heroine', in *Heroic Poetry in the Anglo-Saxon Period*, ed. Damico and Leyerle, pp. 247–64

Benes, Tuska, 2008. *In Babel's Shadow: Language, Philology, and the Nation in Nineteenth-Century Germany* (Detroit, MI: Wayne State University Press)

Benson, Larry D., 1966. 'The Literary Character of Anglo-Saxon Formulaic Poetry', *PMLA* 81, 334–41

Berkhout, Carl T. and Milton McC. Gatch, eds., 1982. *Anglo-Saxon Scholarship: The First Three Centuries* (Boston, MA: G. K. Hall)

Bitterli, Dieter, 2009. *Say What I Am Called: The Old English Riddles of the Exeter Book and the Anglo-Latin Riddle Tradition* (Toronto, Buffalo, NY, and London: University of Toronto Press)

Blair, John, 2005. *The Church in Anglo-Saxon Society* (Oxford: Oxford University Press)

Boyer, Régis, 1981. 'An Attempt to Define the Typology of Medieval Hagiography', in *Hagiography and Medieval Literature: A Symposium*, Proceedings of the Fifth International Symposium Organized for the Study of Vernacular Literature in the Middle Ages, ed. Hans Bekker-Nielson, Peter Foote, Jørgen Højgaard Jørgensen and Tore Nyberg (Odense: Odense University Press), pp. 27–36

Bredehoft, Thomas A., 2004. 'Ælfric and Late Old English Verse', *Anglo-Saxon England* 33, 77–107

Briggs, Julia, 2000. 'New Times and Old Stories: Middleton's *Hengist*', in *Literary Appropriations of the Anglo-Saxons*, ed. Scragg and Weinberg, pp. 107–21

Brooke, Stopford A., 1892. *The History of Early English Literature, being the History of English Poetry from its Beginnings to the Accession of King Alfred*, 2 vols. (London and New York: Macmillan)

Brooks, Cleanth, 1947. *The Well Wrought Urn: Studies in the Structure of Poetry* (New York: Reynal and Hitchcock)

Brooks, Nicholas, 2006. 'From British to English Christianity: Deconstructing
    Bede's Interpretation of the Conversion', in *Conversion and Colonization
    in Anglo-Saxon England*, ed. Catherine E. Karkov and Nicholas Howe,
    Medieval and Renaissance Texts and Studies 318 (Tempe, AZ: Arizona
    Center for Medieval and Renaissance Studies), pp. 1–30
Brown, George Hardin, 2008. 'Ciceronianism in Bede and Alcuin', in *Intertexts:
    Studies in Anglo-Saxon Culture Presented to Paul E. Szarmach*, ed.
    Virginia Blanton and Helene Schecke, Medieval and Renaissance Texts
    and Studies 334 (Tempe, AZ: Arizona Center for Medieval and
    Renaissance Studies), pp. 319–29
    2009. *A Companion to Bede*, Anglo-Saxon Studies 12 (Woodbridge: Boydell Press)
Camargo, Martin, 1981. 'The Finn Episode and the Tragedy of Revenge in
    Beowulf', in *Eight Anglo-Saxon Studies*, ed. Joseph S. Wittig (Chapel Hill,
    NC: University of North Carolina Press), pp. 120–34
Carver, Martin, 2000. 'Burial as Poetry: The Context of Treasure in Anglo-Saxon
    Graves', in *Treasure in the Medieval West*, ed. Elizabeth M. Tyler (York:
    York Medieval Press), pp. 25–48
Cavill, Paul, 1999. *Maxims in Old English Poetry* (Cambridge: D. S. Brewer)
    2004. 'Christianity and Theology in *Beowulf*', in *The Christian Tradition in
    Anglo-Saxon England: Approaches to Current Scholarship and Teaching*,
    ed. Paul Cavill (Cambridge: D. S. Brewer), pp. 15–39
Clark, Cecily, 1971. 'The Narrative Mode of the *Anglo-Saxon Chronicle* before the
    Conquest', in *England before the Conquest: Studies in Primary Sources
    Presented to Dorothy Whitelock*, ed. Peter Clemoes and Kathleen Hughes
    (Cambridge: Cambridge University Press), pp. 215–35
Clark, David and Nicholas Perkins, eds., 2010. *Anglo-Saxon Culture and the
    Modern Imagination* (Cambridge: D. S. Brewer)
Clark, Robert, ed., 2000–. *The Literary Encyclopedia*, www.litencyc.com
Clayton, Mary, 1985. 'Homiliaries and Preaching in Anglo-Saxon England',
    Peritia 4, 207–42
    1994. 'Ælfric's *Judith*: Manipulative or Manipulated?', *Anglo-Saxon England*
    23, 215–27
    1996. 'Hermits and the Contemplative Life in Anglo-Saxon England', in *Holy
    Men and Holy Women*, ed. Szarmach, pp. 147–75
    1999. 'Ælfric's *Esther*: A *Speculum Reginae*?', in *Text and Gloss: Studies in
    Insular Learning and Literature Presented to Joseph Donovan Pheifer*, ed.
    Helen Conrad O'Brian, Anne Marie D'Arcy and John Scattergood
    (Dublin: Four Courts Press), pp. 89–101
    2000. 'Ælfric and Æthelred', in *Essays on Anglo-Saxon and Related Themes in
    Memory of Lynne Grundy*, ed. Roberts and Nelson, pp. 65–88
Clemoes, P. A. M., 1960. 'The Old English Benedictine Office', *Anglia* 78, 265–83
Colley, Linda, 2005. *Britons: Forging the Nation 1707–1837* (New Haven, CT, and
    London: Yale University Press; first edn 1992)
Conner, Patrick W., 1993. *Anglo-Saxon Exeter: A Tenth-Century Cultural History*,
    Studies in Anglo-Saxon History 4 (Woodbridge and Rochester, NY: Boydell)

Corona, Gabriella, 2009. 'Ælfric's Schemes and Tropes: *Amplificatio* and the Portrayal of Persecutors', in *A Companion to Ælfric*, ed. Magennis and Swan, pp. 297–320

Damico, Helen and John Leyerle, eds., 1993. *Heroic Poetry in the Anglo-Saxon Period: Studies in Honor of Jess B. Bessinger* (Kalamazoo, MI: Medieval Institute Publications, Western Michigan University)

Davis, Kathleen, 1998. 'National Writing in the Ninth Century: A Reminder for Postcolonial Thinking about the Nation', *Journal of Medieval and Early Modern Studies* 28, 611–37

2008. *Periodization and Sovereignty: How Ideas of Feudalism and Secularization Govern the Politics of Time* (Philadelphia: University of Pennsylvania Press)

Discenza, Nicole Guenther, 2005. *The King's English: Strategies of Translation in the Old English Boethius* (Albany, NY: State University of New York Press)

D'Israeli, Isaac, 1841. 'Beowulf: The Hero-Life', in his *Amenities of Literature*, 3 vols. (London: Edward Moxon), I, 80–92

Dragland, S. L., 1977. 'Monster-Man in *Beowulf*', *Neophilologus* 61, 606–18

Eagleton, Terry, 1999. '*Hasped and Hooped and Hirpling:* Heaney Conquers *Beowulf*', *London Review of Books*, 11 November, p. 16

Earl, James W., 1978. 'Typology and Iconographic Style in Early Medieval Hagiography', *Studies in the Literary Imagination* 8, 15–46

Elstob, Elizabeth, 1715. *The Rudiments of Grammar for the English-Saxon Tongue* (London: J. Bowyer & C. King)

Foucault, Michel, 2002. *The Order of Things: An Archaeology of the Human Sciences* (London and New York: Routledge; original French edition published 1966, Paris: Editions Gallimard)

Foys, Martin K., 2007. *Virtually Anglo-Saxon: Old Media, New Media, and Early Medieval Studies in the Late Age of Print* (Gainesville, FL: University Press of Florida)

Frank, Roberta, 1992. '*Beowulf* and Sutton Hoo: The Odd Couple', in *Voyage to the Other World: The Legacy of Sutton Hoo*, ed. Calvin B. Kendall and Peter S. Wells (Minneapolis, MN: University of Minnesota Press), pp. 47–64

Frankis, John, 2000. 'King Ælle and the Conversion of the English: The Development of a Legend from Bede to Chaucer', in *Literary Appropriations of the Anglo-Saxons*, ed. Scragg and Weinberg, pp. 74–92

Frantzen, Allen J., 1990. *Desire for Origins: New Language, Old English, and Teaching the Tradition* (New Brunswick, NJ, and London: Rutgers University Press)

2001. 'By the Numbers: Anglo-Saxon Scholarship at the Century's End', in *A Companion to Anglo-Saxon Literature*, ed. Pulsiano and Treharne, pp. 472–95

Frantzen, Allen J. and John D. Niles, eds., 1997. *Anglo-Saxonism and the Construction of Social Identity* (Gainesville, FL: University Press of Florida)

Franzen, Christine, 1991. *The Tremulous Hand of Worcester: A Study of Old English in the Thirteenth Century* (Oxford: Clarendon Press)

Fulk, R. D. and Christopher M. Cain, 2003. *A History of Old English Literature* (Oxford: Blackwell)

Gardner, W. H., 1958. *Gerard Manley Hopkins (1844–1889): A Study of Poetic Idiosyncrasy in Relation to Poetic Tradition*, 2 vols. (New York: Oxford University Press)

Geary, Patrick J., 2002. *The Myth of Nations: The Medieval Origins of Europe* (Princeton, NJ, and Oxford: Princeton University Press)

George, Jodi-Anne, 2010. 'Beowulf in Popular Culture', ch. 8 of her *Beowulf: A Reader's Guide to Essential Criticism* (Basingstoke: Palgrave Macmillan), pp. 115–49

Godden, Malcolm, 1997. 'Wærferth and King Alfred: The Fate of the Old English *Dialogues*', in *Alfred the Wise: Studies in Honour of Janet Bately on the Occasion of Her Sixty-Fifth Birthday*, ed. Jane Roberts, Janet L. Nelson and Malcolm Godden (Cambridge: D. S. Brewer), pp. 35–51

(M. R.), 2007. 'Did King Alfred Write Anything?', *Medium Ævum* 76, 1–23

(Malcolm R.), 2009a. 'Ælfric and the Alfredian Precedents', in *A Companion to Ælfric*, ed. Magennis and Swan, pp. 139–63

(Malcolm), 2009b. 'The Alfredian Project and its Aftermath: Rethinking the Literary History of the Ninth and Tenth Centuries' (Sir Israel Gollancz Memorial Lecture), *Proceedings of the British Academy* 162, 93–122

Godden, Malcolm and Michael Lapidge, eds., 1991. *The Cambridge Companion to Old English Literature* (Cambridge: Cambridge University Press)

Goffart, Walter, 1988. *The Narrators of Barbarian History (A.D. 550–800): Jordanes, Gregory of Tours, Bede, and Paul the Deacon* (Princeton, NJ: Princeton University Press)

Goody, Jack and Ian Watt, 1968. 'The Consequences of Literacy', in *Literacy and Traditional Societies*, ed. Jack Goody (Cambridge: Cambridge University Press), pp. 27–68

Graham, Timothy, ed., 2000. *The Recovery of Old English: Anglo-Saxon Studies in the Sixteenth and Seventeenth Centuries* (Kalamazoo, MI: Medieval Institute Publications, Western Michigan University)

2001. 'Anglo-Saxon Studies: Sixteenth to Eighteenth Centuries', in *A Companion to Anglo-Saxon Literature*, ed. Pulsiano and Treharne, pp. 415–33

Gransden, Antonia, 1992. *Legends, Traditions and History in Medieval England* (London and Rio Grande, OH: Hambledon Press)

Greenfield, Kathleen, 1981. 'Changing Emphases in English Vernacular Homiletic Literature, 960–1225', *Journal of Medieval History* 1, 283–91

Greenfield, Stanley B., 1955. 'The Formulaic Expression of the Theme of "Exile" in Anglo-Saxon Poetry', *Speculum* 30, 200–6

1966. 'The Old English Elegies', in *Continuations and Beginnings*, ed. Eric G. Stanley (London: Thomas Nelson), pp. 142–75

1986. '*Wulf and Eadwacer*: All Passion Pent', *Anglo-Saxon England* 15, 5–14

Greenfield, Stanley B. and Daniel G. Calder, 1986. *A New Critical History of Old English Literature* (New York and London: New York University Press)

Greenfield, Stanley B. and Fred C. Robinson, 1980. *A Bibliography of Publications on Old English Literature to the End of 1972* (Toronto, Buffalo, NY, and London: University of Toronto Press)

Gretsch, Mechthild, 1999. 'Elizabeth Elstob: A Scholar's Fight for Anglo-Saxon Studies', *Anglia* 117, 163–200 and 481–524

2009. 'Ælfric, Language and Winchester', in *A Companion to Ælfric*, ed. Magennis and Swan, pp. 109–37

Griffith, M. S., 1993. 'Convention and Originality in the Old English "Beasts of Battle" Typescene', *Anglo-Saxon England* 22, 179–99

Groom, Bernard, 1966. *The Unity of Wordsworth's Poetry* (London: Macmillan; New York: St Martin's Press)

Gunn, Vicky, 2009. *Bede's Historiae: Genre, Rhetoric and the Construction of the Anglo-Saxon Church History* (Woodbridge: Boydell Press)

Hadfield, Andrew, 2004. *Shakespeare, Spenser and the Matter of Britain* (Basingstoke: Palgrave)

Hall, J. R., 1997. 'Mid-Nineteenth-Century American Anglo-Saxonism', in *Anglo-Saxonism and the Construction of Social Identity*, ed. Frantzen and Niles, pp. 133–56

2001. 'Anglo-Saxon Studies in the Nineteenth Century: England, Denmark, America', in *A Companion to Anglo-Saxon Literature*, ed. Pulsiano and Treharne, pp. 434–54

Happé, Peter, 1996. *John Bale*, Twaynes English Authors Series 520 (New York: Twayne)

Hauer, Stanley R., 1983. 'Thomas Jefferson and the Anglo-Saxon Language', *PMLA* 98, 879–98

Havelock, Eric A., 1986. *The Muse Learns to Sing: Reflections on Orality and Literacy from Antiquity to the Present* (New Haven, CT, and London: Yale University Press)

Heinemann, Fredrik J., 1970. '*Judith* 236–291a: A Mock-Heroic Approach-to-Battle Type Scene', *Neuphilologische Mitteilungen* 71, 83–96

Herbison, Ivan, 2000. 'Generic Adaptation in *Andreas*', in *Essays on Anglo-Saxon and Related Themes in Memory of Lynne Grundy*, ed. Roberts and Nelson, pp. 181–211

2010. 'Heroism and Comic Subversion in the Old English *Judith*', *English Studies* 91, 1–25

Hickes, George and Humphrey Wanley, 1703–5. *Antiquæ literaturæ septentrionalis libri duo*, 2 vols. (Oxford: E. Theatro Sheldoniano); vol. I, George Hickes, *Linguarum vett. septentrionalium thesaurus grammatico-criticus et archæologicus*; vol. II, Humphrey Wanley, *Librorum vett. septentrionalium catologus historico-criticus*

Higham, N. J., 2006. *(Re-)Reading Bede: The Ecclesiastical History in Context* (London and New York: Routledge)

Hill, John M., 1995. *The Cultural World in Beowulf,* Anthropological Horizons 6 (Toronto, Buffalo, NY, and London: University of Toronto Press)

Hill, Joyce, 1990. "'Þæt wæs geomoru ides!" A Female Stereotype Examined', in *New Readings on Women in Old English Literature,* ed. Helen Damico and Alexandra Hennessey Olsen (Bloomington and Indianapolis, IN: University of Indiana Press), pp. 235–47

Hill, Thomas D., 1996. '*Imago Dei*: Genre, Symbolism, and Anglo-Saxon Hagiography', in *Holy Men and Holy Women,* ed. Szarmach, pp. 35–50

Hills, Catherine, 2003. *Origins of the English* (London: Duckworth)

Hines, John, ed., 1997. *The Anglo-Saxons from the Migration Period to the Eighth Century: An Ethnographic Perspective,* Studies in Historical Archaeoethnology 2 (Woodbridge: Boydell Press)

Hofstetter, Walter, 1987. *Winchester und der spätaltenglische Sprachgebrauch: Untersuchungen zur geographischen und zeitlichen Verbreitung altenglischer Synonyme,* Texte und Untersuchungen zur Englischen Philologie 14 (Munich: W. Fink)

Hollis, Stephanie, 1992. *Anglo-Saxon Women and the Church: Sharing a Common Fate* (Woodbridge and Rochester, NY: Boydell)

Hollis, Stephanie and Michael Wright, 1992. *Old English Prose of Secular Learning.* Annotated Bibliographies of Old and Middle English Literature 4 (Woodbridge and Rochester, NY: D. S. Brewer)

Holmes, David M., 1970. *The Art of Thomas Middleton* (Oxford: Clarendon Press)

Horsman, Reginald, 1981. *Race and Manifest Destiny: The Origins of American Racial Anglo-Saxonism* (Cambridge, MA: Harvard University Press)

Hough, Carole, 2004. 'New Light on the Verb "Understand"', in *New Perspectives on English Historical Linguistics, Selected Papers from 12 ICEHL, Glasgow, 21–26 August 2002:* Volume II, *Lexis and Transmission,* ed. Christian Kay and Carole Hough, Current Issues in Linguistic Theory 252 (Amsterdam and Philadelphia: John Benjamins), pp. 139–49

Howe, Nicholas, 1989. *Migration and Mythmaking in Anglo-Saxon England* (New Haven, CT, and London: Yale University Press)

2004. 'Rome: Capital of Anglo-Saxon England', *Journal of Medieval and Early Modern Studies* 34, 147–72

2008. *Writing the Map of Anglo-Saxon England: Essays in Cultural Geography* (New Haven, CT, and London: Yale University Press)

Irving, Edward B., Jr, 2000. '*The Charge of the Light Brigade*: Tennyson's *Battle of Brunanburh*', in *Literary Appropriations of the Anglo-Saxons,* ed. Scragg and Weinberg, pp. 174–93

Jackson, Peter, 2000. 'Ælfric and the Purpose of Christian Marriage: A Reconsideration of the *Life of Æthelthryth,* Lines 120–30', *Anglo-Saxon England* 29, 235–60

Jagger, Holly Elizabeth, 2002. 'Body, Text and Self in Old English Verse: A Study of "Beowulfian" and "Cynewulfian" Rhetoric', Ph.D. Diss., University of Toronto

Jolly, Karen Louise, 1996. *Popular Religion in Late Saxon England: Elf Charms in Context* (Chapel Hill, NC: University of North Carolina Press)

Jones, Chris, 2006. *Strange Likeness: The Use of Old English in Twentieth-Century Poetry* (Oxford: Oxford University Press)

Jones, Christopher A., 2009. 'Ælfric and the Limits of "Benedictine Reform"', in *A Companion to Ælfric*, ed. Magennis and Swan, pp. 67–108

Jurasinski, Stefan, 2004. 'The Ecstasy of Vengeance: Legal History, Old English Scholarship, and the "Feud" of Hengest', *Review of English Studies*, n.s. 55, 641–61

Kermode, Frank, 2001. *Pleasing Myself: From Beowulf to Philip Roth* (London: Penguin)

Keynes, Simon, 1999. 'The Cult of King Alfred the Great', *Anglo-Saxon England* 28, 225–356

Kleist, Aaron J, 2009. 'Assembling Ælfric: Reconstructing the Rationale behind Eleventh- and Twelfth-Century Compilations', in *A Companion to Ælfric*, ed. Magennis and Swan, pp. 369–98

Knowles, David, 1972. 'Introduction' to *Augustine: Concerning the City of God against the Pagans*, trans. Bettenson, pp. vii–xxxiv

Lapidge, Michael, 1975. 'The Hermeneutic Style in Tenth-Century Anglo-Latin Literature', *Anglo-Saxon England* 1, 85–137; reprinted with additions in Michael Lapidge, *Anglo-Latin Literature 900–1066* (London and Rio Grande, OH: Hambledon Press), pp. 105–49, 484–6

    1986. 'The Anglo-Latin Background', in Greenfield and Calder, eds., *A New Critical History of Old English Literature*, pp. 5–37; reprinted with revisions in Michael Lapidge, *Anglo-Latin Literature 600–899* (London and Rio Grande, OH: Hambledon Press), 1–35

    1988. 'The Study of Greek at the School of Canterbury in the Seventh Century', in *The Sacred Nectar of the Greeks: The Study of Greek in the West in the Early Middle Ages*, ed. Michael W. Herren, King's College London Medieval Studies 2 (London: King's College London Medieval Studies), pp. 169–94

    2006. *The Anglo-Saxon Library* (Oxford: Oxford University Press)

Lapidge, Michael, John Blair, Simon Keynes and Donald Scragg, eds., 1999. *The Blackwell Encyclopaedia of Anglo-Saxon England.* (Oxford: Blackwell)

Lavezzo, Kathy, 2006. *Angels on the Edge of the World: Geography, Literature, and English Community, 1000–1534* (Ithaca, NY, and London: Cornell University Press)

Lee, Stuart and Daniel Paul O'Donnell, 2009. 'From Manuscript to Computer', in *Working with Anglo-Saxon Manuscripts*, ed. Owen-Crocker, pp. 253–84

Lees, Clare A., 1999. *Tradition and Belief: Religious Writing in Late Anglo-Saxon England*, Medieval Cultures 19 (Minneapolis, MN, and London: University of Minnesota Press)

    2009. 'In Ælfric's Words: Conversion, Vigilance and the Nation in Ælfric's *Life of St Gregory the Great*', in *A Companion to Ælfric*, ed. Magennis and Swan, pp. 271–96 forthcoming. *Old English Across Time*

Lees, Clare A. and Gillian Overing, 2001. *Double Agents: Women and Clerical Culture in Anglo-Saxon England* (Philadelphia: University of Pennsylvania Press)

Leinbaugh, T. H., 1982. 'Ælfric's *Sermo de Sacrificio in Die Paschae*: Anglican Polemic in the Sixteenth and Seventeenth Centuries', in *Anglo-Saxon Scholarship*, ed. Berkhout and Gatch, pp. 51–68

Lerer, Seth, 2007. *Inventing English: A Portable History of the Language* (New York: Columbia University Press)

Liuzza, R. M., 2002. 'Lost in Translation: Some Versions of *Beowulf* in the Nineteenth Century', *English Studies* 83, 281–95

   ed., 2002. *Old English Literature: Critical Essays* (Hew Haven, CT, and London: Yale University Press)

Loewe, Raphael, 1969. 'The Medieval History of the Latin Vulgate', in *The Cambridge History of the Bible*, vol. 2: *The West from the Fathers to the Reformation*, ed. G. W. H. Lampe (Cambridge: Cambridge University Press), pp. 102–54

[Longfellow, Henry Wadsworth,] 1838. 'Article IV' (review of miscellaneous publications in Anglo-Saxon studies), *North American Review* 47 (no. 100), 90–134

Longley, Edna, 1988. *Louis MacNeice: A Study* (London: Faber)

Love, R. C., 1999. 'Hagiography', in *The Blackwell Encyclopaedia of Anglo-Saxon England*, ed. Lapidge *et al.*, pp. 226–8

Lutz, Angelica, 2000. 'The Study of the *Anglo-Saxon Chronicle* in the Seventeenth Century and the Establishment of Old English Studies in the Universities', in *The Recovery of Old English*, ed. Graham, pp. 1–82

McCarthy, Conor, 2008. *Seamus Heaney and Medieval Poetry* (Cambridge: D. S. Brewer)

MacDougall, Hugh A., 1982. *Racial Myth in English History: Trojans, Teutons, and Anglo-Saxons* (Montreal: Harvest House; Hanover, NH, and London: University Press of New England)

Magennis, Hugh, 2001. 'Audience(s), Reception, Literacy', in *A Companion to Anglo-Saxon Literature*, ed. Pulsiano and Treharne, pp. 84–101

   2006. 'Ælfric and Heroic Literature', in *The Power of Words*, ed. Magennis and Wilcox, pp. 31–60

   2010. 'Germanic Legend and Old English Heroic Poetry', in *A Companion to Medieval Poetry*, ed. Corinne Saunders (Chichester: Wiley-Blackwell), pp. 85–100

   2011. *Translating* Beowulf: *Modern Versions in English Verse* (Cambridge: D. S. Brewer)

Magennis, Hugh and Mary Swan, eds., 2009. *A Companion to Ælfric* (Leiden and Boston, MA: Brill)

Magennis, Hugh and Jonathan Wilcox, eds., 2006. *The Power of Words: Anglo-Saxon Studies Presented to Donald G. Scragg on his Seventieth Birthday*, Medieval European Studies 8 (Morgantown, WV: West Virginia University Press)

Magoun, Francis P., 1953. 'The Oral-Formulaic Character of Anglo-Saxon Narrative Poetry', *Speculum* 28, 446–67

Michelet, Fabienne L., 2006. *Creation, Migration, and Conquest: Imaginary Geography and Sense of Space in Old English Literature* (Oxford: Oxford University Press)

Mitchell, Bruce, 1995. *An Invitation to Old English and Anglo-Saxon England* (Oxford: Blackwell)

Momma, H., 1997. *The Composition of Old English Poetry*, Cambridge Studies in Anglo-Saxon England 20 (Cambridge: Cambridge University Press)

Moseley, Charles, 1997. *J. R. R. Tolkien* (Plymouth: Northcote House)

Murphy, Patrick J., forthcoming. *Unriddling the Exeter Riddles* (University Park, PA: Penn State University Press)

Niles, John D., 2006. *Old English Enigmatic Poems and the Play of the Texts*, Studies in the Early Middle Ages 13 (Turnhout: Brepols)

2007. *Old English Heroic Poems and the Social Life of Texts*, Studies in the Early Middle Ages 20 (Turnhout: Brepols)

O'Brien O'Keeffe, Katherine, 1990. *Visible Song: Transitional Literacy in Old English Verse*, Cambridge Studies in Anglo-Saxon England 4 (Cambridge: Cambridge University Press)

ed., 1997. *Reading Old English Texts* (Cambridge: Cambridge University Press)

Ong, Walter J., 1982. *Orality and Literacy: The Technologizing of the Word* (London: Methuen)

Orchard, Andy, 1994. *The Poetic Art of Aldhelm*, Cambridge Studies in Anglo-Saxon England 8 (Cambridge: Cambridge University Press)

1995. *Pride and Prodigies: Studies in the Monsters of the Beowulf-Manuscript* (Cambridge: D. S. Brewer)

1997. 'Oral Tradition', in *Reading Old English Texts*, ed. O'Brien O'Keeffe, pp. 101–23

Owen-Crocker, Gale R., ed., 2009. *Working with Anglo-Saxon Manuscripts* (Exeter: University of Exeter Press)

Page, R. I., 1999. *An Introduction to English Runes*, 2nd edn (Woodbridge: Boydell Press; first edn 1973)

Palmer, D. J., 1965. *The Rise of English Studies: An Account of the Study of English Language and Literature from its Origins to the Making of the Oxford English School* (London: Oxford University Press)

Pasternack, Carol Braun, 1995. *The Textuality of Old English Poetry*, Cambridge Studies in Anglo-Saxon England 13 (Cambridge: Cambridge University Press)

Patterson, Lee, 2000. 'The Heroic Laconic Style: Reticence and Meaning from *Beowulf* to the Edwardians', in *Medieval Literature and Historical Inquiry: Essays in Honor of Derek Pearsall*, ed. David Aers (Cambridge: D. S. Brewer), pp. 133–57

Plumer, Danielle Cunniff, 2000. 'The Construction of Structure in the Earliest Editions of Old English Poetry', in *The Recovery of Old English*, ed. Graham, pp. 243–79

Powell, Timothy E., 1994. 'The "Three Orders" of Society in Anglo-Saxon
    England', *Anglo-Saxon England* 23, 103–32
Pratt, Lynda, 2000. 'Anglo-Saxon Attitudes? Alfred the Great and the Romantic
    National Epic', in *Literary Appropriations of the Anglo-Saxons*, ed. Scragg
    and Weinberg, pp. 138–56
Pringle, Ian, 1975. '*Judith*: The Homily and the Poem', *Traditio* 31, 83–97
Pulsiano, Phillip and Elaine Treharne, eds., 2001. *A Companion to Anglo-Saxon
    Literature* (Oxford: Blackwell)
Raw, Barbara C., 1997. *Trinity and Incarnation in Anglo-Saxon Art and Thought*,
    Cambridge Studies in Anglo-Saxon England 21 (Cambridge:
    Cambridge University Press)
Remley, Paul G., 2005. 'Aldhelm as Old English Poet: *Exodus*, Asser, and the *Dicta
    Ælfredi*', in *Latin Learning and English Lore: Studies in Anglo-Saxon
    Literature for Michael Lapidge*, 2 vols., ed. Katherine O'Brien O'Keeffe
    and Andy Orchard (Toronto, Buffalo, NY, and London: University of
    Toronto Press), vol. I, pp. 90–108
Reynolds, Susan, 1985. 'What Do We Mean by "Anglo-Saxon" and "Anglo-Saxons"?',
    Journal of British Studies 24, 395–414
Ricks, Christopher, 1972. *Tennyson* (New York: Macmillan)
Riedinger, Anita R., 1993. 'The Formulaic Relationship between *Beowulf* and
    Andreas', in *Heroic Poetry in the Anglo-Saxon Period*, ed. Damico and
    Leyerle, pp. 283–312
Roberts, Jane and Janet Nelson, eds., 2000. *Essays on Anglo-Saxon and
    Related Themes in Memory of Lynne Grundy*, King's College
    London Medieval Studies 17 (London: Centre for Late
    Antique and Medieval Studies, King's College, University of
    London)
Rouse, Robert Allen, 2005. *The Idea of Anglo-Saxon England in Middle English
    Romance* (Cambridge: D. S. Brewer)
Russell, James C., 1994. *The Germanization of Early Medieval Christianity:
    A Sociohistorical Approach to Religious Transformation* (New York and
    Oxford: Oxford University Press)
Salvador, Mercedes, 2005. 'Latin Riddles [Enigmata] (400–800)', in *The Literary
    Encyclopedia* (online publication), ed. Clark
Sanders, Andrew, 2000. '"Utter indifference"?: The Anglo-Saxons in the
    Nineteenth-Century Novel', in *Literary Appropriations of the
    Anglo-Saxons*, ed. Scragg and Weinberg, pp. 157–73
Scott, Margaret, 2007. 'Scottish Place-Names and Anglo-Saxon England', paper
    delivered at Conference of the International Society of Anglo-Saxonists,
    London, 2 August
Scragg, Donald, 2000. 'Introduction. The Anglo-Saxons: Fact and Fiction', in
    Literary Appropriations of the Anglo-Saxons, ed. Scragg and Weinberg,
    pp. 1–21
    2009. 'Manuscript Sources of Old English Prose', in *Working with Anglo-
    Saxon Manuscripts*, ed. Owen-Crocker, pp. 61–87

Scragg, Donald and Carole Weinberg, eds., 2000. *Literary Appropriations of the Anglo-Saxons from the Thirteenth to the Twentieth Century*, Cambridge Studies in Anglo-Saxon England 29 (Cambridge: Cambridge University Press)

Shippey, T. A., 1979. 'Creation from Philology in *The Lord of the Rings*', in *J. R. R. Tolkien, Scholar and Storyteller: Essays in Memoriam*, ed. Mary Salu and Robert T. Farrell (Ithaca, NY, and London: Cornell University Press), pp. 286–316

(Tom), 2000. *J. R. R. Tolkien: Author of the Century* (London: HarperCollins)

(Tom), 2005. *The Road to Middle-Earth*, revised and expanded edn (London: HarperCollins); original edn 1982

Shippey, T. A. and Andreas Haarder, eds., 1998. Beowulf: *The Critical Heritage* (London and New York: Routledge, 1998)

Stanley, Eric G., 1975. *The Search for Anglo-Saxon Paganism* (Cambridge: D. S. Brewer; Totowa, NJ: Rowman and Littlefield); reprinted, with same pagination, in Eric Gerald Stanley, *Imagining the Anglo-Saxon Past: The Search for Anglo-Saxon Paganism and Anglo-Saxon Trial by Jury* (Cambridge: D. S. Brewer, 2000), pp. 1–110

Stanton, Robert, 2002. *The Culture of Translation in Anglo-Saxon England* (Cambridge: D. S. Brewer)

Staver, Ruth Johnston, 2005. 'Modern Adaptations of *Beowulf*', in her *A Companion to* Beowulf (Westport, CT, and London: Greenwood Press), pp. 187–95

Swan, Mary and Elaine M. Treharne, eds., 2000. *Rewriting Old English in the Twelfth Century*, Cambridge Studies in Anglo-Saxon England 30 (Cambridge: Cambridge University Press)

Swanton, Michael, 2002. *English Poetry before Chaucer*, revised edn (Exeter: University of Exeter Press)

Szarmach, Paul E., ed., 1996. *Holy Men and Holy Women: Old English Prose Saints' Lives and Their Contexts* (Albany, NY: State University of New York Press)

Tolkien, J. R. R., 1936. '*Beowulf*: The Monsters and the Critics', *Proceedings of the British Academy* 22, 245–95; widely reprinted

Toswell, M. J., 2007. 'The Codicology of Anglo-Saxon Manuscripts, Especially the Blickling Homilies', in *The Old English Homily: Precedent, Practice, and Appropriation*, ed. Aaron J Kleist, Studies in the Early Middle Ages 17 (Turnhout: Brepols), pp. 209–26

Townend, Matthew, 2001. 'Contextualizing the *Knútsdrápur*: Skaldic Praise-Poetry at the Court of Cnut', *Anglo-Saxon England* 30, 145–79

2002. *Language and History in Viking Age England: Linguistic Relations between Speakers of Old Norse and Old English*, Studies in the Early Middle Ages 6 (Turnhout: Brepols)

Treharne, Elaine, 2006. 'The Life and Times of Old English Homilies for the First Sunday in Lent', in *The Power of Words*, ed. Magennis and Wilcox, pp. 205–40

2009. 'Manuscript Sources of Old English Poetry', in *Working with Anglo-Saxon Manuscripts*, ed. Owen-Crocker, pp. 89–111

Turner, Sharon, 1799–1805. *The History of the Anglo-Saxons: Comprising the History of England from the Earliest Period to the Norman Conquest*, 4 vols. (London: Longman, Hurst, Rees, & Orme); 3rd edn, 3 vols. (London: Longman, Hurst, Rees, Orme, and Brown, 1820)

Tyler, Elizabeth M., 2006. *Old English Poetics: The Aesthetics of the Familiar in Anglo-Saxon England* (York: York Medieval Press)

VanHoosier-Carey, Gregory A., 1997. 'Byrhtnoth in Dixie: The Emergence of Anglo-Saxon Studies in the Postbellum South', in *Anglo-Saxonism and the Construction of Social Identity*, ed. Frantzen and Niles, pp. 157–72

Venuti, Lawrence, 1995. *The Translator's Invisibility: A History of Translation* (London and New York: Routledge)

1998. *The Scandals of Translation: Towards an Ethics of Difference* (London and New York: Routledge)

2004. 'Foundational Statements: Introduction', in *The Translation Studies Reader*, ed. Lawrence Venuti, 2nd edn (London and New York: Routledge), pp. 13–20

Wallace-Hadrill, J. M., 1988. *Bede's Ecclesiastical History of the English People: A Historical Commentary* (Oxford: Clarendon Press)

Whatley, E. Gordon, 1997. 'Lost in Translation: Omission of Episodes in Some Old English Prose Saints' Legends', *Anglo-Saxon England* 26, 187–208

Whitelock, Dorothy, 1950. 'The Interpretation of *The Seafarer*', in *The Early Cultures of North-West Europe (H. M. Chadwick Memorial Studies)*, ed. Sir Cyril Fox and Bruce Dickins (Cambridge: Cambridge University Press), pp. 259–72

Wilcox, Jonathan, 1992. 'The Dissemination of Wulfstan's Homilies: The Wulfstan Tradition in Eleventh-Century Vernacular Preaching', in *England in the Eleventh Century: Proceedings of the 1990 Harlaxton Symposium*, ed. Carola Hicks, Harlaxton Medieval Studies 2 (Stamford: Paul Watkins), pp. 199–217

Wormald, Patrick, 1994. '*Engla lond*: The Making of an Allegiance', *Journal of Historical Sociology* 7, 1–24

Wright, Roger, 1997. 'Translation between Latin and Romance in the Early Middle Ages', in *Translation Theory and Practice in the Middle Ages*, ed. Jeanette Beer, Studies in Medieval Culture 38 (Kalamazoo, MI: Medieval Institute Publications, Western Michigan University), pp. 7–32

Young, Robert J. C., 2008. *The Idea of English Ethnicity* (Oxford: Blackwell)

Zacher, Samantha, 2009. *Preaching to the Converted: The Style and Rhetoric of the Vercelli Book Homilies* (Toronto, Buffalo, NY, and London: University of Toronto Press)

Zacher, Samantha and Andy Orchard, eds., 2009. *New Readings in the Vercelli Book* (Toronto, Buffalo, NY, and London: University of Toronto Press)

Index

Cambridge Introductions to...